Mourning Films

ALSO BY RICHARD ARMSTRONG

Billy Wilder, American Film Realist
(McFarland, 2000; paperback 2004)

Mourning Films
A Critical Study of Loss and Grieving in Cinema

RICHARD ARMSTRONG

McFarland & Company, Inc., Publishers
Jefferson, North Carolina, and London

LIBRARY OF CONGRESS CATALOGUING-IN-PUBLICATION DATA

Armstrong, Richard, 1959–
 Mourning films : a critical study of loss and grieving in cinema / Richard Armstrong.
    p.   cm.
 Includes bibliographical references and index.

 ISBN 978-0-7864-6699-3
 softcover : acid free paper ∞

 1. Loss (Psychology) in motion pictures.   2. Grief in motion pictures.   3. Psychic trauma in motion pictures.   4. Bereavement—Psychological aspects.   I. Title.
 PN1995.9.L59A75 2012
 791.43'6165—dc23   2012029422

BRITISH LIBRARY CATALOGUING DATA ARE AVAILABLE

© 2012 Richard Armstrong. All rights reserved

No part of this book may be reproduced or transmitted in any form or by any means, electronic or mechanical, including photocopying or recording, or by any information storage and retrieval system, without permission in writing from the publisher.

On the cover: Juliette Binoche in *Three Colors: Blue* (1993 France) aka *Trois couleurs: Bleu* (Miramax/Photofest)

Manufactured in the United States of America

McFarland & Company, Inc., Publishers
  Box 611, Jefferson, North Carolina 28640
   www.mcfarlandpub.com

For my sister

Contents

Preface 1
Introduction 7

Chapter 1. Manifestation 37
Chapter 2. Realization 67
Chapter 3. Acceptance 108
Chapter 4. Release 155

Conclusion 193
Bibliography 197
Index 205

Preface

This is a book about the representation and aesthetics of loss and mourning in modern cinema. It is important to stress at the outset that this is not a book about the representation of death in films, but about the representation of the emotional and psychological consequences of death. There have been numerous treatments of death in film books, just as there have been numerous deaths represented in films. But until very recently, the treatment of loss and the films which treat loss and its consequences have been significantly overlooked in cinema scholarship. This is a gap which I hope this book goes some way towards filling.

Significantly, while the theme of loss finds the aesthetics of a film addressing an experience which is very real and very quotidian for many people, and will be very real for everyone in due course, it is also intrinsic to what cinema is as an apparatus. Put simply, the cinema is a space in which we see someone who is no longer there. In its very mechanism, in the furious alternation between presence and absence as the images and their frames rush over the projector beam, cinema technically embodies the play of presence and absence as states, and in consequence of this flicker of presence and absence we gaze up at, and typically adore, a figure who once stood before a camera, perhaps many years ago, yet is now nowhere to be found. By this light, the term "medium," used both to describe the organizing figure at a spiritualist séance, and a mode of aesthetic representation such as film, seems especially apt. The cinema both embodies loss and mediates those whom we have lost, whether they are a dead film star or the deceased relative in a home movie. The aesthetics of loss, therefore, are essential to film history because, literally and figuratively, they chime with what film is, arguably a necropolis of dead souls. Meanwhile, in addressing the consequences of death, what I am calling the "mourning film," that film in which the drama revolves around a loss grieved over, looks beyond the cinema's myriad spectacles of death at the feelings death engenders in the living, and by ghastly implication, the prospect of mine and your own finitude, what the French psychoanalyst and philosopher Jacques Lacan has called the indescribably, unmentionably "Real" of human existence.

I became interested in the representation of loss in the summer of 2005 while preparing a feature article for the American website *Bright Lights Film Journal* on the representation of mourning in a series of British films of the classical and post-classical periods. Rehearsing the theme of the piece with my sister and brother-in-law that summer, little did I know that he would be dead within a year, and she would be embarking upon the long and difficult process of coming to terms with her loss. The autumn found me reviewing Emma Wilson's book *Cinema's Missing Children*, a study of a series of recent European films which treat the theme of the lost child. While in conversation with the author, I wondered aloud why there have been no significant academic treatments of what seemed to me to be a growing range of films addressing loss. She agreed, and urged me to apply to Cambridge University to read for a PhD on the subject. This book is derived from the research which I undertook for my PhD between 2006 and 2009, while the case study of *Genova* is derived from an article which has appeared in the British professional journal *Bereavement Care*.

The complex relationship between European and American cinema has always interested me. It lay behind the theme of my first book for McFarland, *Billy Wilder: American Film Realist* (2000), while many of the directors whom I most enjoy and admire — Wilder, Lang, Hitchcock, Siodmak, Renoir, Tourneur — had careers in Europe and in America. But adopting the optic of grief and mourning to examine a range of European and American films finds this book departing from the auteurist considerations of my first book in order to examine the thematic similarities between a range of films of variously differing provenance, and to explore the light which they throw upon our experience of the end of life. Therefore, I am less interested here in the relationship between, say, Nicolas Roeg's *Don't Look Now* and *Insignificance*, for example, than in that between *Don't Look Now* and Woody Allen's *Interiors*, or that between *Don't Look Now* and Michael Winterbottom's *Genova*. My title, *Mourning Films*, derives from the attempt to see the mourning film as the product of the specific creativity which results when a theme is explored with compassion, discipline and rigour in an artistic medium by the light of a particular inspiration or creative muse. That the "muse" was traditionally conceived of as a female figure chimes with this book's emphasis upon women protagonists facing loss. With this in mind, it could be said that the films which this book analyzes are the children of mourning.

The typical protagonist of mourning in cinema, from Fritz Lang's *Destiny* (1921) to Winterbottom's *Genova* (2008), has invariably, and significantly, been a woman or a girl. In the heyday of cinematic grief in the inter-war and wartime melodramas of the 1930s and 1940s, the representation of this theme took its cue from the massive losses of two world wars, and their impact on a generation of women. Preliminary and exploratory in its aims and form, this book shall proceed with this gender bias in mind. Clearly, many mourning films dwell upon male mourning but that is for another volume and another author to explore. Another precinct of mourning cinema which I touch upon but do not examine is that of the commemorative mourning film. From Abel Gance's *J'Accuse* (1918) to Steven Spielberg's *Saving Private Ryan* (1998), there have been mourning films which explored the generational grief wrought by tragic events of universal dimensions. But since this book takes as its focus the emotional and psychoanalytical repercussions of individual loss, this is another area which may more profitably be covered elsewhere. It could be argued that, if these commemorative films mark cinema's attempt to configure "official" histories of 20th century trauma, bold in their scope, lapidary in their inscription, buried deep within the cinema's generic undergrowth amid the annals of melodrama and the "woman's picture" can be found piercing and everyday accounts of grief's psychological cost.

Part of this book's attempt to theorize a genre or type of mourning film emphasizes the contemporary context of domestic spectatorship which has come to play such a key role in the way in which we view films today, and has become increasingly prominent a subject of scrutiny in academic Film Studies. The final chapter explores this reception context in detail, and seeks to propose ways in which this context might give rise to the identification and extrapolation of a new generic type. So a substantial amount of my research took place before a television screen on which I watched DVD copies of mourning films, and as I see it this book is the product of a very specific era of film reception and analysis. The rest of my research took place in various Cambridge college accommodations in which I pored over works of film theory, psychoanalysis, therapeutic literature and modernist literature borrowed from the Cambridge University Library or the libraries of the faculties of Modern and Medieval Languages and English, to whose staff I proffer my thanks for their time and guidance. A significant number of hours was also spent in my supervisor Professor Emma Wilson's office talking about grief and cinema and if it was not for her this book probably would not have been published. I would like to take the opportunity of thanking Emma for the time and insight she bestowed upon this project. I would also like to thank my friend and colleague Dr. Anna Elsner for sharing my interest in grief and mourning and their literary and cinematic repercussions in long and absorbing conversations while involved in our respective academic projects between 2006 and 2009. On two blissful trips to Paris in 2007 and 2008, I spent mornings revising chapters of my PhD sitting with my coffee outside the Café

Rêve on Rue Caulaincourt, and my afternoons studying funerary architecture in the municipal cemeteries of Montmartre and Père Lachaise. I have fond memories of late summer and early autumn afternoons in the beautiful Ménilmontant cemetery as the leaves turned and fell. I would also like to thank Dr. Catherine Grant of Sussex University and Dr. Pam Hirsch of Cambridge University (my examiners in the autumn of 2009) for their cogent, and delighted, assessment of my thesis and their enthusiasm for its future publication. I hope that the extension and enrichment of my arguments has done justice to their faith in the project.

As if in response to the fin-de-siècle efflorescence of mourning films described in this book, in recent years there have been an increasing number of books and academic initiatives in Europe and America around grief and mourning and their audiovisual representation. In 2010, Boaz Hagin's innovative *Death in Classical Hollywood Cinema* appeared from Macmillan. Extending the study of the work of film theorist Gilles Deleuze, a recurrent figure in this book, David Martin-Jones's *Deleuze and World Cinemas* appeared from Continuum in 2011, and related to the theme of liminality and marginality that mourning representations broach, and in 2013 Routledge will be publishing a special edition of *The European Legacy*, the official journal of the International Society for the Study of European Ideas entitled *The Anatomy of Marginality*. In June 2009, a conference devoted to "Envisaging Death: Visual Culture and Dying" took place at the University of Birmingham, UK. In February 2011, there was an international conference at the University of London entitled "The Carnival of Death: Perceptions of Death in Europe and the Americas." Meanwhile, evolving another important theme in the consideration of mourning representation, the third Annual Yale Film Studies Graduate Conference in April 2011 focused on "Sensing Cinema: History, Theory, Body." April also saw the symposium "Film Philosophy and Death" at the University of York, UK. Religious faith and the turn to secular perspectives and solutions to grief form a key strand in the pages that follow. In October 2011 the Universitat Pompeu Fabra in Barcelona, Spain ran a conference on "Religion and Secularity in Contemporary European Cinema." In February 2010 I co-organized with Anna Elsner an interdisciplinary conference entitled "The Moving Image: Reconfiguring Spaces of Loss and Mourning in the 21st Century" at the Centre for Research in the Arts, Social Sciences and Humanities at Cambridge University. And finally, in late 2012 the academic website *Film Philosophy* shall be hosting a special edition devoted to mourning in modern French cinema, co-edited by Anna Elsner and myself. Each of these events and publications signals a growing interest in death and its artistic and social manifestations and contributes to our understanding of a difficult theme and to our appreciation of its artistic outcomes.

This book has sprung from the conviction that art can constitute a way in which we work though difficult experiences. "What place did the arts have in the process of mourning?" Psychoanalyst Darian Leader asks in his book *The New Black*. "And could the arts be a vital tool in allowing us to make sense of the losses inevitable in all of our lives?" In an era in which we habitually consume televised images of death while eating our evening meal, what happens to the individual's apprehension of the loss of those closest to them, or of the fear of their own finitude, a dread which never goes away while obscured within this nocturnal cycle of mortal imagery dressed as entertainment for our dispassionate consumption. We live in a time in which the rituals and customs surrounding death seem themselves to be in terminal decline, the dying banished to clinical hospital corridors and palliative care wards, the dead to desultory procedures at midweek suburban crematoria. Even the words are changing. We refer to death not by its dreadful name, but as "loss," as if in such a sanitized era we are unable to face the grisly biological facts of human demise and decay but can see death only in terms of a missing person, a void in our lives. It is as though these usages have displaced emphasis from the ghastly event which ends the life of another, one experienced by the dying person yet in a vital sense inexperienced, to the consequences for the living. The dead are not now dead, they are "missing." Somehow the words themselves seem to delete the dead, and the event which causes the dead, in favor of the living. Yet perhaps because of this apparent inability to mourn in the time-honored way, to enter unquestioningly into the weeping, the processions, the dress protocols, the wakes of other eras, our rejection of classical mourning may even be leaving us unable to deal with what we coyly term "loss." In banishing death, are we still able to banish the dead? If once the habit of burying their possessions with the dead, the peculiar behaviors surrounding houses of mourning, were meant to ward off spirits, to keep the dead from returning, how does the loss of these protocols leave us feeling inside? How far is modern mourning, in all its lonely singular complicated misery, the result of being unable to ritually banish the dead and to move on with our lives? And does the endless witnessing of broadcast representations of death, whether true or fictional, signify, as Leader suggests, a compulsion to repeat the prospect of demise in an era without adequate representations of the prospect of loss?

Perhaps, in engaging with and exploring our feelings about material death and emotional loss, the mourning film can offer a space for a dialogue around death and what it means to a society which no longer engages in structured mourning. "It is only in art that a man consumed by his desires produces something similar to a satisfaction of them, and that this game — thanks to artistic illusion — creates emotional effects as though they were something real," Sigmund Freud wrote in *Totem and Taboo*, in part an anthropological study of ancient mourning rituals. I would suggest that this creative dialogue operates on two levels. If such films as *Interiors* and *Three Colors: Blue* offer powerful texts for exploring what modern loss feels like, they and other mourning films also grant spaces for their protagonists to explore creative responses to loss. The essential nature of artworks is so obvious that it is easy to remain blind to it. "Works of art," Leader writes, share something very simple. "They have been *made*, and made usually out of an experience of loss or catastrophe." The need to create on the part of the mourning protagonist, and the need to witness the film, on the part of a spectator who feels the film's effects, has original precedents in the sculpted figures, funeral urns, sarcophagi and mummy cases of antiquity, and for us in the narratives of loss examined in this book. While I have so far encountered little professional testimony of mourning films being used in a therapeutic context, I am convinced that the representation of mourning in certain films has such moral and aesthetic complexity and urgency as to make its appeal to professionals, as well as individuals alone in their grief, cogent and irresistible. Having spent the past five years watching and studying the modern cinema of loss, I recommend these films to the grief counselor, the palliative care worker, the psychiatrist, the cinephile, and the mortal lay reader alike.

Introduction

> "The deafening street was screaming all around me.
> Tall, slender, in deep mourning — majestic grief —
> A woman made her way, with fastidious hand"
> *À une passante*, Baudelaire

A Poem Without Words

In the film *Moonlight and Valentino* (David Anspaugh, 1995) Rebecca Trager Lott, a literature instructor at a New England university, returns to work following the sudden death of her husband. Confronting her students for the first time since her bereavement, she embarks on a discussion of affective fallacy. But her discourse breaks down into a series of fragmented remarks about the properties of words: "Words don't taste good, they don't smell good, they don't keep you warm at night, words don't even leave the mind do they? So my assignment ... to you is to write a poem without words." The assignment is clearly absurd, but the intrinsically limited nature of language is a recurrent theme in films that treat themes of grief and mourning. In *Morvern Callar* (Lynne Ramsay, 2001), the bereft protagonist retreats into a kind of muteness, as do the grievers in *Three Colors: Blue* (*Trois Couleurs: Bleu*, Krzysztof Kieślowski, 1993), *Genova* (Michael Winterbottom, 2008), and *I Have Loved You So Long* (*Il y a longtemps que je t'aime*, Philippe Claudel, 2008). In *Hiroshima mon amour* (Alain Resnais, 1959), the very sound and feel of words in the mouth is emphasized. This "loss" of language has implications for the representation of grief, and for the theorization of the images with which films deal with grief.

The failure of words to communicate the ebbs and flows of grief is a recurring theme in this book. Of course, something of the experience is expressible in language. In the consoling family member, in the funeral platitude, in grief counseling, in religious ministry; in the real world it is primarily through language that grief is communicable. In other words, all we know about grief, we know because we interpret its specificity by interpreting words. In everyday life, subjectivity is a complex of energies and transformations at which language grasps, often ineptly, in order to articulate our desires. But in the event of loss, it can seem as though that which we call subjectivity becomes utterly destabilized by grief. It is not the griever who has the symptoms of grief, but, as with a disease affecting the body, the grief "has" the griever, as it were. As Joyce Carol Oates eloquently puts it: "The widow inhabits a tale not of her own telling" (Oates 2011: 81). This book proposes that filmed images offer more astute ways into the experience of grief than words do. While this may seem a paradoxical ambition in a work which must rely chiefly and importantly on words to express itself, I hope through close analysis of individual films to demonstrate how images can yield more of grief's nature than words alone can. Like the client in group therapy who draws in order to express themselves, the film of mourning pictures this condition in continuous permutations of imagery, color, light, sound and *mise-en-scène*.

Although it is an experience which everyone eventually experiences, death is a stark and remote part of life and its affects are unutterable in everyday terms, unthinkable from the daily context. Everyone knows that they are going to die, but the idea seems academic, a mere notion, vague dread rather than expressible experience. For Michele Aaron "death is everywhere yet nowhere in contemporary life. Corpses litter Hollywood films; the threat of violence propels most television dramas; the recently-recovered or slowly dying make bookshelves groan. But the pain and smell of death, the banality of physical, or undignified, decline, is oddly absent. We are surrounded by the facts and features of mortality, yet try not to mention it" (Michele Aaron: http://www.wellbeingindying.org.uk/pdf/guidebook.pdf). Death, whether my own or that of someone close to me, seems too far away to seem a part of this ongoing life. It seems to exist outside consciousness. Wheeler Winston Dixon puts it graphically: "We move through life in a fever dream, acquiring objects, pursuing goals, engaging in trysts, and surviving conflicts until that day when a car swerves into the wrong lane and crashes into our vehicle head-on, or a blood vessel in our brain bursts, or a button is pushed, or, after a night's sleep, we just do not wake up. The total embrace of nothingness thus becomes the unstated goal of existence, a headlong rush into the abyss" (Winston Dixon 2003: 4). We fear death, but human language seems inadequate before the end of life. No other experience we have matches the conundrum by which something happens to us of which we know so little. And no other experience can seem so awful: "For true horror is fear without a definable or specifiable object" (Doane 1988: 141). Gestures increasingly take the place of words. Elisabeth Kübler-Ross writes of caring for the dying: "Our communications then become more nonverbal than verbal. The patient may just make a gesture of the hand to invite us to sit down for a while. He may just hold our hand and ask us to sit in silence. Such moments of silence may be the most meaningful communications for people who are not uncomfortable in the presence of a dying person" (Kübler-Ross 2003: 124).

The Vicissitudes of Speaking

Moonlight and Valentino initially derives its power from the suddenness of Ben Lott's death. One minute he is jogging, the next he is lying dead after being hit by a passing car. In his essay "The Instant of My Death," Maurice Blanchot tries to approach the knowledge of death in the anecdote of a young man sentenced to death, then summarily reprieved. Blanchot writes, "There remained [...] at the moment when the shooting was no longer but to come, the feeling of lightness that I would not know how to translate: freed from life? the infinite opening up? Neither happiness, nor un-happiness. Nor the absence of fear and perhaps already the step beyond. I know, I imagine that this unanalyzable feeling changed what there remained for him of existence" (Blanchot 2000: 7 & 9). In his commentary on Blanchot's piece, Jacques Derrida speaks of an "inexperienced experience" (Blanchot 2000: 47), describing the conundrum whereby at the moment of my death: "Death has already taken place. Yet this past, to which I testify, namely, my death itself, has never been present" (ibid.: 49–50). Inexpressible, inconceivable, inexperiencable, death leaves a "forgetting" for Blanchot (ibid.: 51), which makes the event of death incommensurable with the events of one's life, with the idea of "event" as we understand it. For Blanchot: "All that remains is the feeling of lightness that is death itself or, to put it more precisely, the instant of my death henceforth always in abeyance" (ibid.: 11).

I shall here illustrate the test which death poses for language. For Blanchot and Derrida, the attempt to describe death exposes a fracture between everyday language and another kind of speaking. There are the metaphysical platitudes of C.S. Lewis, which frustrate even this Christian apologist. While my mortality is unthinkable, the death of another brings feelings which are just as difficult to put into words. In *A Grief Observed*, Lewis writes: "I think I am beginning to understand why grief feels like suspense. It comes from the frustration of so many impulses that had become habitual. Thought after thought, feeling after feeling, action after action, had H for their object. Now their target has gone. I keep on through habit fitting an arrow to the string; then I remember and have to lay the bow down. So many roads lead thought to H…. So many roads once; now so many culs-de-sac" (Lewis 1966: 41). Language itself seems in a kind of suspense before the prospect of finitude. In the cinema of mourning, characters are in limbo — shocked and still — before the loss of those dearest to them. Jonathan Dollimore describes death as "a signifier with an incessantly receding, ungraspable signified" (Dollimore 1998: 127), "the mystifying banality by which we live" (ibid.: 192).

So we fall back on clichés to soothe and console. While in *Cinema's Missing Children*, Emma Wilson describes loss as: "annihilating, immense and nonsensical" (Wilson 2003: 10), such adjectives seem simultaneously apt but overlarge, unsubtle signifiers for a stillness which responds inadequately to the commonplaces of language. For Joan Didion, there is no way of knowing the difference between grief as we imagine it to be, and the actual experience of grief. She struggles to fill "the unending absence that follows, the void, the very opposite of meaning, the relentless succession of moments during which we will confront the experience of meaninglessness itself" (Didion 2005c: 189).

The need to exceed verbal expression is complicated by the relationship between the trauma of losing someone close to us and one's own fear of mortality. This book will explore the role played by one's own fear of mortality in mourning for others. The prospect of the death of another evokes the realization that we too will sooner or later die. This existential knowledge is especially acute for those who witness others dying of wasting illnesses. If traditional funeral ritual appeals to our supposed communion in the hereafter, the anticipation of grief reinforces the notion of solidarity with all the inexpressible pity that goes with it. As Sigmund Freud writes, when someone close to us dies, "our hopes, our desires and our pleasures lie in the grave with him" (Freud 1917: 290). William Worden suggests the link between my grief and my mortality: "As you watch someone deteriorate during a progressive illness, you cannot help but identify with the process, having some awareness that this too might be your own fate" (Worden 1991: 109). To witness this experience is to see something of the incompatibility of life and death, two states which are intimately related yet irreducibly alien from each other. In a testimony written following her husband's death, Gem Duncan writes: "Not being means that there is no interpretation available so it's like living perpetually inside a mystery which I'm never going to solve […] all our lives are mysterious and mysteriously going to end, but the real enigma is that we have no part, or say, or opinion or perspective on the most significant thing we ever do" (Duncan 2009: 1).

The pathological details of terminal pain and bodily decay, the brute reduction of subjectivity to grisly material otherness is a compelling reason why death is something that we find difficult to contemplate. Dollimore writes:

"It could be said that we can begin to understand the vital role of death in Western culture only when we accept death as profoundly, compellingly and irreducibly traumatic" (Dollimore 1998: 126). Putrefaction and decay is a recurring theme in this book, and death's psychological impact is intimately related to the horror of contemplating such decay as one's own. Freud proffers the real conundrum: "It is indeed impossible to imagine our own death; and whenever we attempt to do so we can perceive that we are in fact still present as spectators" (Freud 1917: 289).

How to write about death when language seems so inadequate to describe it? Cathy Caruth writes of "the ineradicable gap between the reality of a death and the desire that cannot overcome it" (Caruth 1996: 95). Psychoanalysis recognizes how grief recalls the characteristic attempt at engagement between psyche and reality, a raw confrontation which is undiminished, un-curtailed and un-consoled by language or reason. The grief-stricken speak of a "scrambled" mental life (Duncan 2009: 2), a diminishing ability to prioritize, remember or think laterally, and the perception that one is stuck in a dream. Worden relates: "One young widow said to me, 'I keep waiting for someone to wake me and tell me I'm dreaming'" (Worden 1991: 26). For Lewis "there is a sort of invisible blanket between the world and me. I find it hard to take in what anyone says. Or perhaps hard to want to take it in. It is so uninteresting" (Lewis 1966: 5).

As a model for that raw experience which confronts the psyche so insistently yet so inexpressibly, Jacques Lacan's notion of the Real is a crucial though difficult psychoanalytical register for our purposes. If the Symbolic register, that of the language through which experience and sensation is mediated, is a realm of words that create a world of things, the Real is that which lies outside language and which resists symbolization absolutely. For Lacan, the Real is "impossible"; impossible to imagine, impossible to integrate into the Symbolic, and impossible to attain. The Real is the object of anxiety, "the essential object which is not an object any longer, but this something faced with which all words cease and all categories fail, the object of anxiety par excellence" (Lacan 2004) It is not difficult to read death as an aspect of the Real, our profoundest fear yet impossible to speak. And like the Real, grief, the consequence of death for those left behind, lacks sense or meaning. It cannot be grasped or engaged with. Like the Real, we struggle to mediate grief through a symbolic system which for Lacan is already inadequate to the expression of human desire. So grief manifests itself in affects, which are too inexpressible, too uncontainable, too awful for verbal articulation. In his recounting of the burning child in *The Interpretation of Dreams*, Freud told of a father's dream in which his dead son appears at his bedside and admonishes the father for neglecting his vigil, causing the child to be burnt by a toppling candle. For Caruth, here lies the very pivot between life and death, the interface between two incommensurable ideas. The father "receives the very gap between the other's death and his own life, the one who, in awakening, does not see but enacts the impact of the very difference between life and death" (Caruth 1996: 106) This pivot informs the differing interpretations which Freud and Lacan confer. While for Freud the dream contains the father's relieved denial of his child's death, for Lacan it embodies the ghastly reiteration of loss and the guilt which presses in upon a father who was unable to save his child. Lacan writes: "But the terrible vision of the dead son taking the father by the arm designates a beyond that makes itself heard in the dream. Desire manifests itself in the dream by the loss expressed in an image at the most cruel point of the object. It is only in the dream that this truly unique encounter can occur" (Lacan 2004: 59). For Wilson, this gross insistence stands for the ineffable absolute of the Real, the "fear, suffering and sensation beyond language" (Wilson 2003: 9). What is represented in Freud's anecdote as dream, a parallel reality which may express the desire to see the child alive, or may express the unthinkable prospect of negligence, in the mourning film is taken beyond this "beyond" of dead facticity, the knowledge that the loved person is no longer alive, to a space more powerful for being more present.

In mourning cinema, the Lacanian Real can be apprehended in the knowledge of unforeseeable decay and unutterable physical squalor. In Western societies naming muck and detritus invites dismay in polite circles. What words, and what moving images try to do in mourning films is to negotiate the emotional consequences of loss as it reverberates through the bereaved, a psychological horror which is physiologically reinforced by the site, and the sight, of death in all of its disgusting nature. Lacan writes: "The real does not wait, and specifically not for the subject, since it expects nothing from the word. But it is there ... a noise in which everything can be heard, and ready to submerge in its outbursts what the 'reality principle' constructs within it under the name of external world" (Lacan 1977: 388). Such "outbursts," beyond the scope of language to protect the polite observer, manifest themselves in shocking images of death and decay in the mourning film, taking the image beyond safe constructs and viscerally affecting protagonist and spectator. This excessive imagery recalls the mourning film's debt to its antecedents in horror cinema, a genre which has traditionally explored death and the afterlife. Such disgusting moments also seem seminal for cinema as form. The spectator's aghast response is a response to the film *as a film*, to the brute facticity of the impression something foul has made on celluloid, reiterating a sense in which the mourning film broaches something of the "natural" status of cinema as a series of arresting images of things which once were unutterably there.

Grounding the discussion of representation in the observations of trauma and counseling literature, this book draws upon the work of a range of theorists. Freud looms prominently in the theorization of grief. His seminal discussion of mourning and melancholia reverberates through the representation of grief in therapeutic literature and in mourning art. Freud acknowledges grief's mystery: "We do not even know the economic means by which mourning carries out its task" (Freud 1917: 255). In his essay "Anxiety, Pain and Mourning" (1926), he writes: "I found that there was one feature about [mourning] which remained quite unexplained. This was its peculiar painfulness" (Freud 1926: 329). The pain of mourning derives, for Freud, from the deep-seated and complex relationship between love and hate which can exist in the mourner. In the essay "Our Attitude Towards Death" (1915), Freud writes of how, behind every person we loved, however familiar, there was a stranger, and behind every profession of love, however ardent, lay a desire to subdue its opposite, an instinct to hate. This ambivalence informs the distinction at the heart of Freud's most important statement on grief. Published in 1917 in light of the huge losses of World War I, *Mourning and Melancholia* contains Freud's attempt to distinguish the behavioral implications of this relationship. He writes of a melancholic ego, dejected, listless, and full of self-reproach. If the mourning individual, having accepted their loss, ideally recovers after a period of time, where there was ambivalence in the relationship melancholia persists: "In mourning it is the world which has become poor and empty, in melancholia it is the ego itself" (Freud 1917: 246). The psychic economy behind melancholia gives rise to a peculiar misery. Freud writes: "If the love for the object — a love which cannot be given up though the object itself is given up — takes refuge in narcissistic identification, then the hate comes into operation on this substitutive subject, abusing it, debasing it, making it suffer and deriving sadistic satisfaction from its suffering" (ibid.: 251). Grief counselors employ the term "complicated mourning" in cases where the mourner's feelings were divided when the person was alive, and remain divided after they are gone, leading to a protracted mourning. For Freud, ambivalent feelings in the survivor need not be overt or even recognized, leading to odd and conflicted moods and reactions: "The complex of melancholia behaves like an open wound, drawing to itself cathartic energies ... from all directions, and emptying the ego" (ibid.: 253). What this complex bequeaths to the mourning film cannot be underestimated, lending extraordinary energies to the performance and resolution of grief. Freud poignantly evokes the demeanor of characters stranded in barren places, alone and steeped in sadness and rage.

In *Beyond the Pleasure Principle* (1920), Freud's delineation of the death drive, the organism's inevitable tendency to return to a state of material decay and inertia can be seen to inform the horrendous inevitability of a demise hovering insistently over both loved one and mourner. In proposing the return to materiality, Freud here anticipates the grisly decay and detritus which the mourning protagonist seems drawn to. The return, whether to inorganic slime or to ancient ways of negotiating the fear of death echoes in Freud's work. In *The Uncanny* (1919), he writes: "There is scarcely any other matter ... upon which our thoughts and feelings have changed so little since the very earliest times, and in which discarded forms have been so completely preserved under a thin disguise, as our relation to death" (Freud 1919: 364). Archaic fears and phenomena link the mourning genre to horror cinema — fear of the dark, ghosts, primitive totems — resonating in the modern mourning film as dementia, hallucinations, and the susceptibility of children. The importance of Freud to an understanding of the mourning film cannot be underestimated. He made death the destiny of all living things, describing a human condition always already in thrall to death and the signs and images with which it is associated. And in charting the impact of loss on the psychology of the individual, Freud showed how grief shapes our ability to negotiate the external world and to relate to others.

Presence/Absence

So the mourner is importantly in two places, here and "there." "Along with ... the teller of ghost stories, the griever is always on the edge of another universe, a cosmos that aches with possibility, like a phantom limb" (Gilbert 2006: 63). Given the difficulties of using language to talk about this interstitial state, the cinema's investment in images seems peculiarly apt to the expression of loss and its liminal consequences, making the mourning film essential to an understanding of how cinema works as an apparatus. Pasolini points to the uniquely obscure nature of the cinematic image: "Cinematographic communication would ... seem to be arbitrary and aberrant, without the concrete instrumental precedents which are normally used by all ... people communicate with words, not images; therefore, a specific language of images would seem to be a pure and artificial abstraction" (cited in Orr 2000: 37). Abstraction, both psychological and visual, is central to the way mourning cinema moves, asserts itself, weaves its spell. From its very beginnings, the moving image seemed to evoke ghosts, the flicker of memory and sorrow in which the mourner lives. Laura Mulvey alludes to this perpetual trembling between life and death, animation and stasis in her book *Death 24× a Second: Stillness and the Moving Image* (2006). She quotes film historian Ian Christie: "Both the Paris papers which reported the first Lumière show ended on the same note ... death will cease to be absolute ... it will be possible to see our nearest alive again long after they have gone" (cited in Mulvey 2006: 46).

Given this fundamental ambiguity, grief is about interpretation and translation. Writers struggle to make sense of loss. Grief has to be re-thought, re-conceptualized, for us to live through it, supposing even this is possible. The films looked at in this book must compensate for the failures of language as a means of talking a way through grief, while some — *Truly, Madly, Deeply* (Anthony Minghella, 1990), *Birth* (Jonathan Glazer, 2004), *Ponette* (Jacques Doillon, 1996), *Three Colors: Blue*— make interpretation part of their dramatic and cinematic project. As the protagonist tries to make sense of what has happened to them, interpretation becomes a metaphor for what we as spectators need to do in order to make sense of the images we are watching. Grief's hermeneutic character cogently links it to cinema, making those films which explore grief helpful texts for the analysis of the experience. Grief and cinema are about making sense of absence.

The relationship between grief and absence has implications for the spectator confronted by an absence on which the apparatus of cinema projects presence. When the spectator sits before the screen, they sit before an image masquerading as something real. The knowledge that what is being looked at, typically adored, admired, longed for in the filmgoing scenario, but is not actually there, evokes the relationship between spectatorship and grief since grief is the emotional consequence of our investment in something that we can "see" in our mind's "eye" but which no longer exists. In the filmgoing scenario emotional proximity is keyed to the spectator's desire that the image be real, that it be there in all its plenitude, satisfying the need to project our desire onto an object which will apparently return our love by simply being there. Adoration of the image is a projection of desire before the fact of non-existence. This makes cinema spectatorship curiously akin to another form of image projection.

If film studies academics have made much of the parallel histories of psychoanalysis and cinema, the rise of the cinema also coincided with the rise of spiritualism in Britain and America in the late–1800s. While spiritualism answered the nineteenth century need for reconciliation between science and faith, it also provides a metaphor for the modern pastime of cinema. This cultural investment in the image conjured from the ether, one which is simultaneously present and absent, reinforces the link between cinema and grief, and emphasizes mourning cinema's claim to integral status in the account of how cinema works. The realization that the image is only an image, and that the image, like the objects we love outside the cinema, eventually perishes, powerfully informs films which trade in the feelings that loss gives rise to, texts, in other words, in which the play of presence and absence is inscribed in the image. As Mulvey writes: "The cinema has constantly ... exploited its ghostly qualities, its ability to realize irrational fears" (Mulvey 2006: 176).

Absence and loss was a common theme in the "woman's picture" strand of classical melodrama, another current which informs the modern mourning film. Writing of the wartime Hollywood melodrama *Tender Comrade* (Edward Dmytryck, 1943), Mary Ann Doane observes: "Each of the women keeps a photograph of an absent husband next to her bed so that the all-female house is laced with reminders of male presence" (Doane 1988: 80).

In their respective theorizations of photography and film, French theorists Roland Barthes and André Bazin were especially aware of the need for memorialization that photographic images satisfy, and the chronicle of presence and absence which they propose. For its status as indexical record of reality, the cinema is a peculiarly privileged medium for engaging with bereaved subjectivity and remembrance. While registering the solidity of the external world, and deploying color, editing and camerawork to explore interiority, cinema crosses the threshold between outer conditions and inner states. And like the objects and evidence coveted by the grief-stricken, the mourning film is a memorial to the passing of a life; for the protagonist that of the person they have lost, and for the spectator that of the survivor figure with whom they have identified. Laura Marks writes: "What this look (the human figure dispersed across the surface of the screen) enacts is something like a perpetual mourning, something like melancholia in its refusal to have done with death" (Marks 2002: 91). Haunting Marks's book is a generalized sense of loss over history's disposal of people and memories. The cinema, its releases fleeting, its archives vulnerable to deterioration, its software endlessly superceded, could almost be read as a history of loss and decay: "Faded films, decaying videotapes, projected videos that flaunt their tenuous connection to the reality they index; all appeal to a look of love and loss" (ibid.: 91).

Memory is intrinsic to the nature and history of cinema. Both as apparatus and as archive, the cinema preserves what is gone, embalms what is dead, recalls what has passed. From the mid–1980s to the late–2000s, a range of fiction and non-fiction films from the multiplex and the arthouse wrestled with questions of memory, a topic which shall ebb and flow throughout this book. While "important" releases such as *Titanic* (James Cameron, 1997), *Schindler's List* (Steven Spielberg, 1993), *Saving Private Ryan* (Steven Spielberg, 1998), and *Shoah* (Claude Lanzmann, 1985) proposed cinema as a form of collective remembrance, the weekly schedules of multiplexes and arthouses were seldom short of movies — *Truly, Madly, Deeply*, *The Bridges of Madison County* (Clint Eastwood, 1995), *Fried Green Tomatoes at the Whistle Stop Café* (Jon Avnet, 1991), *Birth*, *Alice* (Woody Allen, 1990), *Festen* (Thomas Vinterberg, 1998), even *Blade Runner* (Ridley Scott, 1982/1991) — in which micro histories are generated from personal recollection. Some of these films emphasized the role of memory in knowledge, narrative as recollection and testimony.

Woody Allen was a director whose 1980s output, straddling the mainstream and art cinema, foresaw the progressive blurring of these distinctions in the contemporary arthouse. The preoccupation with memory resonates in the words of Marion in *Another Woman* (Woody Allen, 1988): "Is a memory something you have, or something you have lost?"

This book will show how modernist and postmodern film aesthetics generated powerful accounts of aggrieved subjectivity and of the nature of cinema. The wraithlike blues in *Three Colors: Blue*, the rapt looks in *Under the Sand* (*Sous le sable*, François Ozon, 2000), the swirling strobe lights in *Morvern Callar*, the unbidden presence in *Birth*, the "excessive" quality of off-screen space in mourning film after mourning film mobilize cinema's energies to contemplate how film has negotiated a phenomenon central to itself and to each and every one of its spectators' lives.

The 1990s saw widespread experimentation on the cinematic image. From computer-generated graphics to the severe aesthetics of the Dogme movement to the fractious video revelations of *The Blair Witch Project* (Daniel Myrick and Eduardo Sanchez, 1999), the decade saw a wholesale reassessment of the relationship between the image and the object. A hundred years after cinema's first appearance, the 1990s was another film-historical juncture when technology enhanced the magical quality of cinema, its ability to conjure simultaneous presence and absence on a bare wall. It is significant that this time of technological innovation coincided with the widespread exploration of grief. With its play of presence and absence, of what lies just out of reach visually and emotionally, *The Blair Witch Project* seemed to epitomize the era's preoccupation with interiority, a taste broadly exemplified in contemporary American independent cinema's investment in acting and dialogue over the rampant production values and special effects of the 1980s Hollywood mainstream. While the film is conventionally seen as a lodestone of modern horror cinema, its pity for lost children and its interest in psychological dementia cast telling shadows across the mourning genre. Significant, too, is the fact that many of the films examined in this book were based on original screenplays. Like the aesthetics with which they explored grief and mourning, these films were creatures of cinema, less attached to the problematics of language than visually felt attempts to render emotions, to record the results of individual encounters with human demise. These films did not try to *tell* of loss, they tried to *show* it.

One of the most successful arthouse hits of the 1990s was the French film *La Reine Margot* (Patrice Chéreau, 1994), its bloody funereal air tempered with a plea for social cohesion during a key election year in France. Starring the Franco-Algerian Isabelle Adjani and rehearsing the tragedy of religious strife, the film also resonated with the AIDS crisis then at its height in France.

Savage Nights (*Les Nuits fauves*, Cyril Collard, 1992) focused on a young man diagnosed HIV-positive who, in defiance of his death sentence, lives life to the full. Revolving giddily around its protagonist's passion and grief, the film's ethical and stylistic brinkmanship suggested the "death of cinema" discourse, that is of a certain postwar conception of arthouse cinema, current among critics in the 1990s. In hindsight, the death of director Cyril Collard before the film's release adds to its sense of portent. Meanwhile, in America AIDS awareness found expression in the multiplex and arthouse releases *Philadelphia* (Jonathan Demme, 1993) and *One Night Stand* (Mike Figgis, 1997).

Another of the most successful arthouse films of the era was *Three Colors: Blue*, an eviscerating treatment of grief and its affects and the subject of a case study in Chapter 3 of this book. The Danish title *Festen* saw the much-vaunted "DIY" resolve of the Dogme realists break down into a shadowy form of magic realism before the sight of the departed. True to its pragmatic American Protestant roots, the crossover hit *The Blair Witch Project* left us with the brute facticity of abandoned artifacts, more savagely unspeakable for being so crassly matter-of-fact. Appearing in British multiplexes the same autumn as *The Blair Witch Project*, *The Sixth Sense* (M. Night Shyamalan, 1999) not only reinstalled, as had *The Blair Witch Project*, the audience's imagination as a component of horror after decades of literal-minded "slasher" horror, but also reinvested the uncanny with a sense of melancholy.

Owing to considerations of space, case studies in this book focus on a limited number of the films mentioned here. But I hope that by concentrated attention to particular texts, the treatment of grief in these films will resonate with other titles. By drawing antecedents and primary texts alike from the established genres of horror and melodrama, and crossing between the arthouse and the multiplex, Europe and America, this book seeks to propose fresh ways of looking at particular films in a new generic context, and a new spectatorship context with implications for the habitual categorization of films. So the canvas is large, potentially unwieldy, and demands particular organizing principles. The postwar evolution from classical narrative realism to experimental modernisms crucially shapes this book, providing, as that progression did, for an increasingly nuanced account of human interiority. In this regard, *Hiroshima mon amour*, *Cries and Whispers* (*Fiskningar och rop*, Ingmar Bergman, 1972), *Don't Look Now* (Nicolas Roeg, 1973), and *Interiors* (Woody Allen, 1978) mobilized the aesthetic lessons of the postwar decades, making these films key texts in a modern cinema of mourning. Other factors play into the historical progression. The relaxation of censorship in the 1960s facilitated the representation of more "difficult" experiences. Recurring titles in this book are *The Haunting* (Robert Wise, 1963), *The Innocents* (Jack Clayton,

1961), and *Carnival of Souls* (Herk Harvey, 1962), horror films thematically and stylistically informing the emergence of the mourning film, all of which were shaped by the new moral atmosphere of the era.

Private Spaces, Public Rituals

The apparent surge of cinematic interest in grief during the 1990s also resonated more widely. In a world without the consolations of Christian ritual, yet increasingly vulnerable to horrendous, apparently random, instances of public and private violence, grief counseling and trauma therapy became secular methodologies with widespread application. In a post–Christian society, the need to talk and memorialize becomes expressed in cultural artifacts. While the death of the popular British media "princess" Diana Spencer in 1997 saw an unprecedented show of public grief around the world, unusually for a cheaply made British arthouse title, *Secrets and Lies* (Mike Leigh, 1995) won large audiences and Oscar recognition, its portrait of mourning and plea for a compassionate status quo seeming to foresee Diana's death, arguably a key moment in the ethical and political history of modern Britain. Another high profile film of 1997 which made a powerful appeal to contemporary millennial apprehensions was *Titanic*. Both *Titanic* and *Secrets and Lies* effectively extended their portraits of personal grief to broach a more universal emotional atmosphere. Part of the reason for the fabulous profits enjoyed by *Titanic* in 1997–98 was repeat attendance by teenage girls, for whom the film became something akin to a ritual. Some films lend themselves to the expression of community pathos in an age when funeral ritual has become for many just that — a ritual rather than an opportunity to grieve, a symptom of our atomized lives rather than a symbol of our shared condition.

Identification of the big commemorative release opens up an important distinction within the mourning repertoire. *Titanic, Secrets and Lies, Saving Private Ryan, Schindler's List* and *Shoah* are without doubt appropriate titles in the mourning canon. But while they belong there, this book shall focus deliberately on the vicissitudes of individual mourning and its expression. Drawing on major historical events implying a generational suffering and memorialization, the big commemorative release focuses less on the intricacies of bereaved subjectivity and more on cinema's capacity to enshrine generational hurt. Such a project is very different from that of exploring the nuances of subjectivity undertaken in *Three Colors: Blue, Interiors,* or *Hiroshima mon amour,* for example, even given the latter's historical instincts. The film of commemorative mourning is too preoccupied with history's larger narrative, too busy carving their names with pride, to consider the oddness, unpredictable and sometimes subversive attitudes of the mourning protagonist in films constituting the genre's heartland. While *Saving Private Ryan* and *Morvern Callar* are both mourning films, they live in very different precincts of the genre, and if the framing journey to the Normandy cemetery in the former could be seen as a metaphor for a younger generation's dutiful attendance for the film, the melodramas of grief explored or alluded to in this book are psychological case studies commemorating very singular journeys.

This distinction prompts us back to the efficacy of the mourning film's representations for the all-too-mortal spectator. What are we to make of the four women, their faces painted, cavorting in a churchyard on a rainy night in *Moonlight and Valentino*? What does this tell us about the adequacy of contemporary rituals of bereavement and memorialization? Amid an atomized, seemingly irreligious status quo, the performative gesture, emptied of reference to a divinity, apparently carries more weight today than the devotional attitudes of the past. Arguably, this is what makes grief and mourning such a fascinating psychological area, and the mourning film such an unpredictable and enticing type. In a secular world, other sites offer stages for the recognition of grief. The Internet has become another space for commemoration and memorialization. With its characteristic lonely surfer, it recalls the loneliness of the griever, communing in an ether strewn with commemorative websites and appeals for missing persons. Perhaps the devotional attitude of the solitary mourner is all we have left of God. The mourning film, like the woman's picture before it, its typical spectator alone in the dark, perhaps performs the same cathartic function as the rituals of the funeral did for past generations, helping to focus sorrow and vulnerability amid a maze of difficult days.

The Grieving Woman

Why emphasize films representing a woman's grief? Part of the rationale is personal. This book sprang from, and was to some extent made possible by, the sudden death of my brother-in-law, an experience which finds traces in extracts from a testimonial written by my sister that informs some of its observations. In English, my sister is now referred to as a "widow." While in that language the specifically gendered term "actress" is derived from "actor" and "poetess" from "poet," the male equivalent "widower" is a back formation from "widow." This infrequent linguistic construction carries the strong suggestion that the grieving archetype, at least in Anglo cultures, is female (although the pairing "veuve/veuf" in French suggests a similar linguistic and cultural progression in other Western contexts). So the rationale for the gender emphasis in this book is importantly cultural, as well as cinematic. There is a long tradition in Western culture of the suffering or sacrificed woman. Since Renaissance depictions of the Virgin Mary, the assumption that women are more sensitive, intuitive and empathetic than men, more disposed to shows of public suffering and pity, more physically traumatized in their religious devotions, is widely reproduced in the visual arts and in literature. As Ruth Anthony El Saffar shows, in sixteenth century Europe such predispositions led to persecution: "Increasingly from 1517 ... women experiencing raptures, ecstasies, and visions were believed to be under the devil's power" (Anthony El Saffar 1994: 86). Disillusionment with scientific explanations and patriarchal hegemony led many in the nineteenth century to shun official religion in favor of spiritualism and the consolations of the séance. For Colin Davis, this momentous shift led to nothing less than the "supernaturalization" of human consciousness itself. If ghosts were once the external traces of dead souls in limbo before a biblically underwritten Heaven, they were "now inside our heads rather than roaming the outside world, and human subjectivity has been infiltrated by alien, irrational, spectral forces" (Griffiths & Evans 2009: 17). As philosophical rationalism, with all its patriarchal trappings, became entrenched with the Enlightenment, and Europe consolidated into nation states, marginalized or discontented women flocked to the devotional life. The cultural link between gender and moral exceptionality, or delinquency, persists. Classical and post-classical films evince a fascination with "spiritual" women from Bernadette of Lourdes to Sophie Scholl. *Don't Look Now* thematizes the distinction between "masculine" rationalism and "feminine" intuition, to cite just one example. While he, to his peril, rejects the spiritualist gestures in which his bereft wife seeks succor, her grief finds her increasingly drawn to a medium whose innate intelligence makes her the uncanny legatee of Western culture's intuitions, and paranoia, about women visionaries.

This "feminine" temper has fed into official culture in ways which would have far-reaching implications for modernity's investment in representations of women. Victorian melodrama habitually courted audience sympathy for the woman or young girl in distrait. Such a predilection was seen to have a physiological foundation. In the Victorian era, many a female malaise was put down to "nerves." Doane quotes Michel Foucault's observation of the perception that "the entire female body is riddled with obscure but strangely direct paths of sympathy; it is always in an immediate complicity with itself, to the point of forming a kind of absolutely privileged site for the sympathies" (cited in Doane 1988: 68). A feminist writing on melodrama in the 1980s, Doane sees this physiological "sympathy" recalled in the cinema spectator's identification with the suffering heroine. The image of the woman suffering or sacrificed has been a staple of mainstream cinema ever since the *Perils of Pauline* matinee serial in the 1900s, while the woman-in-peril, whether physical or psychological, recurs in a range of cinematic models for female sorrow. A guiding assumption of this book is that the most exemplary protagonist of the mourning film has been female. Not that grieving men do not recur in its annals, but that films revolving around a woman's grief seem so salient that an exploratory work is bound to proceed with this gender bias in mind.

It will be noticed, however, that only one of the films closely studied in this book was directed by a woman. Given the propensity, cultural and cinematic, for women to bear the pain and suffering of grief and mourning, why are there not more films of mourning in the name of the female auteur? Leaving aside the historical truism that it has always been more difficult for a woman to accede to the rank of film director than a man and that, in Hollywood as elsewhere, women directors are few and far between, we must concede that the mourning film has not distinguished itself as a vehicle for women filmmakers. Given its legacy of "feminine" suffering, arguably it has become another vehicle for patriarchal ideas about the feminine temper, more feminine than feminist, perhaps. If in the type's defense we point to the many women involved behind the scenes — Marguerite Duras, Kristi Zea, Jeanne Lapoirie, Lizie Gower, Ellen Simon — of the various projects explored here, we must not forget the actresses before the camera who have shaped modern cinematic mourning, a veritable pantheon of mourning divas. But what makes *Morvern Callar*, the only woman-directed case study here, all the more interesting is the glimpse it offers of a "female" mourning film, an instance in which an arguably masculine cinematic perception of female vulnerability (reinforced in this instance, as the book upon which the film was based was written by a man) has been read through the eyes of a woman director. While this study proceeds with a determinedly thematic, as opposed to auteurist, bias in mind, it cannot help viewing the prospect of further explorations of grief by women filmmakers with great interest. As Robin Wood writes: "[I]t remains unproven that the patriarchal language of mainstream narrative film cannot be transformed and redeemed, that a woman's discourse cannot speak through it" (Wood cited in Erens 1990: 344).

If film history is strewn with the traumatized bodies of women, since its earliest days the cinema has also made a special appeal to women. Early British film star Alma Taylor wrote that "with the invention of the cinema, women secured, for the first time, a form of entertainment which was peculiarly their own" (Taylor cited in Lant 2006: 7). In the classical decades women film writers in Britain and America "wrote of it as a precious refuge of their personal landscape," observe Antonia Lant and Ingrid Periz, "as a force ... for emotional transport: cinema 'makes itself her weepery,' as Dorothy Richardson put it" (ibid. 2006: 1). Cinema's special appeal to women is mirrored by the success of particular formulae in exhibition schedules. Long traditions of filmmaking which treat feelings and subjectivity revolve around female protagonists. As feminist writers in the 1970s and 1980s would show, the mass audiences of the 1930s and 1940s were significantly female, and melodrama came into its own as a palliative for stultifying domestic existences and diminished expectations. The cinema of mourning shares distinctive preoccupations and characteristics with the industry "woman's picture," a staple mainstream genre by the late–1930s and 1940s in Britain and America, distinguished as much by its dedicated generic label as by its preoccupation with charting the travails of female protagonists. Consonant with Victorian perceptions of the female hysteric, pathological and persecutory conditions, "masochism, hysteria, neurosis, paranoia" (Doane 1988: 36), often associated with "the feminine condition" (ibid.: 36), recur in this genre. The mourning film continues this preoccupation with female interiority, making the exploration of pity, empathy, disappointment and longing its own. "There is something extremely compelling about women's films," Doane writes, "with their constantly recurring figures of the unwed mother, the waiting wife, the abandoned mistress, the frightened newlywed or the anguished mother" (ibid.: 3). Significantly, many of these generic archetypes, for their essential condition of abandonment, could be interpreted as the primary protagonist of the mourning genre: the widow. Writing on melodrama, Daniel Gerould draws attention to gender, while emphasizing the plight of a protagonist who, like a widow, becomes the tool of her predicament: "melodrama is devoid of "heroes" possessing free activity who make their destinies for themselves. The dramatic spring is not the character, but the plot with its emotional bases; the characters are only its "tools," and are defined in their character traits only as much as is necessary for motivating the progression of the plot" (cited in Neale 1974: 198). One can see in this description the plight of a figure who does not have, but is "had," by her predicament.

Horror cinema has also fertilized the mourning film in important ways. As C.S. Lewis observed, the links between grief and suspense seem extraordinarily apposite to our purpose, both emotionally and stylistically. If the horror film generates and feeds on fear, its aesthetics are designed to create apprehension: "Grief still feels like fear. Perhaps more strictly, like suspense. Or like waiting; just hanging about waiting for something to happen" (Lewis: 29). Preoccupied with scenarios of loss and sacrifice, animated by themes of masochism, the lachrymal gesture, chance, coincidence and the uncanny, the horror film and the woman's picture together bequeath particular sentiments and attitudes to the mourning film as surely as both genres reproduced such traditional notions of the "feminine" as passivity, emotionalism and intuition. Feminist writing has sought to show how, despite their patriarchal agendas, the excessive emotionalism of these popular genres generated energies which effectively complicate their subscription to the status quo. This book demonstrates how such energies continue to animate a contemporary mourning film which resembles the inadvertent child of horror and the woman's picture. If the dramatization of presence and absence in the mourning film chimes with cinema's essence, its focus on the experiences and emotions of the cinema's most perennial and historically significant audience suggests an important multiplex and arthouse phenomenon.

While fault lines of gender do cut across the mourning genre, the archetypal mourning film, like its forebear the woman's picture of the classical era, remains a female preserve. Some of the most interesting films about grief had women at their heart, irrespective of their cultural and institutional origins. As we shall see, manifestations of mourning in the 1990s and 2000s find women grieving, lost and alone.

A New Genre

The choice of the modest genre multiplex title *Moonlight and Valentino* at the beginning of this Introduction is deliberate. *Moonlight and Valentino* is an example of a practice with particular relevance to the exploration of grief in cinema. Some of the most powerful films about grief sat on the cusp of melodrama and horror. Part of what is uncanny about certain films is the excess of emotion. While melodrama pervades the horror scenario, a kind of horror materializes when melodrama becomes excessively emotional. *The Haunting*, *The Innocents* and *Carnival of Souls*, appearing at the end of Hollywood classicism as European modernist experiments grappled with issues of interiority, all dealt with a woman's loneliness before the prospect of eternity. Illustrating how American and European cinema in the last decade saw moments of generic and industrial cross-pollination, the Gothic horror melodramas *The Others* (*Los Otros*, Alexandro Amenábar, 2001) and *The Orphanage* (*El Orfanato*, Juan Antonio Bayona, 2007) featured British and American actors, were directed and crewed by Spanish filmmakers, and toyed with themes from *The Innocents* and *The Haunting*. They also revolved around women coming to terms with loss. Conversely, *Titanic* and *Festen*, which could be described, despite differing exhibition contexts, as family melodramas, both have an edge of the uncanny. Torn between the effigy of Debra Winger's cancer-ridden form in *Shadowlands* (Richard Attenborough, 1993), and the increasingly lachrymose prospect of her death, upon its release audiences at Cambridge Arts Cinema screenings were visibly upset as they made for the exits. As many mourning films attest, horror often resides in the psychological ravages of extreme sorrow.

Seen through the optic of their relationship with other genres and cycles, many mourning films reiterate older themes and formulae. *The Others* and *A Very Long Engagement* (*Un long dimanche de fiançailles*, Jean-Pierre Jeunet, 2007) both treat the fate of the wartime spouse, anxiously awaiting the return of her husband, perennial themes in melodramas made around the two world wars. *Shadowlands* re-reads C.S. Lewis's relationship with his wife as an oft-told melodramatic staple of undying love. Descending from a novelettish story of a woman's loss, *Hiroshima mon amour* could be read as a soap opera for the atomic age. This would account for its temporal play. If the traditional novelette and its descendant, the woman's picture, told tales in which a woman *happens* to suffer, in *Hiroshima mon amour* the heroine suffers *because* of telling her own tale, the flow of her tears seeming to push the film backwards and forwards in time. *The Sheltering Sky* (Bernardo Bertolucci, 1990) is a modern melodrama transplanted from the American Eastern seaboard to an exotic desert setting, long the catalyst for the housewife spectator's sexual and emotional abandonment going back to the escapism of Rudolf Valentino's *The Sheik* (George Melford, 1921). *Truly, Madly, Deeply, Birth, Under the Sand, The Others, Under the Skin* (Carine Adler, 1997) and *Genova* all declare an interest in an afterlife such as captivated audiences for the Great War melodramas of Russian director Evgenii Bauer and those of Frank Borzage in 1930s Hollywood. Thematic preoccupations and stylistic tropes bring diverse films together in compelling ways.

Other Voices

The film theory used in this book descends from a tradition which is peculiarly alive to the ruminations of the genre under discussion. The work of Gilles Deleuze provides a number of ideas which help us to understand the impact of representations of subjectivity in modernist cinemas, making his writings especially relevant to the analysis of mourning cinema. One of the central ideas in his account of the aesthetic transition from the classical "movement-image" to the "time-image" of post-classical cinema is that of the "un-thought within thought" (Deleuze 1989: 266), the sense in which modernist cinema has, through "irrational" continuity, unmotivated action, purely optical and aural states, given rise to a transcendent representation of time, as opposed to the plot-bounded empirical time of classical cinema. Such a breakdown of the continuities inherent in classical aesthetics encourages mental activity in the spectator which is prior to its resolution as rational, plot-prompted reasoning. As Daniel Frampton puts it, after Deleuze, "The cinematic image takes on what we cannot think; it reflects our initial "incoherent" thoughts (unformulated linguistically) — those thoughts that are powerful but unnamable, uncontrollable" (Frampton 2006: 70). Unavailable to rational linguistic comprehension, death too becomes a kind of un-thought within thought. In their attempt to grasp the un-graspable about death and loss, many moments in the mourning film leave the spectator susceptible to pre-linguistic "thinking."

Deleuze draws examples of modernist expression from the postwar European art film. Representing characters experiencing alienation, dislocation and a generalized ennui before the realities of postwar Continental civilization, works by Alain Resnais and Michelangelo Antonioni among others, provide suggestive precedents for the mourning condition. Even the way Deleuze writes of a protagonist caught in the interstice between classicism and modernism evokes our theme: "suppose a character finds himself in a situation ... that's beyond any possible action, or to which he can't react. It's too powerful, or too painful, or too beautiful. The sensory-motor link is broken. He is no longer in a sensory-motor situation, but in a purely optical and aural situation" (Deleuze 1989: 51). To read recent therapeutic literature on grief is to be reminded of the protagonist of the postwar art film. The mourner's alienation from their feelings and responses, their abstracted reconnaissance with their environment, their complacency before modernity's effects, the characteristic moods of mourning all find echoes in high art cinema. Such are the similarities between protagonists" mental states in high Antonioni and Resnais and the protagonists of *Three Colors: Blue*, *Under the Sand*, *Morvern Callar*, *Interiors* that it could be argued that examination of mourning films reveals a specific elaboration of modernism. Deleuze's perception of modernism as the highest evolution of cinema disposes it to the abstract rumination associated with grief. In this light, the state of macro ennui he describes in *L'avventura* (Michelangelo Antonioni, 1960), *Red Desert* (*Il deserto rosso*, Michelangelo Antonioni, 1964), *Hiroshima mon amour* and *Last Year at Marienbad* (*L'Année Dernière à Marienbad*, Alain Resnais, 1961) suggests a psycho-aesthetic model for mourning cinema's emphasis on mental states. Taking his cue from Deleuze, in a pertinent move for the elaboration of the mourning film, András Bálint Kovács, a recent commentator on postwar modernism, uses the term "intellectual melodrama" to characterize the work of Antonioni's generation. Deleuze's account of the evolution of film style from classical aesthetics to the postwar European art film is a vital context for the exploration of representations of interiority in a variety of texts from classical horror and melodrama, to works by Resnais, Bergman, Allen, Ozon and others. Deleuze's work belongs to a school of film writing which is saliently interested in the concision of the image and consciousness. Not only do his ideas have relevance to classical and post-classical invention in the melodrama and the horror film, but to read Deleuze by the light of post–Deleuzian films such as *Three Colors: Blue*, *Under the Sand*, *Birth* and others is to witness just how pervasive ideas about the layering of consciousness and the protagonist-in-distrait are in modern melodrama.

Like that of Continental antecedents such as Antonin Artaud and Jean-Louis Schefer, even the language Deleuze uses recalls the metaphysical register which persists in mourning cinema. "The soul of the cinema," writes Deleuze, "demands increasing thought, even as it begins by undoing the system of actions, perceptions and affections on which the cinema had fed up to that point" (Deleuze 1986: 210–211). Deleuze evokes the cinema as a kind of consciousness, either psychological or spiritual. The modernist film relies not upon external logics but on internal impressions developing in visions or rudimentary actions. The notion of the movement-image rethinks one of the cinema's fundamental axioms. If in the nineteenth century Joseph Antoine Plateau described that optical phenomenon whereby the eye perceives a succession of images as a continuous flow, Deleuze incorporates movement within the image itself. The classical image *is* an image of movement. Extending this metaphor, the modernist time-image becomes a kind of spiritual automaton: "the highest exercise of thought, the way in which thought thinks and itself thinks itself in the fantastic effort of an autonomy" (Deleuze 1989: 252). In the mourning film there is tension between inside and outside, the daily reflection upon her thoughts going on within the mourning protagonist, and the anguished rubbing of subjectivity against an uncaring, indifferent, hostile world. In *Three Colors: Blue*, Julie Vignon scrapes her knuckles against a bare wall until they chafe and bleed. For Deleuze, after Schefer, cinema "'spreads an experimental night'" over us (ibid.: 194). Pre-Deleuzian writers, and such post–Deleuzians as Frampton, offer an account of cinema which emphasizes its nature as instinctive, intuitive, pre-rational and pre-linguistic, for Artaud a kind of automatic writing which lives on the cusp of the conscious and the unconscious, a form of para-discourse. For Frampton, the film-as-thought enables "a more poetic entry to the intelligence of film" (Frampton 2006: 8).

Aside from revealing a human condition, this "metaphysical" accent reinforces that sense in which mourning films throw light on the cinematic condition. Artaud bears out this mission. The cinema "calls for extraordinary subjects, climactic states of mind, an atmosphere of vision" (Sontag 1976: 181). While Frampton does not address particular states of subjectivity, he does proffer a way of thinking and talking about film as a form of consciousness. Films are "about" something inasmuch as the film is always already "thinking" about what it is showing. The distinction is Heideggerian. In one of the most important philosophical texts of the twentieth century, *Being and Time* (1927), Martin Heidegger sought an account of being which was not about things and subjects, instances of being in themselves, but an account of being as it exists through time. Frampton, too, reaches for an account of film which sees its objects and subjects not in themselves, but already caught up in the film's thinking, this particular film's account of time. Frampton and Deleuze, each in his way, propose an account of experience which is simultaneously an account of time. Heidegger writes: "The central problematic of all ontology is rooted in the phenomenon of time" (Heidegger 1962: 18). For Heidegger, we experience time subjectively, not in terms of clocks, timetables and schedules, but as a continuum in which the present is imbricated with the past and the future. Like a palimpsest, this moment, say the moment of my writing, is overlain with my memories of the past and my thoughts about the future. This layering is a useful notion to apply to the mourning film, with its narrative emphasis on subjectivity and imagery in which recollection, nostalgia and regret co-exist in the present moment. It is not difficult to see the significance of being-in-time to the account Deleuzians offer of cinema, any more than we can ignore the role of time in the experience of mourning and its representation. The phenomenological tradition to which Heidegger belongs is fundamentally useful to a consideration of mourning. Phenomenology challenges the dualism of subject and object which had been central to Western philosophy since Descartes. By theorizing a subject which is always already relating and addressing itself to the environment in which they exist, phenomenology collapses the distinction between subjectivity and objectivity in a way that is especially fruitful to the theorization and aesthetic description of loss. What the mourner faces is the end of an individual dear to them, but they must also negotiate the end of a world which they shared with the lost person. Situated in a world defined by a relationship which gave it sense and meaning, the mourner must reconnoiter being afresh. As many mourners testify, and so many mourning films show, being in mourning is being on the cusp of two worlds; one in which life goes on as though the loss never took place, and one in which the person who defined that world is gone: "When I slip back into the quotidian routine, I also slip into this liminal land where, although I don't expect him to turn up, he hasn't gone either ... until something provides a rude awakening" (Duncan 2009: 1). Seen from a phenomenological perspective, death paradoxically emphasizes the mourner's a priori involvement in the world around them. The sense of dislocation is continually explored in the cinema of mourning.

Heidegger's account of language is also salient to mourning cinema. For Heidegger, thinking can be meditative, poetic, a way of showing rather than telling, evoking rather than describing. "Meditative thinking," Frampton writes, "becomes a poeticising of thought, an attempt to move thinking beyond language, towards a 'primordial poetry' — as all *poeticising* begins with thinking. For Heidegger, meditative, poetic thinking goes some way to revealing the unthought in thought: the unthought ... is the not yet thought, the future of thought which brings the chaos of the "outside" into rational thought" (Frampton 2006: 192). The mourning film also reverts to poetic registers to embody the unspeakable, to resituate the chaos of grief in time, to find and reveal the un-thought in thought. In Frampton's evocation of Heidegger's distinctive sylvan imagery, we detect something of that sense in which the mourning film is most importantly a way of contemplating its subject: "This reflective thinking considers a space, or clearing, where thoughts can be cared for and dwelt on, a space to ponder, allowing thinking to grow and ripen" (ibid.: 192). Writing of his poetry to the editor Jacques Rivière, Artaud emphasizes the uncertain interface between words and the chaos which lies beyond words: "I suffer from a horrible sickness of the mind. My thought abandons me at every level.... Words, shapes of sentences, internal directions of thought, simple reactions of the mind—I am in constant pursuit of my intellectual being" (Sontag 1976: 31). Insofar as such imagery has seemed soothing and consoling to the mourner, it is serendipitous that mourning films evoke the traditional pastoral imagery of heavenly consolation. Yet this is also a reaching beyond language in search of another logic, chaotic and irrational yet beautiful, with which to cope with the senselessness of loss.

The shift in film aesthetics from the classical movement-image, typically the Hollywood continuity scenario with its goal-directed protagonist, pragmatic script, and resolved conflict, to the modernist time-image, with its drifting, inner-directed protagonist and open-ended resolution, is key to the theorization of mourning cinema. As even those theorists who propose a staged model of grief such as Elisabeth Kübler-Ross and Colin M. Parkes acknowledge, grief is not an experience with a set time limit. It is ebb and flow rather than a trajectory with a beginning, middle and an end. It does not lend itself readily to the neat and optimistic solutions of classical filmic storytelling. Even as classically constructed films such as *Moonlight and Valentino, In the Bedroom* (Todd Field, 2001) and *Genova* end, there is scope to reflect on how the protagonist will fare in the future. We like to think, and grief literature bears this out, that grief becomes easier to cope with. But we do not watch mourning films to witness resolution. We watch them to see *how* mourning happens. What we are seeing is not time defined by the project which takes place in it, but time as a project in and of itself. Bálint Kovács writes after Deleuze: "Modern film is the result of cinema's inherent power of articulating time" (Bálint Kovacs 2007: 41). For Deleuze, modernist cinema is *about* time, emptied of the projects and interactions of classical continuity, with classicism's concomitant panoply of shot-reverse shots and economic *mise-en-scène*. By contrast with the classical dramatic trajectory in which a situation is established, disturbed and resolved into a fresh situation, in the purely optical and aural economy of the Deleuzian modernist film, what "happens" is perception, our perception of time's passage becomes the cinematic event, an enveloping and surrounding which breaks down the classical distinction between the spectator and the screen on which pre-modernist film, and its theorization, depended. Echoing throughout Deleuze is the parallel between a consciousness experienced as layered, discrete and abstracted, for our purposes the pure perception of the mourning protagonist, and prior to this the layered consciousness of the grief counseling client, forced to negotiate ongoing macro disorientation amid a sea of prosaic everyday micro-narratives. The Deleuzian account yields much to a project seeking to elucidate the interiority of those facing loss in a world reduced to sensations, intuitions and apparitions. This mental image works out an elliptical universe characterized by symbols, figurality, metonymy and inference. In Frampton's words, it is "drunk because it is blurry in its meaning, loose in its movement, becoming pre-verbal content" (Frampton 2006: 64).

The historical context which Deleuze elaborates is also relevant to the mourning film. He sees the sensory motor schema of classical continuity, with its goal-driven active protagonist, motivated by: "a causal nexus between seeing, feeling, doing" (Elsaesser 2002: 271). Deleuze links the breakdown of the sensory motor schema in modernist cinema to the fractured discontinuous

Interiors. Startling in its blank and unadorned calligraphy of white on black, even the credit sequence of *Interiors* evokes the omnipresent human dilemma of life facing death.

relationships implicit in a European environment facing postwar reconstruction. His description is evocative: "In Europe, the postwar period has greatly increased the situations which we no longer know how to react to, in spaces which we no longer know how to describe. These were "any-spaces-whatever," deserted but inhabited, disused warehouses, waste ground, cities in the course of demolition or reconstruction" (Deleuze 1989: xi). While the main protagonists of this book must negotiate less an overarching sense of socio-aesthetic ennui than a personal crisis with implications peculiar to itself, the confused, aimless, tripping experience of the typical Antonioni or Resnais protagonist offers an important precedent for cinema's exploration of grief. The dislocation felt by characters in *Hiroshima mon amour*, *Morvern Callar* and *Under the Sand* is of the same order as that of the "historical" dislocation of the archetypal Deleuzian modernist character. The wandering women in high Antonioni, Bergman, Resnais are adrift in a strange place, sisters to characters in whom grief has forced a fresh recognition of loneliness and alienation. It is possible to argue that, thematically and aesthetically, the modern film of grief, whether as tribute, imitation, parody or distortion, is a direct descendant of this postwar current.

If modernism proffered a post–Christian realm of man-without-God, in the mourning film this universal crisis devolves to atomic levels, charting the everyday consequences of loss without spiritual consolation. In a world in which loss cannot be explained in divine terms, the pain and sorrow which it causes seem all the more intense for being inexplicable, irrational and unpredictable. Joyce Carol Oates starkly observes: "Though I am writing this memoir to see what can be made of the phenomenon of 'grief' in the most exactingly minute of ways, I am no longer convinced that there is any inherent value in grief; or, if there is, if wisdom springs from the experience of terrible loss, it's a wisdom one might do without" (Oates 2011: 407). Exacting and savage in its affects on the griever, consciousness itself becomes a new metaphysics, drawing the grieving protagonist within themselves and reducing her perspective to the contemplation of the contingent and the abject. Memory is a key theme in this account of solitary recurring pain. Memory can affect the griever on various levels. There is the memory of the departed and the transitory nature of shared moments. There is the memory of how these recollections made the griever feel yesterday, last week, last month, last year. Recollection plays an important role in the Deleuzian account of modernist consciousness. Deleuze could be evoking the mental condition of mourning protagonists Marie Drillon and Morvern Callar when he writes: "Sheets of past and layers of reality correspond, the first emanating from an inside which is always already there" (Deleuze 1989: 199–200). These women live parallel lives in which the dead are constantly present to memory, and in which the protagonist must pursue everyday agendas which exclude the dead yet are imbricated with their memory. The significant other lives within the mourning protagonist, alongside daily intuitions which no longer concern them. Sheets of reality coexist, each overlaying and distorting the other. We are reminded of the scales of a snake, or the endlessly dappled leaves in a tree.

Deleuze writes of the individual shot that "it acts like a consciousness" (Deleuze 1986: 21). For Frampton, a film is always already "thinking" on its subject and themes, each and every shot and camera movement, ellipse and dissolve, color and tone shaping the drama as it unfolds. Frampton's concepts of the "filmind" and "film-thinking" are especially felicitous for the examination of the mourning film. "The 'filmind,'" Frampton writes: "is filmosophy's concept of film-being, the theoretical originator of the images and sounds we experience, and 'film-thinking' is filmosophy's theory of film form, whereby an action of form is seen as the dramatic thinking of the filmind" (Frampton 2006: 6). "Film form is always there, and thus necessarily part of the actions and events, and filmosophy simply, holistically, bonds film's actions to dramatically thoughtful motives and intentions. Film style is now seen to be the dramatic intention of the film itself" (Frampton 2006: 8). Another contemporary film theorist whose ideas recur in this book is Michel Chion, whose work on sound reinforces a similar sense of immanent intentionality. Chion writes: "There is no place of the sounds, no auditory scene already pre-existing in the soundtrack — and therefore, properly speaking, there is no soundtrack" (Chion 1990: 68). Chion reminds us of the ghosts and apparitions of the mourning film; never there but always present. It is not difficult to recognize in a holistic view of filmic intention, in all its complex and exacting effects, the film bound to the mourner's consciousness, her sorrow echoing and re-echoing in its looks, rhythms and energies.

The notion of a theoretical source of a film's visual and aural nature also appeals to the project of describing and classifying films according not to pre-designated personalities and "auteurs," but to the content, form and style with which a particular film manifests its preoccupations, its intentionality. This book identifies a genre from a range of films appearing from differing contexts. Frampton's emphasis on the intuition of a film's flows and energies, as distinct from referring to the rational narrative schemata and overarching heuristics of cognitive, psychoanalytical and auteurist film-theoretical tools, provides a way of talking about cinema which is sensitive to the hidden dynamics of the mourning film. Such a "film-as-*film*" approach also appeals to the way in which many moving image texts are consumed nowadays, a domestic context with implications for the development of the new genre proposed here.

Like Deleuze's, even Frampton's language evokes the delicious suggestiveness of a ghost story, the film "feeling" a relationship between characters and objects, metaphysically "intending" with every shot and camera shift. Frampton's choice of words makes of the film some kind of wraith which appears before the eye and gets into the mind: "Film disrupts principles of reason and judgement, and so becomes a truth with its own will" (Frampton 2006: 200). The film-thought "rests in the filmgoer's mind — it soaks it with its mood, its attention, its movement" (ibid.: 196).

The fluidity of the filmind's intentionality, the way it thinks through the visual and aural concert before the spectator, also enables a more refined approach to the modernist heritage which is so salient to mourning cinema. The indeterminate shifts and mysterious meanderings in Antonioni, Resnais and Kieślowski become explicable, and increasingly desirable, through a filmosophical optic. Like grief itself, the films which chart its convolutions can be difficult to negotiate, demanding a reading which emphasizes their status as consciousness rather than calculation, flow rather than disjunction, the layered heterogeneity which is a persistent theme in therapeutic literature. Quoted by Frampton, the French music critic Emile Vuillermoz wrote in 1918 that film recreates the world as if seen "through a temperament" (cited in Frampton 2006: 196).

The mourning film emerges out of its effects with a world seen through overwhelming regret. This temperamental perspective reiterates its debt to the psychological vicissitudes of high modernism. Unlike the rationalist trajectories of classical scenarios, the modernist film can seem vague and strange, oneiric in its wandering emotionalism. As with Deleuze, many early writers quoted by Frampton were very alive to cinema's magical quality, its status as a conjuring apparatus throwing odd, even unwonted shadows on walls. We are reminded of early film's emergence in the era of sideshow spiritualism. The literature on which Frampton draws not only bears out a correlation between cinema and spiritualism evoked in this book, but the treasuring of cinema's propensity for magic yields much to the identification and analysis of films which discern a kind of magic in the attempt to reconcile death and life. Like a mourning film bounded by death and rebirth, like a dream, "filmosophical thinking is by definition organic. The film thinks with its beginning and end in mind" (Frampton 2006: 84).

Another writer conscious of cinema's original propensity for the irrational is Pier Paolo Pasolini, whose 1988 article "The 'Cinema of Poetry'" sought, like Deleuze, to account for the aesthetic transition from classicism to postclassical art cinema. Pasolini's notion of "free indirect discourse," which he defines as "the immersion of the filmmaker in the mind of his character and then the adoption on the part of the filmmaker not only of the psychology of his character but also of his language" (cited in Orr 2000: 44) offers a way of accounting for neurotic and fractured viewpoints in Antonioni and Resnais. Pasolini's distinction between the "prose" of classical narrative continuity and the "poetry" of the modernist absorption of filmmaker in the protagonist's mindset throws valuable light on modernist aesthetics. Like the film-literary tradition which views a film as consciousness, a "cinema of poetry" dissolves the distinction between human subjectivity, be it protagonist or spectator, and the objective world before the lens that had underpinned classical aesthetics.

Yet while useful to the theorization of the shift from classicism to modernism, Pasolini's demarcation of the prosaic and the poetic image fails to explore fully, beyond some allusions to Chaplin, the possibility of the poetic *within* the prosaic that occurs all too often in classical output. Central to this book is the attempt to discover aesthetic continuities between films made at different moments and in disparate institutional settings. In identifying precedents for a modern mourning cinema, it looks to classical films from Europe and America, works of mainstream providence and from "art cinema" and experimental origins, for the sources and inspirations which have influenced, inflected and shaped an incipient type. The book cites a range of works which show how classical aesthetic norms and commercial imperatives tolerated deviations and experiments from within these paradigms. Many examples, whether intentionally auteurist or not, sat on the fringes of mainstream practice, demonstrating how the "system," in all its collaborations, accidents and serendipities, could give rise to films in which the distinction between "prose" and "poetry" seems ambivalent. Not that so-called "auteur films" do not appear here. They do, but in pursuit of cinema's capacity to explore that specific precinct of fracture that the mourner goes to, these films are seen not as elaborations of a directorial point-of-view but as elaborations in cinema's relationship with death, one as integral to cinema as poetry was to classical prose.

Raising Spirits

This book proposes that films that treat the experience of grief constitute a distinct cinematic genre. To this end, it shall excavate, perhaps more aptly exhume, precedents for a preoccupation which appeared to come into its own in the 1990s. Prior to discussing classical precedents, however, Chapter 1 shall look to the rise of spiritualism in the nineteenth century as a phenomenon coinciding with the development of the moving image, and appealing to the same redemption of loss as the projected but non-existent faces on screen. This examination shall prepare the way for the historical account of representations of grief and loss in film history from the silent era to the early postwar decades. In focusing on classical representations of grief and the afterlife, particular emphasis will be placed on melodrama and the horror genre's investment in loss and its consequences. Drawing upon a range of European and American films from the cinema's first sixty years, this chapter proposes that the related genres of Hollywood melodrama, its sub-generic sister the woman's picture, and the horror movie, furnished especially fertile contexts for cinema's ability to express the inexpressible burden of human mortality. Chapter 1 will argue that the cinema is a singularly effective medium for the depiction of grief and loss.

Subsequent chapters will explore the consequences of classicism for the expression of interiority in postwar cinema. The postwar decades saw a period of cinematic innovation as political polemic, evolving mores, cultural subsidy, changing audience demographics, and fresh critical discourses gave rise to flourishing experimentation across Europe and in America. Continental modernism typically braved the depiction of experiences considered "difficult" or taboo for mainstream cinema. The tackling of issues surrounding sexuality and the meaning of human existence came to be a defining characteristic in distributor rhetoric and critical review alike as moral guidelines became more lax and the mass audiences of earlier decades fragmented. The exploration of interiority in art cinema of this period is crucially exemplified in such works dealing with grief-stricken protagonists as *Hiroshima mon amour, Cries and Whispers, Interiors*, and *Don't Look Now*, which are explored in case studies in Chapter 2.

By the 1970s and 1980s, it was obvious that the exploration of interiority considered high art cinema's privilege since the 1950s had permeated the burgeoning commercial arthouse film, typically in the work of Woody Allen, Nicolas Roeg and Robert Altman, among others. As a particular experience of interiority, by the 1990s grief became a theme common to many films. Knowing allusions to the European art tradition occur in modern mourning films. Emmanuelle Riva, the star of *Hiroshima mon amour*, appears as the grief-stricken protagonist's mother in *Three Colors: Blue*. In *Time to Leave* (*Temps qui reste*, François Ozon, 2005) Ozon knowingly refers to François Truffaut's meditation on death in *Jules et Jim* (1961), in which in an extraordinary passage Jeanne Moreau's freespirited heroine dies, her body is cremated, her bones pounded, and her ashes are scattered. If classically modeled films from the pre–Revolutionary Russian Evgenii Bauer to Hollywood's Frank Borzage reiterated traditional ideas and imagery concerning death and the afterlife, tendencies within classical cinema also foresaw the experimentalism of modernist responses to human finitude. Its pre-linguistic nature descending from tendencies in classical filmmaking and the 1920s Continental avant-garde alike, the visionary register emerging in postwar filmmaking is essential to the way in which modern cinema has evolved. This visionary register shall be explored in Chapter 2. Chapters 2 and 3 contain case studies illustrating the play of modernist aesthetics in the representation of loss in modern cinema. Deploying close analysis of performance and *mise-en-scène*, and a consideration of critical reception, case studies shall examine the strategies of inference and rhetoric which modern representations of grief and mourning use to think this experience anew.

Chapter 4 will propose a taxonomy of aesthetic tropes and effects which find perennial themes and preoccupations elaborated using a rich and consistent set of techniques and strategies. This chapter will pose the question of whether devices used in mourning films reveal anything about popular or therapeutic ideas about bereavement. Or whether by pushing at the boundaries of cinematic representation, they invite us to review our notions of bereavement. Throughout the history of the cinema, films treating grief and mourning appear too frequently to be filed away, perhaps even lost, under vague generic categories such as "melodrama," "woman's picture," "weepie," or "family drama." It is the contention of this book that these films, despite their origins, despite the classifications applied to them, are stylistically too singular, too powerful in their effects, too committed to a specific condition of human existence, to be subsumed beneath such inexact nomenclature. Deleuze writes of "intellectual buggery" to describe his method of rethinking, or "sneaking up behind," a philosophical idea and producing an offspring which is recognizably related but also monstrous and different. This book seeks to "sneak up behind" some canonical films and rethink them in a fresh way in the hope of producing an offspring which is recognizably the film's yet perhaps monstrous and certainly different. I am proposing the mourning film, or to coin a phrase, a "cinéma du deuil," as a type in its own right.

Chapter 1. Manifestation

> "As you grow older, you'll learn to believe in lots of things you can't see."
>
> Miss Spinney, in *Portrait of Jennie*

Cathy Caruth writes of trauma that its narration is "a problem central to the task of therapists, literary critics, neurobiologists, and filmmakers alike" (Caruth 1995: vii). Death, that unknown and unthinkable event, reduces a sentient living personality to a material state, often seeming to manifest itself to those left behind in forms of memory, recollections and sensations which earlier generations would have called spirits or ghosts. Ghosts, apparitions and other manifestations recur throughout this chapter. In the mourning film, the moment of loss is the initial trauma, a dramatic trigger which is unbearable to the protagonist, inexpressible in words, and for the film calls upon a radical rethinking of narrative and the image. In how many other life contexts can the event be so manifest yet so beyond the capacity of language to encompass? Perhaps cinematic imagery offers a fresh set of terms for this moment. Many writers have reached beyond literary metaphor for cinematic analogies for the expression of grief. This chapter will substantially be concerned with seeking precedents for a modern cinema of mourning in the history of cinema. As we shall see, if death has driven literary writing to seek forms of expression outside itself, the representation of grief on screen has taken place most revealingly in marginal practices and fringe cultures. Chapter 1 shall begin with some examples of the literary use of cinematic metaphor from a period during which the cinema was becoming a mass art form with its own specific devices and conventions.

The Moving Metaphor

The twentieth century saw many attempts to frame its devastating events in literature. In the wake of the terrible losses of World War I, and as the cinema came into its own as a cultural force, modernist writing turned to cinematic metaphors to express the inexpressible. In retrospect, it seems paradoxical that historically elaborate public mourning rituals, still closely observed in the nineteenth century and seeming to reach an apogee in Queen Victoria's protracted grief over the death of Prince Albert, fell into decline before the widespread mourning following the sinking of the *Titanic* in 1912 and the international catastrophe of 1914–1918. At the point at which historical events were testing the practicalities of mass interment as well as the ability of language to state the reality of death in the modern era, mourning was increasingly becoming a private affair, the atomized agony of a generation as it turned in on itself, bereft of words, inert and in tears. It was in such a context that cinematic imagery offered a site and a set of effects which could explore differently, perhaps more poignantly, the human horror of extinction, a potential which would be explored by a number of writers. Such usages occasionally bore uncanny reminders of the modern mourning film. In Hilda Doolittle's war novel *Bid Me to Live* (1960), her heroine is a civilian who, like Doolittle herself, was traumatized by the very news of suffering. A vivid precursor of the peripatetic woman whose image animates the mourning film, Julia, a war neurotic, sees the world as "magic lantern slides" (Raitt 1997: 257). Expressed as an odd evocation of cinema's projected imagery, in Virginia Woolf's *To the Lighthouse* (1927), Mr. Ramsay is devastated by his wife's death. Overheard by another character: "('Alone' she heard him say, 'Perished' she heard him say) ... the words became symbols, wrote themselves all over the grey-green walls" (Woolf 1992: 160–161). We are reminded of the chalky inscriptions scrawled over the walls which "call" the demented heroine in *The Haunting*. C.S. Lewis falls back on images. Despite what "might become in the end a snare, a horror, or an obstacle" (Lewis 1966: 55), the writer toys with photographs of his wife before being driven back to the rituals of writing, a fate made increasingly forlorn by his dependence on metaphysical language: "Images of the Holy ... My idea of God ... he shatters it Himself" (Lewis 1966: 55).

The stasis characterizing the war neurotic's sight in *Bid Me to Live* is recalled in subsequent writers' likening it to the cinematic freeze frame. In 1998, Derrida evoked this device for the moment as Blanchot is about to die: "Freeze frame in the unfolding of a film in a movie camera: the soldiers are there, they no longer move, neither does the young man, an eternal instant, another eternal instant" (Blanchot 2000: 74). Duncan writes of stasis: "It is as if the brain can only process forward ... it can only do so one frame at a time; so that one can have the sensation of speed simultaneously with a sense of events being 'freeze-framed' and experienced frame by frame rather than in a continuous flow. It is as if there is a glitch in the reel and the movie is 'going slow' for a spell and then randomly it picks up speed again" (Duncan 2009: 2). As we shall see, the freeze frame and slow motion both take their place in mourning cinema's stylistic taxonomy. The "turn" to the cinematic at moments when literature is challenged by the task of describing death's effects suggests cinema's unique relationship with the transitory moment. Each in their way, these writers liken their experience to cinema's continuity system, a flow of imaged narrative which slows and hastens in tune with the convolutions of narrative. Implicit in literary analogy is the memory of cinema's photographic roots and a primitive era in which the spectator witnessed a technology animated by some mysterious logic of its own.

The Metaphor Moving

What characterizes the manifestation of death in the mourning film is a kind of formal excess of image and sound in which the film reaches for a way of expressing the unbearable and the uncontainable. *Moonlight and Valentino* offers a striking example in which film footage becomes a mobile metaphor for what it expresses. At the moment in the hospital when Rebecca (Elizabeth Perkins) is told by an intern that her husband "didn't make it," this classically made narrative literally slows down, the image going into slow motion, as Rebecca attempts with difficulty to sit down. It is the only time in the film when the film is shot at a different speed. Indeed, it is the only moment when the film employs an unusual device, a "trick" protocol with a long cinematic heritage yet one customarily relegated to the fringes of mainstream practice. At this point, the image could be said to be as "traumatized" as Rebecca is. Such a moment in a mainstream feature seems "excessive," departing from the linear trajectory which is *Moonlight and Valentino*'s overall project, and adopting a vertical trajectory as it plumbs the protagonist's feelings at a particular moment. Throughout film history, the "unbearable" and "uncontainable" expressed in such "extreme" imagery has often been employed to suggest the other-worldly, that is a being or phenomena which is not in any conventional sense really there. The excessive register marks works which thematize the supernatural while exploring the consequences of loss, such as *The Innocents* and *The Haunting*. What is interesting about the moment of decelerated motion in *Moonlight and Valentino* is the way that it distorts the character, the slowing down making Rebecca appear to move in an unnatural way, seeming to "smear" her image so that it looks wraith-like, other-worldly in the wake of her husband's bodily transformation. Thus the suffering woman herself comes to seem supernatural, in some sense not on the same plane as the intern who attends her. This collapsing together of the woman with her malaise has implications for the mourning film as a type. Rebecca refers to herself as disembodied: "I'm not *in* my body, I don't *have* a body." Furthermore, there is a sense in which Rebecca is not *in* the film with the presence and force that other characters are. Recalling the film in retrospect, its other characters, Lucy (Gwyneth Paltrow), Sylvie (Whoopi Goldberg) and Augusta (Kathleen Turner), come more emphatically to mind than its haunted heroine, a quiet presence who seems like a tabula rasa upon which the others inscribe their own preoccupations and troubles. Indeed, *Moonlight and Valentino*'s place in the mourning filmography becomes more assured if we see its bereft protagonist as the namesake of Hitchcock's Rebecca, another suffering chatelaine, more ominous but no less "present" for her very absence. And here was another woman who, like Rebecca, has remained childless. At one point, Rebecca, in a white dressing gown, is seen by a startled dog in the garden burying mementos of her husband. That the mourning woman is the ghost among more substantial "others" seems increasingly vivid. The mourning film is a product of such moments of precipitate presence, the image teetering on the fringes of an ontology, simultaneously calling into question the veracity of what we see, while making it apparent that "something" is present.

The films examined in this book are characterized by moments in which film form bridges the gap between the grieving psyche and the objective world. Such moments see a genre come into its own as a repertoire of aesthetic devices, visual and sonic. Just as writers have turned to cinematic metaphor to express the conundrum of death, such moments see cinema reach beyond language, narrative and the literary in search of its primitive vocation as spectacle. In seeking precedents for the mourning film in the origins of cinema and in the forms of melodrama and horror which cinema took in its classical phase, this chapter will show how the "excessive" image, both in terms of what is represented and how it is represented, is central to the prehistory and evolution of the mourning film.

Excessive Inscriptions

The attempt to inscribe interiority in the image is a persistent theme in mourning cinema and its forebears, testifying to the type's specific mission while also revealing something of the nature of cinema itself. Emma Wilson is alive to that unique property of cinema which can find a film at once able to photographically bear witness, and to provide "reparative, commemorative, knowing illusion" (Wilson 2003: 8). This book will recall moments in which the filmic medium was pushed to recognize loss and its affects, commemorate life, know the place in which life and death meet. Recall that moment in

Under the Skin, as a young grieving woman, encounters her mother's ghost in a lost property basement, the old lady approaching her daughter in a flickering image from among dark aisles of forgotten belongings. Indeed, the very word "medium," both in its artistic and social senses, suggests a site of resurrection and revival. Whenever we watch a film the medium calls up the dead moment, the finished history. Death and life are intertwined in cinema's technological nature as a succession of still images animated by the projector's inner motion, just as the shocking stillness of grief finds the mourner negotiating a succession of stillnesses in time. By proffering a means of moving beyond words to another means of negotiating death, cinema provides another kind of space for consolation and commemoration. For Jean-Luc Godard, this vocation is unique. Cinema is "invariably an operation of mourning and of reclaiming life" (Temple 2004: 367). This consolatory and commemorative vocation relates crucially to the era from which cinema emerged.

The Spiritual Image

There is a historical precedent for the representation of loss and bereavement in films which throws interesting light on the role of the image in cinema. Ever since 1895, when the Lumière train appeared to barrel into the room where spectators sat, various commentators on the cinema have characterized the typical spectator as a rapt and engrossed figure in thrall to the flickering images onscreen. Out of decades of camera obscuras, magic lantern shows, bioskops, phenakistiscopes and zoopraxiniscopes and a variety of optical toys, the final decade of the nineteenth century saw the realization of cinema in a recognizable form. Early manifestations, from the color-tinted extravaganzas of Georges Méliès to the naturalistic exploration of intimacy in *The Kiss* (George Heise, 1896), professed cinema's ambition to push at the boundaries of both visual perception and human interiority. In business from 1896, Méliès's "trick films" derived from his experience in conjuring and theatrical magic, a world which existed, often uneasily, alongside the spiritualist circuit of those days. Decades before postwar arthouse experimentation, Méliès exploited the illusionist properties of cinema from double exposures to jump cuts and time-lapse photography. Works like *La Caverne maudite* (*The Haunted Cavern* Georges Méliès, 1897) and *Le Fantôme d'Alger* (*A Spiritualist Meeting*, Georges Méliès, 1905) traded in spectacles of the afterlife. Meanwhile, the cinema's investment in human interiority rapidly gained notoriety for the new medium. That lingering minute-long record of a couple kissing flush on the lips in *The Kiss* caused such consternation as to prompt the first calls for screen censorship. The film's source text, a successful stage melodrama called

The Widow Jones, hinted at cinema's forthcoming commitment to female desire.

Prospering in the decades leading up to the first Lumière screenings of December 1895, there are uncanny parallels between spiritualism and early cinema. Matthew Solomon hints at their scintillating relationship: "Descriptions of the new medium of moving pictures sometimes suggested that the projected images were ghostlike apparitions" (Solomon 2010: 8). It is a perception borne out in the vivid writings of, amongst others, French journalist Henri Clouzot: "Anxious like spiritualists around a turning table ... they squeeze into the little room where the cinematograph gives its séances. Shhh! The incantation begins. The mysterious device takes off with the click-clacking of a sewing machine gone wild, and the image comes alive. The first impression is stupor" (ibid.: 11). Another French writer, Jean Badreux, catches that strange feeling the modern spectator has that the milling Lumière crowds of 1895–96 are not simply revisited quotidian moments from long ago, but see the dead and the living fetched up in the same room together: "I do not mean to say that the Lumière brothers bring about a resurrection when they revive the dead ... but while leaving the dead to the profound serenity of the tomb, one will be able to see them from henceforth acting, walking, speaking, and singing ... in a word, we will be able to bring those who are no longer in this world back to life before our very eyes. Science has triumphed over death" (ibid.: 11–12).

Spiritualism's claim to revisit the dead provides a suggestive model for the flickering greys and whites of primitive cinema. On March 31, 1848, Kate and Margaret Fox of Hydesville, New York, claimed to make contact with the spirit of a murdered peddler. As their story spread down the Eastern seaboard, mediumship and attendance at séances grew as a popular, and lucrative, form of entertainment and catharsis. Here it is worth making a distinction between two different forms of spiritualism. Jay Winter writes: "First, secular spiritualism encompasses the views of those who explore the supposed existence of human personality after death and the possibility of communication with the dead. It makes little difference whether or not such people believe in God; their quest is psychical and psychological, not theological. Secondly, religious spiritualism describes the attitudes of people who see apocalyptic, divine, angelic, or saintly presences in daily life, and do so at the margins of or outside the confines of the traditional churches" (Winter 1995: 54). This distinction will have a bearing on representations of the celestial in classical cinema, and upon the post-classical representation of mourning.

Lacking the hierarchies and dogmas associated with established churches, secular spiritualism in nineteenth century America and Britain attracted individuals disenchanted on a variety of issues with the prevailing status quo. In

America, it spoke to those who were against the official churches' position on slavery and women's rights. In Britain and in Continental Europe, spiritualism attracted freethinkers critical of Victorian moral norms and the prevailing positivist scientific paradigm alike. Its rise also answered deep cultural needs. For Janet Oppenheim: "There, in the spirit voices, the spirit hands, faces, and bodies, the messages rapped out on walls, floors, and furniture, or scribbled on slate, spiritualists received proof that the human spirit survives bodily death. With that proof, they liberated themselves from the religious anxiety and emotional bewilderment that had afflicted them and continued to torment countless numbers of their contemporaries" (Oppenheim 1985: 2–3). Other episodes seemed more spectacular. Oppenheim writes: "Reports of séances also told of furniture cavorting around the room, objects floating in the air, mediums levitating, musical instruments playing tunes by themselves, bells ringing, tambourines jangling, strange breezes blowing, weird lights glowing, alluring fragrances and ethereal music wafting through the air"(ibid.: 8). Such phenomena carry resonances of cinema's forthcoming potpourri of effects. From Méliès to the "talkies" to postwar widescreen experiments, "odorama," and "The Tingler," and stereophonic sound, down the decades cinema showmen have relied upon sensual entreaties. It should also be remembered that many a medium set up on the fairground, in due course alongside the Kinematograph tent. In France, numerous societies and journals catered to the interest in spiritualism. There grew a thriving market for crystal balls and medium's tables. In 1858, celebrated spiritualist Allan Kardec founded the *Revue spirite*, a periodical committed to the idea that science and religion both answered deep human needs. In France, as in Britain and America, the popular interest in spiritualism chimed with more official intellectual currents. In the 1880s, Jean-Martin Charcot's work on hypnotism and trance states at the Pitié-Salpêtrière hospital in Paris not only anticipated Freud's work in the same area but appealed to the spiritualist mindset.

The mid–nineteenth century also saw the theorization of a characteristic of human sight vital to the comprehension of cinema and which, arguably, played some role in the gullibility of the séance attendee. In 1836, Joseph Antoine Plateau discussed the "Stroboscopic Effect": "If within one second, a series of images showing successive movement can be seen with the eye, and if these pictures are shown in succession, the laggard sense of sight causes these pictures to be seen as movement and not as single pictures" (Plateau cited in Burns 1999). While the spiritualists flourished, work on the mechanical facilitation of "persistence of vision" continued in Europe and America through the middle of the century: "As early as 1849 Plateau suggested the use of Daguerreotypes with a Phenakistiscope; but none of a number of patents and proposals of the 1860s and 1870s reached a solution to the problem of how to take a series of photographs in the rapid succession necessary to reconstitute the appearance of a moving image of an action" (Robinson 1973: 13). The 1860s saw the earliest projection of moving images using a magic lantern zoetrope. In 1875, John Roebuck Rudge developed the Rudge projector, capable of the most fluid projection of images thus far. Using seven posed photographic slides Roebuck exhibited what appeared to be the prospect of a man removing his own head. The trade name Rudge proposed was "Phantascope," a word with all too obvious metaphysical connotations.

Parallels between spiritualism and the rise of the moving image seem compelling. Even on the linguistic level, in French the word "séance" refers to a meeting or session. A "séance de cinéma" refers to an assemblage of persons at a film. While in English the term has retained the nineteenth century sense of those gathered around a table awaiting some emanation of the afterlife. Spiritualism and the cinema depend for their appeal on the conjuring of images, people, the beloved from the ether. Both institutions saw groups of the convinced gather in darkened public rooms for reasons of pleasure and consolation. Both began as fairground pastimes and by the onset of a devastating world war would provide comfort for thousands of bereaved mothers, wives, sweethearts and sisters. What distinguished the Fox incident in Hydesville was that, unlike the claims of those "visited" by dead souls while in trance, sensual evidence of the afterlife came to the sisters via audible rapping on wood. This objective characteristic lent credence to the often maligned work of mediums. As Oppenheim argues, the rise of spiritualism responded to the disorientation many in the nineteenth century felt before the findings of science with its strictly materialistic God-less mapping of experience. The empirical note struck at Hydesville suggested that the human need for spiritual consolation and the scientific requirement of physical evidence could be reconciled. The evidence of the senses thus became as vital to those taken in by spiritualism as it was to the scientific establishment: "Observation, not Scripture, was the source of wisdom" (Winter 1995: 56). The need to believe was one shared by the séance attendee and, in due course, the cinemagoer.

Writing on early cinema, Tom Gunning discusses "an aesthetic which was defined by the goal of astonishing viewers with sensational displays and direct address" (Cook 1999: 370). In pre-classical films of the 1900s, Gunning and André Gaudreault identify moments of "monstration" when a single shot exceeds the requirements of narrative and characterization. If their word suggests the monstrous apparitions of spiritualism, the similarities between spiritualism and the moving image also occur to Oppenheim. She observes that, to those seeking proof of a transcendent realm, the drawing room séance resembled the role television would come to play in secular society (Oppenheim 1985: 9). For their entertainment function "domestic séances may have offered something of the escapism so abundantly supplied by soap operas today, but with one important difference: In the spiritualist home circle, the medium was not simply an outside observer; she was the crucial participant in the unfolding drama" (Oppenheim 1985: 10). Spiritualism appealed crucially to women. Kudos attached to mediums or "trance lecturers," providing an early forum in which American women could address mixed audiences. The concurrent rise of spiritualism and cinema emphasized the public display of female interiority, a display which would become all the more visible and significant as cinema evolved. While mediumship attracted bored middle-class matrons and drudging servant girls alike, women would be a key demographic in the classical cinema audience. If the fraught interiority of the female protagonist crucially shaped post-classical art cinema, by the 1990s films revolving around a woman's grief would engage powerfully with subversive public behavior. If Solomon argues convincingly that the link between spiritualism and cinema did not lead to "spirit-cinema" in the way that photography's development in the nineteenth century had led to "spirit-photography," nevertheless the cinema's narrative investment in ghosts and in mourning over the decades may offer scope to characterize mourning cinema as a generic form of spirit-cinema analogous to that precinct in early photography.

Melodrama and Horror

As the cinema passed into its classical phase from around 1917, the relationship between the lachrymose and the uncanny, so crucial to the spiritualist's trade, found expression in the growing popularity of the screen melodrama and the horror film. As Steve Neale has ably described it, "melodrama" is a term which has traditionally embraced high adventure and what we now deem "action genres," as well as the lachrymal drama, rather than exclusively signifying the preoccupation with floridly expressed emotional states by which theorists came to define it during the 1970s. For our purposes, that the term has come to mean different things at different times seems almost serendipitous. Like the term "genre" itself, around which a number of ideas and interests cluster, melodrama can be a fluid concept, a quality which perhaps lends it to adaptation to the project of this book.

It is within melodrama and horror that the roots of a contemporary mourning cinema can be found. In the silent and early sound eras, the melodrama imbued with metaphysical themes flourished in Europe and America alike. In Czarist Russia, the melodramas of Evgenii Bauer rehearse a link between the heroine's inner life and the afterlife, trading in the consolations of the hereafter and making vivid appeal to those who wished to believe in a love that never dies, a stock theme in stage and screen melodrama. In *The Dying Swan* (*Umirayushchii Lebed*, Evgenii Bauer, 1916), Vera Karalli magnetized audiences as a soul torn between life and death. In *After Death* (*Posle smerti*, Evgenii Bauer, 1915), in which a photographer is haunted by the ghost of a young woman who kills herself out of love for him: "Bauer confronts the audience with the wraith-like Karalli in a way that reminds us of cinema's capacity to conjure apparition in darkness" (Armstrong 2007: 36). The secularization which shaped both classical melodrama and the horror film could already be felt in Bauer. While *After Death* makes much of the afterlife, interestingly in a Russia still beholden to the Czar as God's representative on Earth, there is no mention of God or the clergy. Bauer was more interested in the philosophical problem of presence and absence, of the reconciliation of life with death, than in the appeal to consensual attitudes. This had innovative consequences for the image. Like the Méliès films, *After Death* was shot in black-and-white with color tints. Summarizing Bauer's work, Richard Taylor finds his aesthetics, rather than embracing the naturalism underpinning early American *mise-en-scène*, create a distinctive sense of screen reality. For actor and director Ivan Perestiani: "Bauer had a gift for using light. His scenery was alive, mixing the monumental with the intimate.... A beam of light in his hands was an artist's brush" (Vincendeau 1995: 34). Bauer's work emerged out of a late nineteenth century theatrical form described by commentators as "modified melodrama," a mode characterized by "high-voltage emotionalism, examination of soul-states, and the observation of manners.... The unhappy end became common" (Cook 1997: 166). Appearing against a backdrop of the bloodiest war in history, Bauer's fraught heroines answered the need for models of grief while becoming potent emblems for Allied outrage over the German invasion of Belgium, the sinking of the *Lusitania*, and the execution of nurse Edith Cavell, regularly cited at the time as symbols of "femininity" violated by German excesses. (Raitt 1997: 247). Arguably "the nineteenth-century melodramatic ideal of reducing dialogue in favour of music and pictorial *mise-en-scène*" (Gledhill 1997: 169) echoes across the cinema of mourning.

The visual and aural evidence that seemed crucial to spiritualism's credibility was satisfied by classical melodrama, which located extreme emotions in everyday contexts with a naturalism that bore out its ontological justification. Cinema's first three decades saw many international examples convinced of the existence of a spiritual realm transcending life's vale of tears. World War I and its aftermath saw a boost in spiritualism's fortunes as women sought succor for their losses. Winter writes: "The upheaval of war led not to a rejection or recasting of attitudes about spiritualism, but to the deepening of well-established Victorian sentiments and conjectures concerning the nature of the spiritual world" (Winter 1995: 76). Melodrama's aesthetic invention derived from the theatricalism of the nineteenth century séance. By the 1910s, the imagery thrown up on the nickelodeon wall and in the suburban séance must have borne uncanny resemblances.

Prewar Continental cinema provides fertile contexts for the exploration of pathological forms of interiority. "European cinema," Deleuze writes, "at an early stage confronted a group of phenomena; amnesia, hypnosis, hallucination, madness, the vision of the dying, and especially nightmare and dream. This was an important aspect ... of German expressionism and its various alliances with psychiatry and psychoanalysis; and of the French school and its various alliances with surrealism" (Deleuze 1989: 53). In Weimar Germany, the new Expressionist films explored traumatic inner states with widespread aesthetic consequences for world cinema. For Paul Wells, *The Cabinet of Dr. Caligari*, *Nosferatu* and *The Golem* (1920) were early masterpieces that proved influential elsewhere, largely because ... they progressed aspects of cinema itself and were motivated by an artistic seriousness that was soon to dissipate in the Hollywood model" (Wells 2000: 44). While Deleuze sees the various Continental modernisms as attempts to break with the "'American' limitations of the action-image" (Deleuze 1989: 53), classical Hollywood was famously enriched by exposure to European experiment. The Germanic legacy can be felt in *The Mummy* (Karl Freund, 1932), a highly inventive work so imbued with the material circumstances of death that it could take its place as a lost ancestor of recent films of mourning such as *Morvern Callar*, *Under the Sand* and *Kissed* (Lynne Stopkewich, 1996). John Baxter writes: "The mummy's revivification, its crusted eyes creeping open ... the slow extending of a bandaged hand with fragments of rubbish trembling on the fingertips to suggest the rotting nature of the body, an exit shown by unravelled bandages dragging across the tomb's floor" (Baxter 1968: 76). Appearing from Universal, a "poverty row" studio practiced at making low budgets and low "Germanic" lighting conjure strange frissons, *The Mummy* remains a strong example of "excessive" aesthetics in the Hollywood mainstream. Such excesses were encouraged by the fact that the Hollywood "Production Code," setting forth guidelines on "good taste" and instituting a set of recommendations governing the representation of sex and violence, did not come into force until July 1934. The early–30s were a rich era in the American horror film's exploitation of audience susceptibilities. Other historical factors play into this golden age of horror. *The Mummy*, *Frankenstein* (James Whale, 1931), *The Mystery of the Wax Museum* (Michael Curtiz, 1933), *Freaks* (Tod Browning, 1930): so much of Hollywood's horror output of the interwar years featured deformed creatures that we may discern the delayed reaction to a public legacy of the recent war, its disfigured and maimed survivors inhabiting street corners and bars in cities across Europe and America. In one of the most powerful scenes in the Continental cinema of the time, and one which undoubtedly influenced Hollywood's horror cycle, in the antiwar film *J'Accuse* (Abel Gance, 1918) the war dead rise from a French cemetery to reproach those complacent civilians who let them die in vain.

Other Continental films also inform cinema's interest in mourning and grief. In *Destiny* (*Der müde Tod, Between Two Worlds*, Fritz Lang, 1921), Death sequesters a young girl's lover behind a windowless wall surrounding the annex to a cemetery. When she begs to have him back, Death offers her three chances to save him. With its extraordinary lighting and architectural sense, this hauntingly beautiful melodrama finds its heroine longing to break the binds of earthly existence to reach the "other side." We are reminded of the desire of the séance attendee and the yearning of modern mourning heroines such as Marie (*Under the Sand*), Laura (*Don't Look Now*) and Julie (*Three Colors: Blue*). In Lang's one French film *Liliom* (Fritz Lang, 1934), a dead criminal is allowed a day on earth to console the little girl who misses him. The similarity with the bereft Ponette in *Ponette* (Jacques Doillon, 1996) is suggestive. While Lang's notorious account of the child murderer in *M* (Fritz Lang, 1931) concentrates on the pursuit of the killer and its political implications, its investigative scenario is framed by the loss of Elsie Beckmann and her mother's forlorn voice calling for her is one of the film's most powerfully narrated scenes. In France, Abel Gance's melodrama *Mater Dolorosa* (*Sorrowful Mother/The Torture of Silence*, 1917) amply trades in the "suffering woman" scenario endemic to melodrama, here making death her only route to happiness. The film charts a woman's guilt over her affair with her husband's brother and subsequent pregnancy. She attempts suicide, but, doubly cheated by death, she loses her lover who is killed trying to save her. Writing with reference to the director's use of superimposition, Deleuze observes: "As Gance says, superimpositions are the images of feelings and thoughts by which the soul 'envelops' bodies and 'precedes' them" (Deleuze 1986: 86). For Deleuze, "with Gance the French cinema invents a cinema of the sublime" (ibid.: 49). The superimposed image will take its place in mourning films to come. In a film which understands the eventual condition of all men and women, the heroine of *Mater Dolorosa*, stricken with grief and longing for release, dramatizes the Freudian death drive, the urge animating all desire. In the prewar decades, imagery foretelling the cinema of mourning also appears from avant-garde contexts. In the surrealist classic *Un Chien Andalou* (Luis Buñuel and Salvador Dalí, 1928), there appears an image which seems essential to the mourner's attempt to reconcile life and death, the ego and the lost object. A man is shot and falls to the ground. As he does so, he reaches out and strokes the back of a nude woman crouching in front of him who disappears as he expires. The image is full of contemporary resonances. Winter shows how the image of the war widow crouching before a grave, whether in flesh or in stone, became a familiar sight in the post–1918 era. Meanwhile, as Winter observes, Freud's account of inconsolable melancholy also evokes the need to touch as a way of mediating loss, to establish its limits amid "a forest of loss, unable to focus on what had been torn from their lives" (Winter 1995: 115). The image of the woman reaching out and touching the world around her will recur in modern mourning films. For collapsing the present and the past, the absent and the present, this image also resonates with the mourning film's preoccupation with time. Deleuze writes of how the experiments of prewar European cinema attempt to reach "a mystery of time, of uniting image, thought and camera in a single 'automatic subjectivity'" (Deleuze 1986: 53). Death and loss proffer compelling actual and aesthetic imagery in the early decades of cinema. Responding to the horrors of war while inheriting lachrymose and fantastical tendencies from theatrical melodrama, sideshow obscurantism, spirit photography and the trick film, classicism learned early how to manipulate a susceptible public with the eternal drama of presence and absence.

High Melodrama

Death and its effects have often been most poignantly realized in films which broach the limitations of conventional practice in their aesthetics. David Bordwell characterizes Hollywood classical conventions as a kind of filmic holy writ: "the film studio (resembling) the monastery's scriptorium, the site of the transcription and transmission of countless narratives; that unity is the basic attribute of film form; that the Hollywood film purports to be "realistic" in both an Aristotelian sense (truth to the probable) and a naturalistic one (truth to historical fact); that the Hollywood film strives to conceal its artifice through techniques of continuity and "invisible" storytelling; that the film should be comprehensible and unambiguous; and that it possesses a fundamental emotional appeal that transcends class and nation." (Bordwell 1988: 3). The Hollywood model constitutes an accessible, easy-to-read, "excessively obvious cinema" (ibid.: 3) which does not challenge the spectator's ability to follow the narrative. According to Annette Kuhn, this model was established by the mid–1930s, at which time sound technology had been introduced and narrative had become the backbone of studio output and fundamental to audience expectations: "The era of classic cinema may be regarded as a period in which the cinematic image remained largely subservient to the requirements of a specific type of narrative structure" (Kuhn cited in Cook 1997: 40). Despite local differences, the classical Hollywood model was widely adopted in European commercial cinema. The effect of this classical model is, ideally, one of uninterrupted immersion. Susan Hayward writes, "In this cinema, style is subordinate to narrative: shots, lighting, color must not draw attention to themselves any more than the editing, the *mise-en-scène* or sound.... Ambiguity must be dissolved ... the spectator must know where she or he is in time and space and in relation to the logic and chronology of the narrative" (Hayward 2006: 66). For Valerie Orpen, the obviousness of the match between aesthetics and content is importantly a trick of the editing: "Since classical cinema's main purpose is supposedly to tell a story ... it follows that continuity editing is not intended to be noticed ... should never be obtrusive without good reason. It appears "invisible" and "seamless" and therein lies its strength." (Orpen 2003: 16). Robert Kolker stresses self-evidence and the compelling nature of the continuity system for audiences: "an unfolding story that seems to be unfolding on its own; that the audience be embraced by that story.... They liked what they saw and wanted more. We want more still" (Hill 1998: 18).

Yet while accounting for the essential parameters of classical practice, Bordwell's taxonomy of Hollywood classicism obscures the often startling stylistic experimentation that could be achieved in the classical studio film, heterogeneity with implications not only for a future cinema of mourning, but for the essence of cinema's very "hypnotic monstrum" (Orr 2000: 42). If for Pasolini the dominant "tradition of film language," of which Hollywood was the major exemplar, "is primarily naturalistic and objective" (ibid.: 42), beneath the hegemony of mainstream narrative cinemas, cinemas of "prose" as Pasolini sees it, lies the medium's essential mysteriousness, its poetry. He writes, "In other words, all its irrational, oneiric, elementary, and barbaric elements were forced below the level of consciousness; that is, they were exploited as subconscious instruments of shock and persuasion" (ibid.: 42). Classical Hollywood history is incomplete without those moments when the dominant style of narrative prose came under the influence of cinema's capacity for the poetic. Such poetic impulses often emerged out of the straitened economics of the studio second feature. Deleuze writes, "The B movie [was] an active centre of experimentation and creation" (Deleuze 1986: 167)

Spiritual Gestures

In the years of the transition from silent to sound cinema, a cycle of Hollywood melodramas appeared which sought to reconcile classical realism with metaphysics. Underwritten by a compelling story, increasingly sophisticated technology, and the German influence on lighting and *mise-en-scène*, the scenarios found in *7th Heaven* (Frank Borzage, 1927), *Street Angel* (Frank

Borzage, 1928) and *A Farewell to Arms* (Frank Borzage, 1932) combined naturalistic narrative with a spiritual dimension. The celestial implication of Bordwell's "scriptorium" seems most apt. In these elegant, polished and moving films, transcendent sentiments found legitimacy in a transparent accessible form. One of the assumptions of classical Hollywood melodrama was the idea that mortality and human tenderness bring individuals together and legitimize a modern sense of community. Romantic love and death are intertwined themes in Borzage's spiritual dramas. Jessica Winter writes, "Love does not conquer all ... but it is the sole transcendent value in an ugly world, a protective but permeable bubble.... Amid the ravages and enforced separations of war and the hardships of poverty, Borzage's lovers find safety and redemption in each other's arms, a rapturous solace that even death can't kill. Framed in loving close-ups and swathed by soft, flat lighting, his lovers glow with a sensuous, mysterious purity that's not quite of this earth. His melodramas posit love as a secular religion, and many of his films imply a spiritual continuity between this world and the next, allowing the dead to speak in voiceover ... or appear in double exposures ... Borzage's universe also permits returning from the dead" (Armstrong et al., 2007: 56). For Ephraim Katz, "[Borzage] pioneered in the use of the soft focus, and the gauzed photography of his films, combined with a fluid, caressing camera movement, gave his lovers an idealized halo" (Katz 1998: 154). Such devices saw classicism broaching the possibility of human transcendence in technologically innovative ways, a celestial legacy which will recur in Hollywood treatments of grief and mourning.

The Borzage cycle illustrates how the rapt and tearful spectator at the spiritualist séance resonates with the engrossed, often female, Hollywood spectator of the 1930s and 1940s. The promise of blissful transcendence which underwrote the medium's work also animated the munitions workers, housewives and shop girls who flocked to the cinema. Jay Winter writes, "Cinema was a kind of semi-private séance, bringing old images to millions through 'modern' technology" (Winter 1995: 138). Theorizing that strand of classical melodrama known in Hollywood and to audiences and critics as the "woman's picture" or "weepie," Molly Haskell identifies the appeal in terms familiar from the séance: "the mesmerized absorption, the choking, the welling up of tears" (Haskell 1979: 163). By 1938 and the release of the characteristically metaphysical *Three Comrades* (Frank Borzage, 1938), melodrama had lost much of its celestial quality. Yet the era saw the heyday of a genre which realized what the nineteenth century spiritualists had envisaged; strong female heroines, transcendent passion, and a very willing audience. As Haskell writes, "For the woman's film, like other art forms, pays tribute at its best (and at its worst) to the power of the imagination, to the mind's ability to picture a perfect love triumphing over the mortal and conditional" (ibid.: 188). Designed for the matinee audience and dedicated to depicting a woman's point of view, the woman's picture not only evokes earlier moments of lachrymose excess at the afternoon séance, but contained potential for contemporary ideological subversion. And in these *women's* films, as in Bauer, female desire and female stars shaped both narrative and aesthetics: "Fontaine's and Darrieux's obsessions become leaps into immortality. The lovers in *Back Street* are finally united — in the resurrection of filmed time. In *Peter Ibbetson*, Ann Harding and Gary Cooper, separated by prison walls, live their love in their dreams and in the bowery radiance of Lee Garmes' cinematography" (ibid.: 188).

A director closely associated with Garmes was Josef von Sternberg. Sternberg's was a practice which notoriously breached the boundaries of narrative in search of aesthetic excess. Known more for the tantalizing pictorialism of the melodramas he made with Marlene Dietrich between 1930 and 1935 than for the coherence or credibility of their plots, Sternberg's Dietrich cycle privileged the poetry of light over the prose of narrative and did so for the sake of a woman's interiority, however mysterious her motives. In *Shanghai Express* (Josef von Sternberg, 1932) and *The Scarlet Empress* (Josef von Sternberg, 1934), "the visual form itself rather than a conventional plot express the content" (Katz 1998: 1306). Sternberg and Garmes juxtaposed "shadow and light to express shifts of mood and inner action" (ibid.: 1306). The Sternberg-Dietrich films revolved around her feelings, however elliptically and metonymically put. Indeed, the more minimal Dietrich's acting seemed, the more contrived the script, the more banal the dialogue, the more she seemed to make the very light the vehicle for the film's affects. If the archetypal woman's pictures of their day put Mrs. Average America at the heart of a Main Street novelette, Sternberg made Dietrich the exotic medium of a thousand perfume counter fantasies. He fastidiously shaped the light around his star, replete with "the ever present scrims, veils, nets, fog, or smoke between subject and camera" (ibid.: 1306). As Deleuze realizes, Sternberg's preoccupation with the image descends less from archetypal German Expressionist interactions of light and shadow than with "light's adventure with white" (Deleuze 1986: 96), a legacy putting Sternberg closer to the metaphysics of Borzage, even the apparitions of spiritualism, than commentators have acknowledged. Central to the Sternberg-Dietrich melodrama is a form of spiritual choice, a device animating the narrative and providing motivation for the "lyrical abstraction" (ibid.: 115) of the film's visuals. For Deleuze, this aesthetic, like the desiring woman enhanced by its allure, is all about transcendence, a making-possible, virtuality beyond the natural and empirical state of things. The cycle's importance to the evolution of the mourning film is inscribed in this aspiration to another place. For Dietrich's ethereal heroines, death is not just inevitable but a kind of blessed release to be courted and even prepared for; in *Dishonored* (Josef von Sternberg, 1931), her Mata Hari figure is shot for espionage, but not before applying her makeup.

Death is made meaningful in the woman's picture because for its protagonist it is consequent upon the instinct to love. The event of death validates a romantic conception of love for the characters on screen, while underwritten for the spectator by a naturalistic diegesis inflected by blissful effects of light and metaphysical suggestion. Love, earthly, contingent, a seemingly chance encounter, becomes immortal, transcendent and celestial through its association with the end of life. A skilful blending of Gothic horror and the woman's picture, and a seminal instance of how such miscegenation can give rise to a fresh generic configuration, *Rebecca* (Alfred Hitchcock, 1940) finds love and death indissolubly related. The film is usually seen as a melodrama charting its naive young heroine's transition from girl to woman via marriage. Less often discussed is the fate of the housekeeper Mrs. Danvers (Judith Anderson). Mrs. Danvers was devoted to Rebecca, her employer's late wife. After we first meet her, the camera moves into a close-up of her face before the image dissolves into a clock face reflecting a window streaming with rain. There is the suggestion of unremitting sorrow hidden beneath a controlled visage. Deleuze's characterization of the close-up as a device which tears the image away from spatio-temporal coordinates (Deleuze 1986: 99) is neatly borne out here. As character and as humor, Mrs. Danvers resists both space and time. Dressed in plain funereal black, she is a mournful presence, inexplicably appearing in rooms and startling the second Mrs. de Winter (Joan Fontaine), detailing with sensual relish the contents of Rebecca's room, now a shrine to the dead woman. We see Mrs. Danvers appear behind billowing lace curtains. The effect of this gaunt middle-aged presence beneath lace could be seen as a subversive, perhaps cruel allusion, to celestial moments in Bauer, Borzage, Sternberg's Dietrich beneath gauze. In this cinema of the celestial, light's adventure with white becomes a harbinger of the metaphysical.

Haunting *Rebecca* like the absent figure of its title, Mrs. Danvers seems to occupy some limbo between the past and the present, this world and the next, prevented from a normal life by her obsessive passion for her mistress. On the discovery of Rebecca's final illness and her subsequent fate, Mrs. Danvers sets fire to the house and herself with it. Earlier, Maxim de Winter (Laurence Olivier) relates how he disposed of Rebecca's body by punching holes in the planks of a boat. The final image of Mrs. Danvers is a low angle of the ceiling from which burning planks fall on her. It is as though by laying the ghost of Rebecca, de Winter lays the ghost of Mrs. Danvers, who will follow her mistress into eternity. The fact that we see the burning planks from Mrs. Danvers's perspective suggests, like the clock face earlier, a film which is ambivalent in its patriarchal allegiances. Feminist writers have applauded the way *Rebecca* establishes an excess of desire which is not exhausted by the expository police investigation of the film's second half. Tania Modleski writes, "For if death by drowning did not extinguish the woman's desire, can we be certain that death by fire has reduced it utterly to ashes?" (Modleski 1998: 133–134). Mrs. Danvers's baleful shadow looms across such modern mourning films as *Interiors*, *Under the Sand* and *I Have Loved You So Long*.

Evincing a dual heritage of nineteenth century theatrical histrionics and the aesthetic contrivances of the parlor séance, if classical melodrama traded in tears, certain trends in the classical horror film were also marked by an investment in pity and sadness. In the 1940s, the low budget Hollywood horror picture remained a site for Continental-style innovation and invention. Alexander Nemerov details the ways in which a cycle of cheap horror films made by Russian-born producer Val Lewton at RKO invested themes of monstrousness and the uncanny with a poignancy usually associated with melodrama. As during World War I, for British and American women the mid–1940s was a time of anxiety as their men went far away, perhaps never to return. Nemerov writes of Lewton's work: "Though none of them is about the war, it appears in them all the same, even if we never catch a clear glimpse of it. Like a ghost moving through the house, it slams doors and tips over the pottery, inverts pictures on the wall, and shatters windows with rocks never thrown. In movies celebrated for their portrayal of the unseen, the war is the singular invisible beast, the Damned Thing, that stalks around and bends the grass as we look in vain for shade of hide or hair" (Nemerov 2005: 1). Edmund Wilson explains the historical appeal of horror: "The longing for mystic experience which seems always to manifest itself in periods of social confusion, when political progress is blocked: as soon as we feel that our own world has failed us, we try to find evidence for another world" (cited in Nemerov 2). Releases such as *Cat People* (Jacques Tourneur, 1942), *I Walked with a Zombie* (Jacques Tourneur, 1943), *The Curse of the Cat People* (Robert Wise and Gunther von Fritsch, 1943) are suffused with a melancholia all the more powerful for its elusive nature. The sudden apparitions, which may or may not be intimations of another realm, link Lewton to Bauer while foretelling the ellipses of modern mourning cinema. As a textbook moment in the horror film's evolution, what distinguishes the Lewton horror cycle is the hiding of the horror, the habitual non-disclosure of a ghastly thing which cannot be imaged. Lewton films exploit "the phobia attached to the truth of the unseen" (Doane 1988: 50). This brinkmanship of the frame line recurs in the mourning film's play with off-screen space. For Nemerov and other commentators, the Lewton RKO cycle is as much a riposte to the oblivious optimism of wartime Hollywood releases such as *Mrs. Miniver* (William Wyler, 1942), *Meet Me in St. Louis* (Vincente Minnelli, 1944) and *Going My Way* (Leo McCarey, 1944), all high profile high prestige productions, as it evinced a fringe precinct of classicism straining to express extremes of human longing. Paul Wells writes, "The horror film was a pertinent and persuasive model of the darker underbelly of American culture" (Wells 2000: 51).

Lewton's relevance to the mourning film can be felt in the periodic manifestation of human icons, images of statuesque figures within which is concentrated telling complexes of emotion. For Nemerov, they represent "an infinity of connotation. They are versions of his belief in the suggestive power of darkness, the allure of the unseen over what is plainly visible.... These minor figures visualize the murmurs of grief and lost gestures of mourning, transient and sensuous as the touch of a finger on nylon" (Nemerov 2005: 4). Following the death of her mother (Simone Simon) in *Cat People*, in its sequel *The Curse of the Cat People*, Amy (Ann Carter) does not mix with other children, frequents a mysterious mansion, and insists that she has a "friend," invisible to her parents but not to Amy. As though charmed, Nicholas Musuraca's camera returns to Simon's iconic spectral figure alone in a snowbound garden. A caped medieval angel standing in a cemetery singing a lullaby, this projection of a child's grief becomes a metaphor for feelings too powerful for literal representation during stoic wartime, as well as a rapt model for mourning women in *Interiors* and *Don't Look Now*. For its indulgence in metaphor, its emphasis on interiority and its poetic view of the afterlife, *The Curse of the Cat People* seems persuasively European. Indeed, appearing a little under two years apart, the Lewton film is remarkably redolent of Marcel Carné's *Les Visiteurs du soir* (Marcel Carné, 1942), with its reconciliation of Earth and Heaven, and a plea for compassion in a divided and occupied wartime France.

Another powerful image in Lewton's work is that of Jessica Holland (Christine Gordon), the woman possessed by voodoo spirits in *I Walked with a Zombie* who sleepwalks to a native ceremony through a sugar cane field by moonlight. Mute and melancholy, Jessica offers an archetype for that recurrent figure in the cinema of mourning; the wandering woman. While she is not in mourning for the death of another, in losing her agency and vitality because of the curse she is under, Jessica is in mourning for the loss of her own life. She embodies that grief for the self which is a part of grieving for the Other. Nemerov also identifies in Lewton a trope of "kinetic immobility" (ibid.: 7). He refers to the scene in *Cat People* in which a charcoal drawing is swept along by the wind. The still figure and the image of kinetic immobility have implications for future mourning films. Lewton's output contains uncanny portents of the type. Death, whether as material finitude or the living death of the zombie, is thematically highlighted in *I Walked with a Zombie* by the words of Paul Holland (Tom Conway) to his wife's nurse. Looking out to sea, he observes, "And that luminous water. It takes its gleam from millions of tiny dead bodies, the glitter of putrescence. There's no beauty here—only death and decay." Foreshadowing suggestions of the abject which disparately mark *Three Colors: Blue*, *Morvern Callar* and *Kissed*, the sugar cane field is dotted with skulls, while a decaying animal hangs in the moonlight. The sea is a key motif in *I Walked with a Zombie*, the milieu in which the innocent nurse Betsy (Frances Dee) is introduced to the immanence of death and the site of the somnolent Jessica's supposed drowning. The sight of the sea foreshadows the significance of water and sea in mourning films. Over the issue of fear and loss, in Lewton's work the horror movie and melodrama come into fluent concision with consequences for postwar treatments of grief.

Also atmospherically shot by Musuraca was *The Spiral Staircase* (Robert Siodmak, 1946), another film of significance to the archaeology of the mourning film, not least for its allusion to cinema's prehistory. The opening scene finds the heroine, a lady's maid in turn-of-the-century New England, sitting rapt at a screening of *The Kiss* at a local bioscope. Helen (Dorothy Maguire) saw both parents die in a fire ten years before and was so traumatized that she has become mute. The sense in which Helen is "stuck" in her grief is alluded to in conversations with her suitor, the local doctor, while her experience of the single night in which the action plays out is neatly mirrored in Lewis's observations of grief: "Tonight all the hells of young grief have opened again; the mad words, the bitter resentment, the fluttering in the stomach, the nightmare unreality, the wallowed-in tears. For in grief nothing 'stays put.' One keeps on emerging from a phase, but it always recurs. Round and round. Everything repeats. Am I going in circles, or dare I hope I am on a spiral? But if a spiral, am I going up or down it?" (Lewis, 49). In this light, the film is aptly named. Its action takes place amid local panic following the murders of several young women, all of whom had some physical defect. Key scenes find Helen disoriented by what she sees. Following a reverie in which she fantasizes marriage to the local doctor, she searches for the now dissolved *mise-en-scène* of her happiness. After she locks the man she believes to be the killer in the cellar, Helen runs from room to room seeking help, the scene viewed from a high angle by Musuraca's watchful camera. Earlier, we saw the camera pull back along a landing as it appeared to "watch" Helen looking at herself in a mirror. The prospect of the film "happening" around a disoriented wandering protagonist will recur in mourning cinema. At the time *Variety* magazine alluded to the camera's agency: "Fascinating use is made of the camera to make it nearly as potent a force as action itself in creating [an] eerie background" (Lazaroff Alpi 1998: 144). Meanwhile, the prospect of death occurring beyond sight, mind and language, what the killer ominously refers to as "the quiet that I can give you," recurs in scenes in which, as his victims are strangled, we see only hands clutching at the air, their voices clamoring for breath, while they are elided into darkness. In hindsight, *The Spiral Staircase* seems blithely aware of the various cinematic currents which have formed the cinema of mourning, containing eerie effects in which the suggestion of prewar horror is occasionally inflected with an avant-garde sensibility, as Charles Higham and Joel Greenberg show: "An eye lurking deep in a cupboard; a face that swims out of focus as the dumb mouth blurs into a hole" (Higham 1968: 24). We have only to recall the moment in *Un Chien Andalou* less than two decades earlier in which a man clutches his face, removing his hand to reveal that he has no mouth, to feel the resonance of Continental surrealism for classical American horror.

Responding perhaps to news of the massive loss of life as World War II entered its final stages, the Hollywood melodrama staged a revival of metaphysical themes. *The Song of Bernadette* (Henry King, 1943) put a young woman at the center of one of the most celebrated cases of religious hallucination in modern history. Relying on rhetoric rather than the visual frissons associated with Lewton's work, the film now seems a pale recollection of Borzagian celestial melodrama. A prologue enlists trust in Bernadette's "visions," while assuring the non-believer that they had no business being in the cinema. Coded with classical lighting and *mise-en-scène* to reconcile earthly strife with heavenly consolation, the sight of the Virgin Mary provided solace for those seeking religious and emotional succor in hard times. While nostalgic for an earlier moment in screen aesthetics, *The Song of Bernadette* also evoked the era of high spiritualism. When the hallucinations supposedly occurred in 1858, thousands flocked to Lourdes: "Women and especially children brought the supernatural into everyday life and the everyday into the supernatural" (Winter 1995: 121). Winter evokes droves of women at the wartime matinee: "There arose a vast pilgrimage movement, active to this day" (ibid.: 121). Integrating the celestial with wartime stoicism was the British woman's picture *Millions Like Us* (Frank Launder and Sidney Gilliatt, 1943). There a young factory worker learns of the loss of her airman husband. Cue for a beseeching gaze heavenwards as the angelic Celia (Patricia Roc) hears another bomber squadron set off for an uncertain future. This brief moment of soft focus seems all the more affecting for the solace it provides from the stridently documentary look and pace of the film.

The celestial register can be felt in other mourning films of the period. Another vehicle for the star of *The Song of Bernadette*, Jennifer Jones, was *Portrait of Jennie* (William Dieterle, 1948), in which a phantom girl appears to a lonely artist in late–40s New York dressed in garb of the early part of the century. The girl lived in the city in the 1900s and died many years before in a storm off the New England coast. At each meeting she appears older than at the last. There is something Heideggerian about the way in which *Portrait of Jennie* juxtaposes the living artist and this long-dead figure, overlaying the quotidian details of his present with old newspapers and, most poignantly, his memories of her. The artist is left with nostalgia for someone nobody he knows ever knew, his mourning coalescing around a liaison which happened for him alone: "Few films toy with cinema's capacity for absence and presence with such lingering, happy melancholy" (Armstrong 2007: 139). *Portrait of Jennie* is an allegory of grief, positing the time mourning takes on a metaphysical plane in which the timeless and the contingent are intertwined. Reflecting this juxtaposition, the film's most novel characteristic as a film was the infusion of contemporary New York locations with an ethereal sense derived from a combination of color, monochrome and sepia images. The phantom girl's song is haunting —

> "Where I come from
> Nobody knows
> And where I'm going
> Everything goes,
> The wind blows,
> The sea flows —
> And nobody knows."

— catching the sense in which life is transient and every being is bound towards death. While pushing emotive buttons in the high-40s, issues of transience and ineffable continuity, as well as imagery — the sea — recur in Jennie's song which echo throughout mourning cinema. Another British film, *A Matter of Life and Death* (*Stairway to Heaven*, Michael Powell and Emeric Pressburger, 1946), re-imagined the possibilities of monochrome within a realist tradition and remains one of cinema's most felt articulations of the competing claims of love and death. While Technicolor scenes on Earth lend an English village a visionary luminosity, grey monochrome images of Heaven suggest modernity's religious skepticism, the diminished imagery even anticipating the dour looks of modern mourning films such as *Interiors* and *Birth*.

Postwar Excess

One of the most iconic images of 1950s American cinema is that of Jane Wyman's widow sitting apparently alone in her suburban lounge, her form spectrally reflected in the screen of a television set as the off-screen voice of a salesman assures her that this far-seeing apparatus will bring all of life back to her. The title of the film from which the image comes is not inapposite: *All That Heaven Allows* (Douglas Sirk, 1955). Working in melodrama, Sirk made use of postwar technology to invest the image with the excessive emotions of his protagonists. "While the coming of sound meant the dominance of the verbal register ... development of new technologies in the 1950s — colour, widescreen, deep-focus, crane and dolly ... made a complex *mise-en-scène*" (Cook 1999: 158). As the Hollywood studio system and the narrative-driven continuity system on which it was founded began its decline, *mise-en-scène* in the 1950s melodrama became the site for some uncontainable emotions.

Geoffrey Nowell-Smith has drawn on Freud's notion of "conversion hysteria" for an idea of the excess of music, color, movement and *mise-en-scène* in the work of postwar melodrama practitioners Sirk, Max Ophüls and Vincente Minnelli: "Such 'hysterical' moments can be seen as a breakdown in realist conventions, where elements of the *mise-en-scène* lose their motivation and coherence is lost" (ibid.: 160). Theorized by Freud and Charcot in the 1880s, in cases of conversion hysteria acute psychosocial stress is converted into physical symptoms such as a twitch or a muscular spasm. By disabling or impairing a bodily function, the brain would relieve the patient of experiencing such stress again. The analogy with a film in which an excess of emotion leads to imagery which is distorted in relation to the demands of realistic narrative seems clear. The florid "hysterical" musical *Carousel* (Henry King, 1956) inscribes extreme grief across the image. Made earlier by Borzage (*Liliom*, 1930) and Lang (*Liliom*, Fritz Lang, 1934), *Carousel* bathed its tale of the carnival barker given reprieve from Heaven in the lush colors of Charles G. Clarke's cinematography. Free of the high bright optimism of other 1950s Hollywood musicals, King's rendition of Ferenc Molnár's tragic play saw undying love taking on a macabre tinge as the implications of death and loss were played out amid a riot of compensatory hues.

Thomas Elsaesser identifies a melodrama protagonist constrained from self-expression by circumstances, the resulting emotional energy exploding across the screen. Elsaesser writes, "Because of the restricted scope for external action determined by the subject and because everything, as Sirk said, happens "inside." [This] sublimation of dramatic conflict into décor, colour, gesture and composition of frame ... in the best melodramas is perfectly thematized in terms of the characters' emotional and psychological predicaments" (cited in Gledhill 1987: 52). In *Imitation of Life* (Douglas Sirk, 1959), extremes of emotion find histrionic expression as the acting competes with the theatricality of a big community funeral. A daughter's reconciliation with her mother at the mother's funeral finds Sarah Jane (Susan Kohner) hysterically attempting to bridge the gap between life and death amid an overripe widescreen set piece of auspicious dimensions. Excess becomes the very theme of the scene and its visual rendition. So resplendent is the mother's funeral that, as James

Harvey remarks, it appears to have "little to do with the character of Annie" (Harvey 2001: 421). Modleski emphasizes how unique this sequence is: "It is notoriously difficult to find tragedies that deal with the subject of an aging, ailing or dying woman. But if the subject has not lent itself to high drama it is the very stuff of the "debased" form of tragedy, melodrama" (Modleski 1999: 196). Appearing in the year commonly consecrated by film historians for its flowering of modernist cinemas, *Imitation of Life* is regarded as the high water mark of 1950s Hollywood melodrama. The mourning film owes much to the theorization of late classical melodrama's excessive sentiments and *mise-en-scène*.

The postwar horror film drew as much of its energy from its protagonist's inner life as from the revelation of monster, ghoul or specter of more literal-minded traditions. Like the cinema itself, horror has its roots in an earlier era. Carlos Clarens wrote, "As the capacity of religion and its equivalents to fill the need receded with the advance of rationalism and technology in the nineteenth century, the simultaneous discovery of the unconscious and the cinema released a new source of imagery for rendering unto film ... the immanent fears of mankind: damnation, demonic possession, old age, death, in brief the nightside of life" (Clarens cited in Cook 1999: 196). Concurrent with modernist European cinema's explorations of alienation and spiritual malaise, postwar American horror became a site for investigations into the modern psyche. Films marketed and critically described as "horror" are steeped in the horror of loss and bereavement.

The following case studies focus on titles appearing as the Hollywood studio system was giving way under the pressure of dwindling audiences, artistically invigorating currents from abroad, and the relaxation of censorship. These examples are drawn from mainstream studio output and its client productions, and the burgeoning independent sector, established and novice directors, and feature actors of earlier generations alongside fresher sensibilities. In their attitudes and aesthetics, these films bridge a transitory moment between classicism and modernism, culturally and cinematically imbued with ancient preoccupations while searching for modern ways of expressing and elaborating them.

Case Study: *The Innocents*

> "In the old park frozen and alone
> Two shapes passed by a while ago
> Their eyes were dead, their lips weak...."
> "Exchange of Feelings," Paul Verlaine

Produced under the aegis of 20th Century–Fox, *The Innocents* (1961) was directed by Jack Clayton, a British filmmaker famously associated with the

1960s British New Wave. Though set in the past and based on a canonical literary source, *The Innocents* responded to the contemporary relaxation of censorship, offering an unsettling portrait of metaphysical portent and sexual obsession. Anticipating the mourning film in many ways, it revolves around a woman who drifts to a liminal space and is brought face to face with the point at which life and death meet. While trading in the imagery of the Gothic mansion common to the 1930s Universal horror cycle, *The Innocents* found an ambiguous protagonist attempting to negotiate uncanny feelings and phenomena. Two women restlessly wander the baroque corridors of *The Innocents*. The sexually naïve governess Miss Giddens (Deborah Kerr) learns from her charges of the passion of two servants who exerted a baleful influence upon the children. Miss Jessel (Clytie Jessop) committed suicide after her lover died. The housekeeper Mrs. Grose (Megs Jenkins) describes her: "She grieved till there was something crazy in her eyes. Never slept, never ate. I used to hear her wandering all over the house, sobbing.... Finally, she died." Languishing in a destructive relationship with Peter Quint (Peter Wyngarde), Miss Jessel, whom we see indistinctly as a vague apparition crossing a corridor, across a lake, is the suffering soul of the film, with all the knowledge of love that Miss Giddens lacks but steeped in the masochism of the woman's picture's characteristically lovelorn protagonist: "Bad she was, but no woman could have suffered more."

The conspiracy between Quint and Miss Jessel, and the children Miles (Martin Stephens) and Flora (Pamela Franklin), generates a strange energy in the house, becoming expressed in a sexual suggestiveness which permeates the film, being both pathological and, as the boy invokes the dead Quint, in Miles precociously sexual. As in *Portrait of Jennie*, a sense of regret is played out in a song with which the children summon the dead. The film's chilling atmosphere comes as much from the specters which appear to Miss Giddens as from a sense of melancholy which overcomes her, and overwhelms a house which inhabits a place somewhere between here and eternity. Heaven and earth become one in the scene in which she bends down over Flora's tortoise and in the ornamental lake behind her the sky becomes reflected in the water. Meditating on the role water plays in French cinema, Deleuze identifies a uniquely clairvoyant quality which is relevant here. He writes, "It is in the water that the loved one who has disappeared is revealed, as if perception enjoyed a scope and interaction, a truth which it did not have on land" (Deleuze 1986: 82). The shimmering image of a servant standing in the garden in a black dress, what Michael Dempsey, comparing her with the increasingly substantial apparition of *Don't Look Now*, refers to as a "gossamer ghost" (Dempsey 1974: 42), is far from the set piece statuesque of Simone Simon's reassuring angel in *The Curse of the Cat People*. The servant resembles more

The Innocents. In an image so degraded as to evoke a macabre satire of the stiff Victorian portrait photograph, Miss Jessel here hovers above the waters of an ornamental lake, summoned by a little girl's song...

the ghostly apparition of nineteenth century spirit photography, an image so degraded as to emphasize transience, while its subject is so pitifully alone as to echo Miss Giddens's own loveless isolation. As Jeremy Dyson writes, "Because the shot is so wide and seemingly composed of shifting layers of foggy grey, the viewer is forced to peer into it, trying to make sense of what they are seeing" (Dyson 2006).

At the behest of its uncontainable emotions, the film's ostensible realism gives way to a visual experimentation which is all the more shocking for being sudden and infrequent. The apparition of a woman passes through a wall in front of Miss Giddens. She sees a woman crying but when she reaches her, all that is left are teardrops on a piece of furniture. Such moments recall the atmosphere of a Magritte painting. The strangeness emerges out of the commonplace detail of nineteenth century interiors corrupted by a bizarre ontological twist in the dominant plot of realist surfaces. Bazin recognized that photography, hence realist cinema, can give rise to this surrealist "twist" in what we are looking at: "Because it produces an image that is a reality of nature, namely, an hallucination that is also a fact" (Bazin 1970: 16).

Dissolves draw attention to the frailty of that which Miss Giddens witnesses. The film itself appears to collude with her projections. Deleuze writes, "The cinema can, with impunity, bring us close to things or take us away from them and revolve around them, it suppresses both the anchoring of the subject and the horizon of the world" (Deleuze 1986: 59). Frampton's filmosophical approach is peculiarly relevant to the way the mourning film accommodates its protagonist's interiority and what this does to the look and atmosphere of the film: "The film may feel a relationship between the character and the object, may think associations beyond 'rational narrative schemata'" (Frampton 2006: 109). Conjured up by the children's song, one which we seldom witness them actually singing, the horrific moments in *The Innocents* are elicited by the film as a film, the soundtrack conspiring with the image track to subvert the spectator's gaze. Coming amid quotidian moments of Miss Giddens's existence, they recall the traumas which erupt across future mourning films.

The Innocents also foretells the mourning film's preoccupation with the abject. Flora presents Miss Giddens with her tortoise. Miss Giddens gasps as a beetle falls out of the gaping mouth of a nude cherub in the garden. Flora sees a spider eating a butterfly. As the children entice spirits into the house, it is gradually invaded by wildlife: insects, reptiles, pigeons, a fly buzzing. That the dead are accompanied by these extraneous horrific elements suggests closeness, even complicity, between the dead and the earth which echoes across mourning cinema. Miss Giddens hints at these visitations as she attempts to investigate what the children know: "There are still the others." With hindsight, we feel her words inspiring another moment in the evolution of mourning cinema. The scenario of the lonely, fraught, possibly insane woman isolated in a house with two precocious children will be revived in *The Others*.

Case Study: *The Haunting*

"Because I could not stop for Death —
He kindly stopped for me...."
"Because I could not stop for Death," Emily Dickinson

The interaction between the woman's film and the horror film becomes increasingly obvious on close examination of certain titles. If *The Innocents* traded in the emotional distrait of the female protagonist and the Gothic tensions of the traditional horror movie, *The Haunting* (1963) saw another impressionable and inexperienced woman torn between innocence and depravity when she becomes the conductor of restless spirits in a haunted house. The minute Eleanor Lance (Julie Harris) appears, it becomes a woman's picture, from the potted account of the narrow compass of her suburban existence, to the dour Mrs. Dudley (Rosalie Crutchley), the caretaker's wife at Hill House, a character resembling the mysterious Mrs. Danvers in *Rebecca* to a degree which suggests *The Haunting* as almost a parodic revision of the classical baroquerie of Hitchcock's film. This evolution is borne out in the narrative. Despite the studiedly skeptical "scientific" framing premise, an interesting ploy in the film's attempt to attract a fresh audience for classical horror, *The Haunting* takes up a curious distance from the characters, appearing to be happening "around" them. This atmosphere is reinforced by Crutchley's rather arch performance. Mrs. Dudley's instructions are rehearsed irrespective of whether or not anyone is listening. At one point, the camera moves around a room while the characters are asleep or absorbed in their thoughts. Such distance has implications for a film which stealthily balances its scientific rationalism against the increasingly hysterical inner voice of its protagonist.

Much is made of Eleanor's loneliness. Chosen to take part in a scientific experiment, she reacts as if having won an exotic holiday among a new set of friends. But if the romance consists mainly in a fraught tryst with a Greenwich Village lesbian as both cower under the sheets, Eleanor becomes the medium for powerful narratives of lust and longing from beyond the grave, forces which drive her to her own death. The film's conceit finds a professor, Dr. Markway (Richard Johnson) gathering a focus group to research supernatural phenomena in an old mansion. By contrast with Markway's rationalist if sympathetic approach, Eleanor's behavior — wandering around the house at night, talking of how the house wants her to stay — characterizes her as deranged. Eleanor herself seems to cause the supernatural disturbance within the house, one linked to the disturbance within Eleanor. The horror movie is traditionally a vehicle for exploring the conundrums of female sexual desire. In *The Haunting*, supernatural disturbance has its earthly correlative in Eleanor's emotional state. In common with Mrs. Rand, Miss Giddens, and other "wandering" female protagonists in the mourning film, we find out little about Eleanor beyond a voice-over which teeters between the obsessively self-righteous and the demented. Is she in love with Markway? Is she in love with Theodora (Claire Bloom)? Did she kill her mother? Hill House could even be a figment of Eleanor's deranged imagination. Echoing the description in Markway's initial exegesis, Eleanor's sensibility may itself be "a house of Hades." We know that she cared for her mother for eleven years until her death, but as the psychic Theodora points out, she was not sorry when her mother died. Neurotic and lacking in self-esteem, it is easy to surmise in Eleanor the melancholic Freudian griever. Ambivalent about the love object, one with which she nevertheless narcissistically identifies, Eleanor constantly debases and abuses herself. At one point the paranormal investigators discover Eleanor's name scrawled in chalk on a wall. That this will be a premonition of Eleanor's fate suggests the ancient prohibition against uttering the name of the deceased. And the film is very much hers. As Frampton would have it, this fraught film has a mind of its own, but one in tune with Eleanor's. A panning shot across the nursery from her to Markway as they sleep is a fluid way of showing that some intelligence, Eleanor's or some other, is manipulating them. In *The Haunting* the revisionist attempt to make old ideas appeal to a new generation found the horror film regurgitating the concerns of melodrama while imbuing its supernatural unease with the complexity of modern mourning.

Case Study: *Carnival of Souls*

> "Fumey, spiritous mists inhabit this place
> Separated from my house by a row of headstones.
> I simply cannot see where there is to get to."
> "The Moon and the Yew Tree," Sylvia Plath

True to a tendency to gloss mainstream genres in the postwar American avant-garde, the independently made *Carnival of Souls* (1962) put female subjectivity at the center of a discussion of the line between life and death. The restless blonde protagonist of this low-budget film bears an uncanny resemblance to Monica Vitti in Antonioni's contemporary chronicles of alienation. Mary (Candace Hilligoss) survives a car wreck and tries to assume a normal life in a small town. But she is haunted by odd moods and tempers. A strange man keeps appearing to her. Is this image something she has or something she has lost? The film's experimental use of sound and unconventional camerawork and editing evoke a peculiar kinship between the European modernist evocations of female disorientation and the American surrealism of Maya Deren. Its use of monochrome stock evokes the realist connotations of black-and-white, yet offers the world as one occupied by someone on the edge of her wits. Mary wanders around a department store before realizing that, although she can see them, no one can see her. The ethereal "heavenly" tones of her organ playing suffuse the soundtrack, simultaneously tinting its world with the protagonist's neuroticism and mocking the celestial associations of church music and perhaps classical era celestial melodrama alike. Like *The Haunting*, *Carnival of Souls* belongs relentlessly to its protagonist. Pasolini could be writing of it when he observes of the cinema of poetry that "it is based on the totality of those film stylemas that developed almost naturally as a function of the anomalous psychological excesses of the pretextually chosen protagonists" (Orr 2000: 51).

Mary's experience recalls perceptions of the undifferentiated, miscellaneous world of the grieving individual which recurs in accounts of grief. Duncan writes, "It is difficult to recognize some events or pieces of information as being more significant than others" (Duncan 2009: 2). The mood of dislocation, incommensurability and ontological confusion evokes Deren. A shot at the film's primary location, a fairground pavilion, finds Mary resembling the famous still of Deren seen peering through a gauze screen in *Meshes of the Afternoon* (Maya Deren and Alexander Hammid, 1943), a film which, for Stephen R. Bissette "can be seen as the true "midwife" to a whole series of later horror "trance" films" (Mendik 2002: 42). The fairground setting seems peculiarly apposite. As noted, the cinema's own earliest manifestations were witnessed in fairground sideshows, while traditionally the fairground was a space of carnivalesque abandon, a world turned upside down which here resonates with Mary's sense of dislocation. The fact that this place is now disused only adds to the film's funereal air.

Mary's car fell into a river, and at the start of the film she appears to return from water to land. In Deren's *At Land* (Maya Deren and Alexander Hammid, 1944), a strange amphibious woman fetches up "at land," her odyssey, like Mary's, eventually driving her back to the water. We are reminded of a being forced to live outside its natural element, and mourning women such as Julie Vignon and Marie Drillon who are drawn back into the water. The words of the perplexed priest who tries to save Mary — "You cannot live in isolation from the human race, you know" — echo generations of churchmen and mental health specialists' attempts to retrieve the mourner from their searching.

Grief and mourning have been fundamental to cinema as a set of aesthetics and as an experience of spectatorship. The representation of grief and the afterlife throw unique light on the evolution from classical to post-classical filmmaking. Emerging from spiritualist effects and the yearning for metaphysics into an era marked by skepticism, mass carnage and widespread loss, the cinema has proved to be a poignant site for the revelation of interior states to which grief gives rise. Such a project has had manifestations in Europe and America, in commercial filmmaking and in arthouse and avant-garde practices alike. In commercial cinema, the overlap between melodrama and the horror film afford a unique space for the exploration of this subject matter. In Chapter 2, the legacy of this engagement with grief and loss shall be traced into more recent films.

Chapter 2. Realization

"He didn't 'make it'? ... Are you telling me that he's dead?"
Rebecca, in *Moonlight and Valentino*

Chapter 2 shall explore the ways in which a series of films appearing in the post–World War II period proposed innovative aesthetics for the post-classical exploration of grief and mourning. There will be case studies of individual releases highlighting particular accommodations of aesthetic and theme. The aim of Chapter 2 is to extend the discussion of aesthetic premises for a genealogy of mourning films begun in Chapter 1, from which a contemporary cinema of mourning can be proposed.

In grief counseling language, "realization" is the stage through which the bereaved individual passes on their way to acceptance of their loss (Lake 1988: 29). According to those theorists who utilize a staged model of grief and its affects, in a normal "uncomplicated" case the initial shock of bereavement is followed by realization of what has occurred, from which stage the bereaved individual begins to assimilate the loss. Chapter 2 is informed by the idea of "realization" in its description of the ways in which those uses of film language which deviate from or "exceed" the confines of strictly narrative exposition, "realize" or make credible, the extraordinary condition of subjectivity which is the film's theme. Building on the emergent modernist sensibilities explored in Chapter 1, this chapter will show how the representation of this stage of loss was progressively facilitated by developments in postwar cinema.

Grief is a complex experience, making the commonly theorized model of shock, realization and assimilation appear, however useful a therapeutic hypothesis, overly schematic in the light of real experience. Parkes writes: "Grief is not a set of symptoms which start after a loss and then gradually fade away. It involves a succession of clinical pictures which blend into and replace one another" (Parkes 1996: 7). Parkes's imagery is fortuitous for the analysis of cinematic representations. We are reminded of a series of dissolves fading one into the other, distinctive yet integrally related. Worden writes of how "grieving does not proceed in a linear fashion; it may reappear to be reworked" (Worden 1991: 18). The cinematic realization of grief can find the aesthetically "excessive" moment in complex relationships with the rest of the film, recurring, reverberating and coloring more conventional narration as it records the ebbing and flowing of emotions. In Chapter 1, the identification of a mourning cinema involved the excavation of film history in search of tendencies and paradigms which deviate and fissure the "official" stylistics of mainstream output in a manner we may describe as analogous to the way in which death fissures everyday experience. In Chapter 2 Deleuze, Pasolini and Frampton will be deployed to account for the shift which took place in film aesthetics from the classical era to a postwar period of modernist experiment. Academic accounts of classical film style will be utilized to identify the norms against which modernist explorations of grief and mourning defined themselves in the 1960s and 1970s.

The mourning film involves the interaction between inner states and outer realities, making the account of real space and psychological space a running theme in the films explored in this chapter. The experience of grief and mourning provides cogent material for films to explore these conditions. Accounts of hallucinations, mis-identifications, cognitive failures, inconsolable wandering recur in therapeutic literature, becoming a serendipitous legacy to the sympathetic and imaginative filmmaker. If Chapter 1 identified a pre-1960 archaeology out of which a modernist mourning cinema emerges, postwar European and American art cinema provided seminal examples of expressive potential for a contemporary cinema of mourning. Chapter 2 will highlight a range of films from the postwar decades which contain particularly bold and affecting treatments of loss and its psychological consequences.

Classicism/Post-Classicism

The postwar period witnessed a growing atmosphere of experiment in European and American cinema. Avant gardes in Continent Europe and in North America explored the conundrums of subjectivity within the contexts of consumerism, the erosion of traditional community structures, changing film-industrial structures and cinema-going demographics, and the threat of nuclear annihilation, conditions which demanded a new understanding of the relationship between the individual and the world at large. If secularization led grieving individuals to turn to mental health practitioners rather than the church, the postwar art film proposed itself as a compelling refuge for thinking subjects confused by the atomization of modern existence. *Voyage to Italy*

(*Viaggio in Italia*, Roberto Rossellini, 1953) is sensitive to transience, mortality and the perambulations of bereft individuals. Dudley Andrew writes: "Rossellini's film defines the modern by clinically analyzing postwar European values and by inventing a form to do so. A meandering essay, a sort of "ba(l)ade," in Deleuze's term ... it ignores the classicism of narrative cinema and the hermeticism of the avant-garde to thrust cinematography up against a reality that is both material and spiritual" (Hill 1998: 176). As usefully charted by Laura Mulvey (Mulvey 2006: 110), this film's conflicting energies, torn between the goal-driven desire for narrative sense embodied in the husband Alex (George Sanders) and the lingering contemplative attitudes of his wife Katherine (Ingrid Bergman), *Voyage to Italy* seems to emphasize a gender dichotomy which has informed the mourning film from its generic roots to its modernist manifestations. Katherine, the wandering protagonist of Rossellini's film, is the descendent of wandering women from Bauer onwards.

Parkes describes the experiences of mourners who have sought succor from spiritualism. "Their reactions were mixed: some felt that they had obtained some sort of contact with the dead and a few had been frightened by this. On the whole they did not feel satisfied by the experience and none had become a regular attender at spiritualist meetings" (Parkes 1996: 55). Such ambivalence reflects how archaic the procedures of spiritualism seem in a culture marked by the decline of metaphysics, the rise of technology, and the increasingly marginalized place death has in public life. In an age which questions the consolations of spirituality, post-classical film aesthetics broached new ways of articulating the certainty of physical death in a world without God and the spiritual social contract which His name underwrote. In a world without God, moral solutions become relative and the films explored here contain peculiarly affecting moments of human tenderness amid grief's turmoil. Such moments, contingent, rare, and often confused with other emotions, only complicate the thematic and stylistic terrain of the modernist mourning film.

Theorizing the transition from prewar to postwar cinema, Deleuze acknowledges a modernist image which is less globalizing and consensual than the Hollywood model and more dispersive and multiple, plotting something of the loss of a transcendent moral narrative and the erosion of belief systems. The representation of the atomized subject has precursors in prewar art cinema. Deleuze writes of King Vidor's *The Crowd* (King Vidor, 1928), a classical Hollywood film which dramatizes the tension between the modern urban environment and the fortunes of the individual over which modernist films will characteristically fret: "The city and the crowd lose the collective and unanimist character which they have in King Vidor, the city at the same time ceases to be the city above ... in order to become the recumbent city, the city as horizontal ... where each gets on with his own business" (Deleuze 1989: 211). A celebrated shot in Vidor's film finds the camera moving horizontally across New York's skyline to settle on an office building in which the hero sits amid a sea of desks. In 1960, Billy Wilder famously repeated this urban pan in *The Apartment* (Billy Wilder, 1960) as he homes in on the New York skyscraper in which his modern Everyman toils in an exposé of corporatism (the very title of which bespeaks dispersal and atomization). Deleuze returns the individual to the paradox of an atomized collective "since they are all caught in the same reality which disperse them" (ibid.: 211). In the absence of traditional narratives of community and faith, the mourning film will home in on figures alone and adrift amid the turmoil of their feelings. In a world without faith, death seems even more dispersive and multiple. Parkes writes, "To accept the fact that death can strike anywhere and that illness is no respecter of persons or desserts undermines one's faith in the world as an ordered and secure place" (Parkes 1996: 85). Dislocation and despair are perennial symptoms of grief in the modern mourning film.

Classical narrative cinema seeks to validate the notion of an ordered existence. The trajectory of the classical realist film subscribes to the pattern whereby a state of affairs is established, disrupted, and then reaffirmed in a modified condition. Bordwell writes of "the undisturbed stage, the disturbance, the struggle, and the elimination of the disturbance" (Bordwell 1985: 157). Such a pattern appealed to the popular conviction that real experience is like this. Ideologically, it recommends a rational status quo based on the subject citizen's full engagement with values of adaptability, pro-activity and optimism. Post-classical films elaborate more complex accounts of the journey from realization to the acceptance of loss. A recurring motif in case studies here is that of the sea. An age-old metaphor for the travail through which individuals pass in order to gain self-knowledge, for our purposes the sea could also be seen as a metaphor for looser, heterogeneous, and more multiple relationships between form and meaning, relationships with implications for the way modernist mourning films can be viewed and read.

The interaction between experience and selfhood is the ground over which classical realism and art cinema typically differ. For Bordwell, "In the art cinema ... shifts between 'objective' action and 'subjective' moments are often not signalled by the narration" (ibid.: 152). What distinguishes the art film is a mélange of interior and exterior record. "Whereas art-cinema narration can blur the lines separating objective diegetic reality, characters' mental states, and inserted narrational commentary, the classical film asks us to assume clear distinctions among these states" (ibid.: 162). For Deleuze, disorientation in the modernist film is fundamental: "We no longer know what is imaginary or real, physical or mental ... not because they are confused, but because we do not have to know and there is no longer even a place from which to ask" (Deleuze 1989: 7).

Representations of dispersal and dislocation characterize modernism from its earliest manifestations. Italian neo-realism, the first postwar European film movement to have an international critical impact, typically chronicles the re-emergence of life from amid the rubble and turmoil of wartime Italy. Even its most salient titles, such as *Rome: Open City* (*Roma, Città Apertá*, Roberto Rossellini, 1945) and *Germany: Year Zero* (*Germania, Anno Zero*, Roberto Rossellini, 1947), suggest the disorientation of modern life. Like the modernist novel, modernism in the cinema calls into question the spatial and temporal systems structuring experience: "That is, narration is no longer the most important aspect of plot; other structures can compete for our attention. Hence these films often pose problems of how to unify themselves" (Bordwell 1985: 381). This leads to a characteristically discrete quality: "a dynamic of unity and fragmentation is set up within the text" (ibid.: 381). This dynamic operates in modernist mourning films, texts characteristically ruptured by the excessive unpredictability of grief.

The Deleuzian commentary on modernism ponders the breakdown of narrative, spatial, psychological and temporal causality. By contrast with the unifying concepts and protocols of classicism, this heterogeneity is informed by Deleuze's reading of Henri Bergson, principally Bergson's notions of multiplicity and duration. For Bergson, quantitative multiplicity is the attempt to reconcile similarity and difference. In his example, the flock of sheep is simultaneously a collectivity and consists of singular spatially specific animals. While resonating with the urban scenes of postwar modernist cinema, this image bears vivid recollections of twentieth century genocide imagery. To illustrate the notion, Bergson describes our experience of sympathy, an apparently homogenous one which actually consists of a number of different emotions. As Freud suggests, the mourner, too, can have complex attitudes towards the dead. Sympathy for dying relatives, and that for attendant mourners, is complicated by other emotions: "All human relationships have ambivalence (love-hate features). Bereaved individuals often have to deal with feelings of guilt because they loved the person who died, but also disliked him or her at times. In conflicted grief the degree or intensity of ambivalence is much stronger and more difficult to resolve" (Humphrey 1996: 152). Mourning cinema abounds with instances in which imagery may be "conflicted." Complexes of tension and tenderness emerge in *Hiroshima mon amour*, *Cries and Whispers*, and *Interiors*. What makes mourning films interesting is that they often leave us alternately sympathetic towards and alienated by protagonists. Grief is so overwhelming that the mourner often thinks and behaves in contradictory ways. Mental life becomes scrambled and intentions become obscure. Grief can demonstrate how unknowable the other can be, a perception borne out by Humphrey and Zimpfer: "It can never be assumed that the innermost reality of another human being can ever be fully understood" (ibid.: 171). Some of the best scenes in mourning films find us torn between perspectives amid fragile and uncertain dramatic situations. All the more moving are those moments in which seas of despair and longing are transcended by moments of tenderness between characters. Instances of sympathy emerge like epiphanies amid an atmosphere of mutual recognition and brief solidarity.

Themes of duration and multiplicity shape the Deleuzian account of modernist cinema, and will figure increasingly in mourning cinema. Descending from the phenomenological philosophical tradition, as Elsaesser and Buckland argue, for Deleuze cinema is "the most philosophically rich instance of the inseparability of matter, temporality, and consciousness, which in his view is as decisively indicative of our modernity as, say, binoculars or the *camera obscura* were for Cartesian philosophy" (Elsaesser 2002: 250). If traditional film theory characterized cinema as images that move, grounded in the material and mechanical circumstances of image production and perception, Deleuze reverses the emphasis, characterizing cinema as movement-images and time-images. Forming the basis of classical realism, the movement-image, or "action-image," integrated character, locale and action in a unified time and space. The postwar decades mark a transition towards the "time-image": "Why did the war make possible ... this emergence of a cinema of time, with Welles, with neo-realism, with the new wave ... the cinema has undergone a much more important change here than the one which happened with the talkie" (Deleuze 1986: xii). Deleuze theorizes an aesthetic evolution with implications for the articulation of inner states. Orr writes, "What is crucial for the time-space image here is its need to combine four elements which have no absolute internal boundaries, the real and the oneiric, the recollected and the imaginary" (Orr 1993: 99). Passages of the modern mourning film also incorporate matter, temporality and consciousness.

The exploration of inner states was crucial to the postwar European art film. Art cinema "is a highly subjective cinema.... Dreams, memories and fantasies abound, and are transcribed by means of optical point-of-view shots" (Cook 1999: 109–110). This blurring of interior and exterior perceptions is motivated by a particular philosophical attitude towards modern experience. At the Cannes premiere of his quintessentially modernist *L'avventura*, Antonioni reflected on an alienated modern subject lacking the moral postulates to match her competences in an urbanized technological world. For Julian Petley, characters in the high modernist art film "are incapable of authentic relationships with each other or with their environment because they carry within them a fossilised value system quite out of step with modern times" (ibid.: 109). Pasolini relates how Antonioni's style shifted in emphasis between *L'avventura* and *Red Desert*. "In *Red Desert* Antonioni no longer superimposes his own formalistic vision of the world on a generally committed content (the problem of neuroses caused by alienation), as he had done in his earlier films in a somewhat clumsy blending. Instead, he looks at the world by immersing himself in his neurotic protagonist, reanimating the facts through her eyes ... *because he has substituted in toto for the world view of a neurotic his own delirious view of aesthetics*" (Orr 2000: 48, Pasolini's italics). If this protagonist is frequently a bourgeois woman, the idea that the postwar art film is a viable precursor of the mourning film becomes all the more persuasive. Like its antecedents in mourning literature — Woolf, H.D., Isabel Allende, Joan Didion — the protagonist of the mourning film is such an intelligent and articulate, though lost, soul.

Writing on Pasolini's "Cinema of Poetry," Orr summarizes: "Form is born out of the intensity of theme and the irrational, not the aesthetic, remains the raw datum on which the filmmaker works" (ibid.: 137). Modern cinema, for Pasolini, is characterized by the departure from mainstream narrative method and its rationalist assumptions. As already noted, for Pasolini the loosening of conventional narrative and its revelation of objective experience as a condition of subjectivity led to a modernist image more hospitable to the "oneiric" and "barbaric" impulses to which film is naturally prone. Glossing, Orr writes, "The film image is irrational. This does not move the image away from the Real but towards it" (ibid.: 134). If the Lacanian Real cannot be mediated through language, classical narrative too, so driven by the script and dependent on objective causality, could not readily accommodate the tangled states which modernism made its subject matter, despite interesting attempts in that direction. Martine Beugnet evokes whole histories of cinema which repudiate the classical dependence on language-based narrative: "Even when confronted with the incredibly fertile field of non-narrative, experimental cinema, the tendency for film theory has been to focus on experimental practices as processes of "deconstruction" (of the classical techniques and apparatus) rather than as independently and specifically affective modes of artistic expression" (Beugnet 2007: 29). Embracing conventional narrative syntax and experimental instincts alike, the modern mourning film could be seen to deconstruct classicism while in its way reinventing cinema.

The post-classical image of bereaved subjectivity is characterized by the attempt to realize a fresh ontology of grief. The visionary quality that Pasolini describes is echoed by Deleuze, for whom the modern cinematic image is less bound by its material postulates, becoming an indeterminate reality flowing wraith-like across the eye: "Part of the energies, the flux and intensities that embed thought and the material world in what might be called the "super-

supermedium" of multi-layered durations and coextensive temporalities" (Deleuze cited in Elsaesser 2002: 250). An example of the Deleuzian time-image can be found in *Interiors* as a mature woman gazes through a window at herself as a child playing on the beach she is looking at. First we see her looking, then the children, then her again, contributing to a Deleuzian sense of "sheets of time" lain one across the last, successive and contemporaneous durations in which matter, temporality and consciousness find fractured visionary expression. Laboring under temporal and emotional complexes, mourning imagery often transcends the narrative, evoking the interiority of the mourner.

The Visionary Image

The term "visionary" is so apt for mourning cinema that it requires further elucidation. It is here understood as that which exists in a vision or in a hallucination. This may be the spectral visions found in *Carnival of Souls* and *Under the Skin*, premonitions of another temporal space in *Don't Look Now*, or the hallucinatory distortions of reality in *Interiors* or *Under the Sand*. It could also result from the manipulation of an image which is apparently independent of a character's perspective, giving rise, as at the end of *Morvern Callar*, to imagery which is there in itself and for itself, an instance of the image "speaking," the film having eventually adopted the singular perspective of its protagonist. In this instance, the image, determined in classical cinema by the strictures of narrative and character, exceeds the requirements of plot to become imagery as such, an un-anchored vision rather than the visual revelation of plot. Deleuze's "supermedium" becomes visionary insofar as the visionary register transcends the utilitarian requirements of classicism to become in the psychological modernist tradition the concision of thought, movement, time and light.

According to Deleuze, what cinema achieves that literary narrative cannot is "the kinetic modulations of movement and the potential infinity of images, their rhythms and plasticity" (ibid.: 251). The visual is intrinsic to the visionary register. If classical aesthetics equated the camera with the eye of the spectator, a tradition perhaps coming to its celebrated apotheosis in Hitchcock's late-classical *Rear Window* (Alfred Hitchcock, 1954), Deleuze makes visibility intrinsic to the image. In modernist cinema "the eye is already there in things, it's part of the image, the image's visibility.... The eye isn't the camera, it's the screen" (Deleuze 1995: 54–55). The reversal from the camera/eye of classical cinema to the eye/screen of modernist practice can be felt in the scene in *Carnival of Souls* in which Mary's body is inscribed with slats of shadow as she passes beneath a boardwalk, making her appear and disappear before us. This scene, with its rhythmic flow of presence and absence, recalls the crude technology of cinema's prehistory in which the flickering materiality of the apparatus was intrinsic to the spectator's experience, an effect which in turn recalled the visionary intermittences of the séance. In this scene, narrative is not so much visual as visuality becomes narrative. The film becomes film as such, its narrative a story of light and shadow, the narrative of vision. The film has a "mind" of its own.

The prospect of visuality-as-narrative resonates across postwar modernism. In *Carnival of Souls*, a film which inhabits the muddy interstice between commercial filmmaking and left-field experiment, the play of light over the figure of the protagonist suggests the inseparability of the objective record from the subjective experience. This dance of black shadow and white sunlight is a metaphor for Mary's state of flux between the world of mortals and the realm of the dead. It is an instance of Deleuzian lyrical abstraction, in which the protagonist is torn between this world and another. The imagery seems to "think" through this condition in purely visual terms. The use of gradations of light is a strategy widely used in films of mourning to inscribe the image with a protagonist's feelings, as well as expressing the point where life and death meet.

Hallucinatory and aesthetically "excessive," the visionary register sees a film mediating the gap between life and death, the protagonist and the world, the self and the other. Since they offer an uncertain space from which to gauge the verisimilitude of the image, the power of these films resides in this visual and narrative ambiguity. Frampton finds in art cinema a celebration of ambiguity: "Cinema doesn't become reasoning and arguing. It gives us access to non-concepts or non-philosophy as some people would call it, it gives us indistinct ideas or vague concepts, it gives us just an idea of something" (Frampton 2006: 21). Frampton's filmosophical approach emphasizes how apt film is for the expression of grief: "The film tells us the unknowable, the impenetrable, lost love, forgetting, it is an uncertain something" (ibid.: 21). For the spectator confronted with the mental states of the mourning protagonist, death becomes the ultimate un-thought thought.

Mourning cinema finds its protagonists seeing or experiencing things which we must attribute to grief. Therapeutic literature backs up such epistemological uncertainty. Worden sets out the characteristics of normal grief reactions which include disbelief, confusion, hallucinations, preoccupation and a sense of presence: "This is the cognitive counterpart to the experience of yearning. The grieving person may think that the deceased is somehow still in the current area of time and space" (Worden 1991: 26). Uncertainty also characterizes the spectator's negotiation of the film. In *The Innocents*, we are not sure whether the ghosts are there, or are figments of Miss Giddens's imagination. In *Interiors*, we are not sure whether Joey is seeing her mother or whether this is a trick of nocturnal light. Such scenarios appear to unfold in a realistic space, but they are also saliently happening *for this protagonist alone*. Lake observes a splitting of the mourner's subjectivity: "There may also be times when you feel completely disassociated from your own feelings, as if you are watching yourself from outside your body, looking down from a high position" (Lake 1988: 114). To the accompaniment of a wailing voice, the scene in *The Sheltering Sky* in which a caravan passes across the desert seems awash with the "voice" of its lonely wandering protagonist. Grief is unpredictable because it happens inside the protagonist, in "the indistinction between fiction and reality that the unconscious appears to bring in its wake" (Lebeau 2001: 64).

While the visionary register lends itself to the representation of grief and mourning, surprisingly few releases of the high modernist period, roughly from 1955 to 1975, tackled mourning. It is intriguing to trace the evolution of style from postwar studies in beleaguered subjectivity, whether mainstream, modernist arthouse or avant-garde, to recent mourning cinema. Classical horror cinema notoriously invested in images of the terrorized or sacrificed woman, while the Suffering Woman has enjoyed a genre all of her own. It seems interesting that the protagonists of four high modernist explorations of grief were women, and women who suffer for their experiences. *Hiroshima mon amour*, *Cries and Whispers*, *Don't Look Now* and *Interiors* all revolve around female protagonists coming to terms with loss. In each film, women are traumatized and in two of them they actually die. All the films involve innovative explorations of visual style. The personal crisis takes center stage, with implications for what the spectator sees and hears. These seminal mourning films chart moral and epistemological distrait prompted by an acutely personal experience. While the fruit of high art modernism, *Hiroshima mon amour* and *Don't Look Now*, take their inspiration, respectively, from the novelette and female-centered melodrama, a legacy consciously alluded to in the former. For critics, the postwar art film came freighted with the fears and paranoia associated with the Cold War. In *Hiroshima mon amour*, grief is the place where the personal life and this public legacy meet. Indeed, the personal breakdown which loss involves has been a gift to filmmakers fixated on wider questions of meaning in a society without faith, ethical values in a consumerist universe, or a sense of identity in a place without moral and epistemological absolutes. To watch mourning films from the high modernist period now is to witness the cinema, in an era dissatisfied with God and the ersatz consolations of spiritualism alike, broach a fresh set of illusions with which to chart the psychological vicissitudes of sorrow and, however tentatively, the possibility of consolation.

The instances of film technique discussed in the following case studies represent the continuation of modernism's quest for meaning by other means. They also contribute to the identification of the type "mourning film" which this study proposes. Therapeutic literature recognizes that grieving itself can be a way of acknowledging loss, but also a way of adapting to it. Using similar terminology to my own, Lake writes that "the most important relationship that has changed is that with the person who has died. Grieving is the continuation of this relationship by other means" (Lake 1988: 39). The films discussed here offer paradigmatic cases of a cinema of mourning the influences of which ripple across recent manifestations of the type. *Hiroshima mon amour* involves an exploration of narrative and memory. *Cries and Whispers* and *Interiors* propose experimental uses of color and *mise-en-scène* to explore psychologies. *Don't Look Now* reworks narrative continuity in the search for the enigma of death.

Case Study: *Hiroshima mon amour*

> "If suddenly you did not exist,
> if suddenly you are not living,
> I shall go on living."
> *Dead Woman*, Pablo Neruda

Hiroshima mon amour (1959) remains a key moment in the evolution from classical to post-classical, or modernist, cinema. In his documentary *Hiroshima le temps d'un retour*, Luc Largier observes that "with the birth of the 1960s, Alain Resnais's first feature opened the way to what we call modern cinema" (Largier 2004). Focusing on the affair between a French actress (Emmanuelle Riva) and a Japanese man (Eiji Okada) in contemporary Hiroshima, the film explores the way in which wartime experiences continue to shape her life years later. In the occupied French town of Nevers in 1944, the woman had an affair with a German soldier who was killed by the French Resistance. Following the liberation of France, she was branded a collaborator and imprisoned. Now she is an actress in Hiroshima to make a documentary commemorating the dropping of the first atomic bomb in 1945. Melding a rich record of the contemporary city with an interior monologue in which its ghastly history becomes intertwined with the fraught recollections of a mourning woman, the film's imagery broaches the play of public history and private interiority, public space and private feelings, in resonant and visionary ways. For Vincent O'Connell, Hiroshima and Nevers are "places on a map [which] become suffused, confused with the emotional history of the people who live there" (O'Connell 1996: 59).

Hiroshima mon amour traces an interior journey during which the woman tries to come to terms with her past and learn to live for the future. Recalled in memory, the flashback images of Nevers are inscribed with the events and feelings she experienced there. Resnais's representation of these locations is in both cases shaped by the twin poles of human consciousness: the continual play of interiority and an objective world of objects and other experiences. The woman's recollections of Nevers suggest less a place than a state of mind, an internal account made of memories and recollections, rather than an external geographical space. Siobhan Craig writes: "Her subjectivity as we see it in the Nevers flashbacks challenges the epistemological categories by which we are accustomed to ordering experience. The woman's selfhood — the trace of which is expressed in everything that surrounds her, just as she herself echoes and mirrors walls, rivers and cat, in a boundariless commingling, her world without stable delineation of time or seasons, gender or even life — has collapsed into conceptual rubble" (Craig 2005: 34). Confronted with death, language becomes limited and distorted. Yet the grieving individual must talk about their grief: "That talking helps her to come to grips with the reality of the death.... The verbalizing can include memories of the deceased, both current and past" (Worden 1991: 43). The film was based on Marguerite Duras's exquisite screenplay, and for Penelope Houston at the time, "the text relies so much on repetition, alliteration, the sound as well as the sense of words" (Houston 1960: 20). The actress — Riva herself came from the theatre — savors the word: "'Ne-vers' ... Nevers is just a word like any other," suggesting less an objectively present geographical location, more a subjective emanation. The sound — "Ne-vers" — literally comes out of the character, a noise specifically made by this person. For William Van Wert, Riva's voice contributed to the effect: "a measured, accumulative, self-conscious and slightly hysterical *plain chant*" (Van Wert 1977: 32). Her observations of Nevers suggest a fount of originating consciousness for this woman, a kind of primal scene which continues to haunt her feelings and her outlook. We might read the line "I learned to read in Nevers" in terms both of her having actually learnt to read language, and having been presented the script of her biography, the template of her life. Caruth writes, "Traumatic memories are the unassimilated scraps of overwhelming experiences, which need to be integrated with existing mental schemes, and be transformed into mental language" (Caruth 1995: 176). By analogy, we might argue that the difficult experiences which mourning films contend with give rise to excessive aesthetic moments, posing a challenge to critical accounts of these films. For approaching the challenge of arraying visual tropes and schemas in a context in which verbal language is left so wanting, *Hiroshima mon amour* remains a key exemplar of mourning cinema. Its seminal status consists in its fluid play with topographies of exteriority and interiority.

The woman's interior journey is interwoven with a geographical journey, an interweaving recalled in the film's opening credits in which we see what appears to be the aerial shot of some ghastly scar, a traumatic rhizome growing across the landscape, and reaching into the past and into the future. It is an effective metaphor for the bleeding together of places exterior and interior around which mourning films become stylistically organized. Deleuze writes of the place of landscape in the modernist film: "Landscapes are mental states just as mental states are cartographies, both crystallized in each other" (Deleuze 1989: 199). This crystallization can be seen in the way in which, while the Hiroshima of the present is characterized through documentary realism, a busy account of a city always already evolving despite the protagonist's interior distraction, we are prompted to see Nevers via her own static memories, a loop of recollection which never ends but never changes. For O'Connell, in what is less a story of passion, more a tale of obsession, these lovers "are doomed to wander the museum of emotions and to keep coming back to the same room, the same glass cabinet: The Human Heart, Please Do Not Touch" (O'Connell 1996: 59). We see nothing at Nevers which did not happen to the woman. Deleuze graphically suggests the interface between self and world. The point at which they meet "this membrane which makes the outside and the inside present to each other is called memory.... [Memory] makes sheets of past and layers of reality correspond, the first emanating from an inside which is always already there, the second arriving from an outside always to come, the two gnawing at the present which is now only their encounter" (Deleuze 1989: 199–200).

There is something spare, even stylized, about Resnais's images of Nevers which reiterates the metonymy of recollection rather than the plenitude of objectivity. The title of his film *Private Fears in Public Places* (*Coeurs*, Alain Resnais, 2006) returns to the fraught concision of self and world. Reviewing it, critic Richard Combs recalls other places of the mind in the director's work, their "fragility ... wistfulness ... essential nowhere-ness" (Combs 2007: 43). By comparison with Nevers, Hiroshima is full of the facticity of urban modernity, an incidental street demonstration, the distant flashing of neon, taxis arriving as if from other appointments in the city, the whole suggesting multiple layers of being and temporality. Nevers feels homogenized, a dreamscape in grey and green, curiously dreamlike, as if nobody inhabits it aside from the people the woman speaks of. It exists only because it is being remembered. Indeed, comparing the plenitude of Hiroshima with the metonymic space of Nevers, we are reminded of the amplitude of color, its "fullness," as against the shades of monochrome cinematography, its "moodiness." We know that the woman's story of Nevers is going to be sad, lending these somber images the inevitability of a desultory personal imprint, always a *mise-en-*

scène of emotion rather than a real town existing through space and time. We are reminded of a grave; its ageing stone greying and greenish, its words, its historical claim to attention, now weathered and indistinct. Only the occasional mourner or interested passerby can make the inscription meaningful again. Buried amid the rush of contemporary Hiroshima, and as it were stumbled upon by the domestic spectator, the space of Nevers seems increasingly memorialized and lapidary. The intercutting of objective space with subjective space features often in mourning cinema.

Resnais's protagonist observes that she dreams about Nevers most often, yet thinks of it least often. We are reminded of the "tomb" theorized by Nicolas Abraham and Maria Torok, incorporated within the mourner who is unable to reclaim that part of them which they lost upon the death of the Other. Unable to contemplate or speak of the loss, as we shall see in forthcoming case studies, it is in the night that the tomb affects baleful reminders. Here the woman is not so much in possession of the tomb as she is possessed by it. It is fitting, perhaps, that she has no name, for the complexities of experience that make us the individuals we are have for this woman eroded her status as a knowing agent of singular identity. Like Hiroshima in 1945, her identity has been obliterated by a single act. Caruth observes that "to be traumatized is to be possessed by an image or event" (Caruth 1995: 4–5). The deliberately metonymic quality of Nevers's vale of tears is all that is left of this character's ravaged identity. It is the film's stony metaphor for her buried suffering. Both the actress and the city harbor horrendous histories, Hiroshima's museum of twisted bottle tops, bikes and frazzled hair the film's mute actual equivalent of the hidden repository of pain which she tries to vocalize. It is as though Hiroshima's museum artifacts make obvious by analogy the damage that she has suffered, the irrefutable evidence which counters years of denial.

The pain hurts most when the woman is unconscious, unaware, asleep. For Deleuze, the archetypal Resnais protagonist is like Lazarus: "[He] returns from death, from the land of the dead; he has passed through death and is born from death" (Deleuze 1989: 200). Resnais's protagonist wanders — from Nevers to Paris, from her German lover to her Japanese lover, around and across Hiroshima — in the attempt to grasp and assimilate her trauma, to possess rather than be possessed. Wilson describes her odyssey as "blind, mnemonic pacing" (Wilson 1999: 63). We recall bereft wandering women from Bauer, from Lewton, from *Carnival of Souls* and *The Innocents*, sleepwalkers traversing some insistent grey landscape of turmoil and melancholy. This "wandering" condition is borne out in real life accounts of grief. Joyce Carol Oates recalls, "In public places I seem to be searching for someone who is missing—I wonder if for the rest of my life I will be searching for someone who isn't there" (Oates 2011: 243). Erich Lindemann, a celebrated commentator on grief states, wrote: "There is a restlessness, inability to sit still, moving about in an aimless fashion, *continually searching* for something to do. There is, however, at the same time, a painful lack of capacity to initiate and maintain normal patterns of activity" (cited in Parkes 1996: 50). Searching is a common characteristic of the woman in the mourning film. The evolution of this searching protagonist was facilitated by the appearance of a new generation of women in world cinema. Deleuze acknowledges a new kind of post-classical actor: "'actor-mediums' capable of seeing and showing rather than acting" (Deleuze 1989: 19). Nevers is a projection of this actor-medium. Largier describes *Hiroshima mon amour* as being "like a kind of ghost that gently haunts contemporary cinema" (Largier 2004), while haunting mourning films to come. He could be describing the actor who plays the film's protagonist. In the 1960s, Riva gained a reputation for portraying women who must live through the consequences of social transgression. As the radical who is seduced by a priest's faith, in *Léon Morin, Prêtre* (Jean-Pierre Melville, 1961), Riva evokes a passion reminiscent of the "possessed" women of cinema's past. In *Thérèse Desqueyroux* (Georges Franju, 1962), she recalls the moment when she poisoned her boorish husband. Houston witnessed "a kind of awareness likely

Hiroshima mon amour. Condemned to search for some inner solace, the mourning heroine is forever mobile, uncertain, amidst the spaces through which she drifts, her life, like her peripatetic progress, seeming to be nothing but an accident.

to disturb those who like their responses to be more directly aroused" (Houston 1960: 20). Writing in the 1970s, Roger Manvell said of Riva that she had a "special gift for creating an atmosphere of uneasy quiet around her characters" (Manvell 1972: 419). Her distracted searching foresees rehearsals of wandering women from Julie Christie in *Don't Look Now* to contemporary manifestations such as Samantha Morton, Juliette Binoche, Charlotte Rampling and Nicole Kidman.

Distracted wandering shapes *Hiroshima mon amour*'s fluid imagery, too. In the opening scene of intimacy between the woman and her Japanese lover, their entwined bodies seem to melt together as they are covered in the ash which covered the dead following the atomic blast which destroyed Hiroshima. It is hard to tell the man's body from the woman's in this scene. Skin seems to search for skin in a scene which brilliantly exemplifies that sense in which film can simultaneously record surfaces and plumb depths. For O'Connell, it is a "perfect cinematic landscape, both exterior and interior" (O'Connell 1996: 59). Compare it with the celebrated lovemaking scene in *Don't Look Now*. If that was a film which attempted reconciliation, between the dead and the living, a mother and daughter, a husband and wife, a project uneasily informing its fractured editing and constant distinguishing between protagonists, *Hiroshima mon amour* is much more about merger and indistinctness, a project vividly played out in the opening scene. The sense of events and forms flowing one to another, which this scene suggests, recalls Deleuze's notion of multiplicity. Recollecting her German lover as he died, the woman's words suggest flow rather than unitary form: "I could see no difference between this dead body and my own." At one point, she sees her Japanese lover asleep with the palm of his hand upturned, like the German's hand as he lay in the road. For the mourner, reminders of the dead come at any moment, triggering pangs of grief in convoluted time-scales. Parkes characterizes the stages of grief as initial numbness, followed by pining, then disorganization and despair, followed by gradual recovery. Like the convoluted time structures in mourning films, these phases flow into one another: "The discovery of a photograph in a drawer or a visit from an old friend can evoke another episode of pining" (Parkes 1996: 7). *Hiroshima mon amour* is a film of becoming. Largier observes, "She is in transit, between two countries, between two love affairs ... she is not absent, but no longer quite there" (Largier 2004). With its peripatetic camera and wandering heroine, *Hiroshima mon amour* comes to resemble the Deleuzian "ba(l)lade," a play on words suggesting a song or round and a strolling motion, to evoke the lyrical meandering motion of a modernism reduced to its optical and sonic elements. For Deleuze, "there emerges a cinema of pure optical and sonic signs, a narrative form that is lyrical in its meandering distractions combining both elements of the song and the circular route ... and a Nietzschian concern with the past within the present" (cited in Orr 2000: 9). The significance for the depiction of the mourner reduced to continual searching and recalling is not difficult to surmise.

In *Hiroshima mon amour*, the fraught individual sensibility is at odds with the documentary record which Resnais's film initially proposes. The film at times recalls a postwar cinema travelogue, an impression gradually giving way to ruminative ambient drama much as, for the mourner, numb witnessing of an unfolding reality gives way to ambient yearning. Resnais's travelogue presages the opening scenes in the Moroccan port in *The Sheltering Sky*, their strenuous account of a postwar colonial town diminishing into an aimless travelogue into the protagonist's interiority as the film progresses. In *Hiroshima mon amour*, we see the fiction film as realist record give way to the interior account of modernism. The film explores the ebb and flow of interiority for the individual adrift in a modern context in which she literally and metaphorically feels abroad, a Frenchwoman in Japan, exposed in a foreign world. Far from the spiritual peace which is the heroine's reward in the celestial melodramas of Borzage, itself a kind of comfort by other means, Riva's character is less comforted than disconnected, less at home than dislocated. We are reminded of Duras's *India Song* (Marguerite Duras, 1975), in which a woman's distracted languor, played out in off-screen voices, eventually leads to her own utter dislocation in death. Because we see Hiroshima through an abstracted gaze, it becomes fragmented, rife with loose connections as the past erupts into the present, its spatial content simultaneously providing context and non-context

Using performance, editing and narrative space, *Hiroshima mon amour* pushed traditional melodrama to critique the classical relationship between protagonist and world in ways that continue to shape contemporary mourning cinema. It often goes unmentioned that in the late–1950s modernist innovation occurred within examples of commercial cinema as well as in art and avant-garde production. The similarities between *Hiroshima mon amour* and Hitchcock's *Vertigo* (Alfred Hitchcock, 1958) are worth recalling. Both are films in which mourning characters attempt to reclaim and somehow "correct" the past. Both take place in distinctive locations which are so vividly present as to emphasize the protagonist's disconnection and distrait. The cinema's romantic legacy hangs heavy over both. In response to the shift in cinema characterization at this time, in 1962 the distracted protagonist of *Carnival of Souls*, herself perhaps a left-field riposte to *Vertigo*'s Madeleine Elster, wanders aimlessly between life and death. Describing a perception voiced at *Cahiers du cinéma* around the time of *Hiroshima mon amour*, Orr comments on that journal's identification of the emerging modernist cinema with changing cinematic representations of womanhood: "The portrayals of the modern woman by Riva, Jeanne Moreau, Anna Karina, Monica Vitti and Harriet Andersson, which go beyond the idealizations of Hollywood and its forms of stardom, are for them vital signs of the arrival of the modern cinema" (Orr 1993: 9). While Vitti became the archetypal wandering protagonist in Antonioni, Andersson appeared in Bergman's *Cries and Whispers*, the subject of the next case study.

Case Study: *Cries and Whispers*

> "We die with the dying:
> See, they depart, and we go with them.
> We are born with the dead:
> See, they return, and bring us with them."
> *Four Quartets*, T.S. Eliot

In Ingmar Bergman's chamber melodrama *Cries and Whispers* (1972), a narrative of alienation and dislocation is inscribed in vivid and visceral terms. In melodrama, both in its mainstream and "intellectual" manifestations, color plays a key role in the evolution of postwar cinema. Its use in mourning cinema adds resonance to the realization of inner states. Color brings extraordinary incandescence and vigor to *Cries and Whispers*. Bergman's film explores two sisters' and a servant's grief as a sibling dies of cancer in a mansion in turn of the century Sweden. The stock used by cinematographer Sven Nykvist was Eastmancolor, a brand of high speed film with less graininess and more sensitivity to color, lending imagery a livid, slightly oneiric quality. *Cries and Whispers* starts as credits appear against a bright red backdrop. Later the women seem to drift from room to room in white nightgowns like ghosts against red decor. Nykvist separates scenes using red washes which flood the frame like blood, or like pain floods consciousness. In view of the film's time setting, such an image evokes pre-classical imagery from the contrivances of the spiritualist séance to Bauer's use of color tints.

Bruce Kawin is another theorist of cinematic modernism who draws an analogy between the eye and the screen. For Kawin, "the image field of *Cries and Whispers* is retinal: that of all the blood in this film, the most inescapable is that which, analogously, gives colour to the eyelids closed against intense light" (Kawin 1978: 17). Kawin links the film's bloody fades to characters' recollections and reveries, "which is to introduce a sequence of private 'vision'—as well as useful in suggesting that the screen is itself retinal" (ibid.: 17). This use of color was noted by commentators at the time of the film's release. Philip Strick wrote of "a stunning Bergman experiment in the uses of red and white, its rooms upholstered in membranous scarlet, its occupants like brightly costumed ghosts" (Strick 1973: 110). Strick may have been influenced by Bergman's contemporary commentary on the film in which he referred to the red field as signifying the "moist membrane" of the soul (cited in Orr 2000: 85). In *Cries and Whispers*, over-determined reds express the traumatic subjectivity of distressed women "bleeding" across its ontological reality.

The film begins on Monday morning as a series of clocks strike four. Gaunt and in dreadful pain, Agnes (Harriet Andersson) wakes and writes in her diary. Watching a film which constantly teeters between life and death, presence and absence, we recall that dawn is allegedly the time chosen by suicides to end their lives, while the dying fear the dawn most of all. Karin (Ingrid Thulin) summons the servant Anna (Kari Sylwan) to listen to the night but Anna hears nothing. As the sisters flit through the house with their oil lamps in response to Agnes's howls, they seem more like spirits than living beings. Grief puts the grief-stricken in a liminal space between themselves and the world around them, between now and what comes after. In this universe set on the cusp of day and night, light and dark, life and death, we are reminded that the space between living and not-living can be very slight, divided only by the red of a wall, Nykvist's divisive red washes evoking the fecund but fragile symbol of life.

This liminality finds an echo in *Interiors*, a film haunted by Bergman's influence, in which we are unsure of the veracity of the protagonist's vision. Both films toy with the hallucinatory possibilities of grief and the image, putting us simultaneously inside *and* outside the scopic and aural fields of the film's characters. In a visionary conception of cinema, a tension is set up between what may be seen and what may be imagined, what may be real and what may be the residue of memory or affect. By playing with our traditional fear of the dark and our compulsion to look, drives traditionally defining the cinema spectator, at such moments these films recall cinema's links with spiritualism and the classical horror film's play with spectatorial apprehension. Of all Bergman's chamber dramas, *Cries and Whispers* encroaches most emphatically on the horror canon.

The dying Agnes rises from her death bed to embrace her sisters once more. As Strick notes (Strick 1973: 110), it is not important whether this is a dream, an imagining or a remembrance. Consonant with the mourning film's characteristic blurring of ontological and epistemological boundaries, what the film articulates is pure intensity. Less a coherent event, "experience" in the conventional sense of the word, what happens here is defined by the circulation of the non-corporeal, the unformed, what Deleuze and Félix Guattari call the "Body without organs" (cited in Elsaesser 2002: 271). Elsaesser and

Buckland account for the uncertain status of this scene. The Body without organs "may also allow us to understand how in much contemporary cinema the dividing line between inside and out, but also the boundaries between bodies, have become difficult to draw" (Elsaesser 2002: 272).

Cries and Whispers reiterates the frailty of language before death and pain. From the opening scene of Agnes's pain, Elaine Scarry extrapolates "a sustained attempt to lift the interior facts of bodily sentience out of the inarticulate pre-language of 'cries and whispers' into the realm of shared objectification" (Scarry 1985: 11). Existence becomes an illusion, characters evoking a state on the verge of becoming something other. Karin's life and marriage is "nothing but a tissue of lies." As Agnes rises, she speaks: "For you it may be a dream, but not for me." As a filmmaker, Bergman perennially explores illusion and *Cries and Whispers* compares this or that character's alienated subjectivity with this theme in mind. Prior to Agnes's apparent resurrection, Anna wanders alone around the house chasing a sound: "Someone's crying all the time." The modernist protagonist is prey to a vision, less an actor than acted upon. As noted, it is widely acknowledged that in the late–1950s and 1960s, Bergman contributed significantly to modernizing the cinematic representation of women. The characters portrayed here by Thulin, Andersson and Liv Ullmann descend from a cinematic tradition of women possessed by unearthly longings nourished less by mainstream aspirations than by tendencies on the fringes of mainstream practice. We are reminded of the aural imaginings of Miss Giddens and of Amy in *The Curse of the Cat People*. The mourning film involves the exploration of precincts of subjectivity to which people normally do not venture.

In mourning films, as in life, grief leads to congeries of emotion. The scene of Agnes, embracing her sister Maria (Ullmann) carries intimations of the dreadful and the sexual. Joan Mellen's unsparing description of Agnes spells out what is at stake in being close to a dying person: "Her lips are bitten, her skin sallow, her hair lank, her teeth yellow, her nostrils distended with pain. She is woman stripped of allure, bared to the repellent essentials of a body in decay" (Mellen 1973: 10). While the contrast with the vibrant Maria's facile affections, her "wet smiles" (ibid.: 10), could not be starker, the confusion of feelings could not be more macabre. In *Persona* (Ingmar Bergman, 1966), Bergman explored another ambivalent relationship between two women, one an actress (Ullmann), the other her young nurse (Bibi Andersson), as their interaction teeters between trust and resentment, friendship and hatred. Both films acknowledge that we go through life responding to others in complex ways, reconstituting them just as we reconstitute ourselves. Verbal language and body language can be schizophrenic. The scene between Agnes and Maria catches something of the buried desire between close friends or the envy of sisters. But it also elicits ancient horror at the thought of intimacy with the dead. Like real grief and mourning, mourning films open up fissures and schisms between individuals and between individuals and their perceptions, while blurring the borders between propriety and indecency, health and decay, themes taken up in *Morvern Callar, Under the Sand* and *Kissed*.

Bereft after the death of her own child and now enduring the loss of her child surrogate Agnes, Anna speaks the sadness that is an irreducible part of death's horror. If this were a lesser film, Anna's maternal presence might propose her as the film's moral conscience. But here she is dumbstruck before the prospect of eternity. *The Innocents* proposed spirits summoned by characters (and by the film), but simultaneously explicable by reference to its protagonist, whose maternal instincts are undermined by the confusion of fear and desire. Like Miss Giddens, who may be reporting genuine evidence of spirits or may be going insane, Anna wishes only to care and nurture and the longing makes her especially sensitive to human loneliness before the prospect of death. Hence the scene in which Anna offers her surrogate child her breast is especially moving. In Anna's reverie, Agnes speaks of the loss of bearings as life ends: "It's so empty all around me." Emptiness, darkness, ambiguity are all characteristics of grief. It is there, assailed from all directions, in the "open wound" of Freudian melancholia, in the fraught rhizome at the start of *Hiroshima mon amour*. Therapeutic literature speaks of disorientation: "So that you can no longer sleep as you did, feel safe in the street the way you used to, or be secure in your own home" (Lake 1988: 73). This emptying-out also characterizes the film's account of physical pain. Few mourning films encounter so vividly the pain which can accompany death, an inexpressible sensation bringing disorientation in its wake and leaving language behind. Pain "actively destroys [language], bringing about an immediate reversion to a state anterior to language, to the sounds and cries a human being makes before language is learned" (Scarry 1985: 4).

In a film punctuated by temporal interruptions, we see Agnes, her sisters and Anna out for a picnic on some spring day in the past. The sense in which this is Agnes's recollection and her happiness alone which is being recalled is emphasized by the way the sisters do not interact. We do not even see Maria and Karin's faces. This is less the comfortable ellipses of familiarity than the awkward silences of disconnection and alienation. Memories, like dreams, are *about* the emotion that has given rise to them. Just as Resnais's protagonist's memories of Nevers reduce Nevers, and recollections of the beach in *Interiors* will reduce the milieu of childhood to feelings, so Agnes's recollections reduce the past to an emotion, a metonymy of happiness. Ostensibly, this spring scene is a relief for the audience after the studied claustrophobia of the film's impeccably anguished interiors. Yet the prospect of young women in white frolicking in sylvan meadows also seems an inauthentic echo of the ghostly figures flitting through the house earlier. Agnes's and the film's final words ring hollow: "This really is happiness." The forced note recalls the prospect of a life of blissful fleeting pleasures followed by a dreaded agonized conclusion. Of Bergman, Dorota Ostrowska observes: "He was fascinated by the ways in which film gradually transformed a present moment into a past one. He wanted to capture in the present moment that which was the most fleeting in it and extend it to make it feel like eternity" (Ostrowska 2007: 59). For the poignancy of its desperate perspective, this scene embodies Bergman's preoccupation with time's passage and his legacy to modern mourning cinema.

Case Study: *Don't Look Now*

"You come upon me,
tiny, swept aside, rejected,
and just as desperate as yourself."
Letter to the Clairvoyant, Antonin Artaud

If Nicolas Roeg's *Don't Look Now* (1973) derives something of its dramatic tension from the dispute between "masculine" rationalism and "feminine" intuition, its account of a couple's responses to their daughter's death highlights two distinctive experiences of grief. Yet its celebrated narrative conceit and its reputation as a key modern horror film have tended to emphasize the man's story rather than the woman's, resulting in readings such as Milne (1973), Kolker (1977), and Sanderson (1996). This is appropriate since *Don't Look Now* is crucially a film about the inevitability of death, its premonitory trajectory strewn with clues and suggestions as to the fate of the male protagonist. As Dempsey writes, "Visions and hallucinations disturb...; bleeding red stains appear everywhere; water and broken glass form sinister link-chains; portents and mysteries, cries and whispers" (Dempsey 1974: 40). The theme of death as a fated destination was explored in Roeg's previous films: *Performance* (Nicolas Roeg and Donald Cammell, 1970), and *Walkabout* (Nicolas Roeg, 1971). At the time of *Don't Look Now*'s release, the director stressed his interest in death as an inescapable condition of identity: "The fact that we seem to go directly towards it, however much we avoid it. It's something that does obsess me, the idea of where and how we approach, and where we finally reach our personal death scenes. At one time people used to go to funerals.... But today death has become a taboo thing; again this getting away from identity" (Roeg cited in Milne 1973: 7). In tracing the downfall of the skeptical John Baxter (Donald Sutherland), *Don't Look Now* proffers not simply death's inevitability, but its consequences for those who survive. With hindsight, the film comes to embody debts to melodrama and the séance, Dempsey calling it "an occult melodrama" (Dempsey 1974: 39), making *Don't Look Now* seem a highly seductive prototype for the modern mourning film: "Few horror films have explored the hurt at the heart of the uncanny with such a sense of sorrow" (Armstrong 2007: 469).

Don't Look Now's place in the cinema of mourning becomes increasingly obvious if we contemplate the emotional devastation which underwrites its characteristically generic play with notions of premonition and the afterlife. What is intriguing about this modernist film, slickly appearing in the wake of a 1960s cultural (and, importantly, cinematic) revolution secure in the benefits of secular life, is the way in which it can so convincingly entertain the notion of a metaphysical space to which the dead go and from which they communicate to the living. This faith is intimately bound up with the film's exploration of personal loss and its consequences. John is rational; his resolute conviction is that "my daughter is *dead*, Laura! She doesn't come peeping back at me with messages from the fucking grave. She's dead dead *dead*!" (Scott 1997: 66). It is a denial of metaphysics which is also, the film proposes, a denial of death itself, one asserted in the bereft rationalist as a reluctance to face the consequences of his daughter's death. John's refusal to countenance a metaphysical dimension of human finitude seems strange for a character making his living restoring Byzantine churches, prompting a reading which is less cultural than psychological. It could be argued that John's work constitutes a sublimated attempt to restore the past, to pretend that it has not gone, that nothing has changed.

The psychoanalytical notion of incorporation is relevant here. What is effectively incorporated in the inability to reclaim that which has been lost is loss itself. The psyche becomes determined by loss, the mourner possessed by it, in this case without realizing it. Abraham and Torok write: "There can be no thought of speaking to someone else about our grief under these circumstances. The words that cannot be uttered, the scenes that cannot be recalled, the tears that cannot be shed — everything will be swallowed along with the trauma that led to the loss" (Abraham and Torok 1994: 130). Unable to come to terms with the passing of the little girl whose corpse he held in his arms, John is literally unable to revert to terms, of any kind, to describe how he feels. Hence he never speaks of Christine (Sharon Williams), whereas her mother Laura (Julie Christie) speaks of little else.

John's psychology remains as mysterious as his eventual fate. Is he the victim of the notion that men are incapable of showing their emotions? Does he feel responsible for Christine's death? Given the inextricable relationship between the death of the other and one's own mortality, the scenario the film proposes is one in which John's refusal to emote is related to his refusal to entertain clairvoyant premonitions of his own death. Put in Heideggerian terms, John is in denial of his being-towards-death, a denial which will eventually throw into doubt his acknowledgement that he has or will lose anything that is dear to him. By contrast, Laura's response to loss is a form of introjection. Abraham and Torok describe introjection as an everyday phenomenon: "a constant process of acquisition and assimilation, the active expansion of our potential to accommodate our own emerging desires and feelings as well as the events and influences of the external world" (ibid.: 9). However, in this instance her ability to "come to terms" with loss leads Laura into distorted, even subversive waters. For Abraham and Torok, introjection is the "psychic counterpart" (ibid.: 9) of the individual's normal trajectory from childhood into adulthood, except that Laura's trajectory takes her from adulthood into a form of childhood. The difference in outlook between husband and wife is played out on the level of the film itself. John's stoicism is neatly analogized in the sharp cut from Laura's stifled scream on first seeing Christine's corpse, the sound of her voice covered by the edit, to John diligently working at a building restoration in Venice, the cut signalled by the din of a power drill as it drowns out Laura's shock. From the start, Laura's voice, the means by which the individual explains and comes to terms with loss, is denied her, leaving Laura to look for, or revert to, another kind of speaking. Her search is a quest for assimilation and continuity amid a contingent experience which is interpreted by the editing as the resolution of a fractured surface into a kind of set piece grandeur.

However elusive and obscure their lives seem to John and Laura and to the spectator, the film's characteristically splintered continuity serves the paradoxical purpose of thematizing continuities by "showing" without showing. In a film about absence, the ellipses between shots become parts of what the film seeks to reveal. For Deleuze, editing highlights the actual and the virtual aspects of the image, the sense in which an image contains and is anticipated by absence. In this reading, the editing table becomes a metaphor for the Deleuzian crystal, its ability to highlight images like the differing refractions of light available as the crystal is turned. This play of actual and virtual, presence and absence is central to *Don't Look Now*. The film proposes the search for a resting place, a continuum from restless edit to resolved scene, from a moment of consciousness to another, from the physical world to the metaphysical, from life to death. Michael Riley writes, "The film suggests that beyond what one conventionally sees and hears there is another "world" that can be apprehended not so much by sight as by vision" (Riley 1995: 15). Riley's distinction resonates with mourning cinema's perennial preoccupation with "thereness" and presence, as well as that between seeing and premonition explored in this example. What *Don't Look Now* realizes is the sense in which these continuities contain the contingent, whether edit, moment of consciousness, physical detail, within the larger picture, while the larger picture can be surmised in the detail. What makes it a difficult though convincing apologia for the metaphysical is the way in which it teases the spectator with visions and imports which may be there or may be "present," proposing Bazinian solidity or arousing the faculty of clairvoyance in the spectator. This suggestiveness is famously exploited in an assortment of clues set up in the film's opening sequence — Christine's red mackintosh, broken glass, a spillage of red, water. True to its modernist heritage of fracturing, or rethinking, narrative, such images are less intended to make sense in classical narrative terms than to linger pregnantly in consciousness. Relationships may be elusive but they exist. *Don't Look Now* is well named, for its juxtapositions are truly shocking, as well as symptomatic of the film's modernist sensibility. Deleuze writes, "The cinematographic image must have a shock effect on thought, and force thought to think itself as much as thinking the whole. This is the very definition of the sublime" (Deleuze 1989: 153). It is as though *Don't Look Now* "proves" the existence of the metaphysical by proposing a quasi-causal trajectory, played out in vivid clues, from Christine's death to her father's, from earthly turmoil to celestial calm. The film privileges a kind of speaking about death which intuits and acknowledges design while finding a space for succor amid a realm of sorrowful contingency. Despite its eccentric underlying ethos, *Don't Look Now* may be the most conventionally religious of modern mourning films.

That the film seeks continuities between the solidity of earthly spaces and the ideal spaces of a transcendent perfection resonates with its film-historical lineage, linking the postwar Gothic Anglo thriller tradition to the European arthouse. Visually and thematically, *Don't Look Now* seems the most "Continental" of British films. Again, Deleuze writes of an "expressionism [which] keeps on painting the world red on red; the one harking back to the frightful non-organic life of things, the other to the sublime, non-psychological life of the spirit" (Deleuze 1986, 56). *Don't Look Now*'s Venetian setting and its preoccupation with the ancient chimes with the film-cultural legacy from which it emerged. The mood of irrevocability permeating John's story links it to a popular tradition in British cinema which by the early–1970s was in decline. The Gothic literary tradition is concerned with the relationship between fate and contingency, death and life, vitality and morbidity, relationships also explored in cinematic manifestations of the Gothic. *Don't Look Now* appeared as the Hammer cycle of British horror films was reaching its visceral apotheosis amid a climate of liberalization in screen representations of sex and violence. Under this impact, Hammer output came to seem increasingly ironic and denatured, as Roeg recognized: "Nowadays, when people talk of the Gothic cinema they're really talking about camp. It's very sad, because the Gothic is a tremendous cultural influence, not a funny thing at all. And I wanted *Don't Look Now* to have a Gothic feeling" (Milne 1973: 7). Seen today alongside such releases as *Lust for a Vampire* (Jimmy Sangster, 1971) and *Frankenstein and the Monster from Hell* (Terence Fisher, 1973), *Don't Look Now* sees the reinvigoration of British Gothic by an infusion of European attitudes to color and space exemplified by *Cries and Whispers* (1972), and a play with time and interiority looking back to *Hiroshima mon amour*. Such reinvention can be surmised in the film's title. Unusually, and alone among the titles explored in this book, while "*Don't Look Now*" may describe John's ambivalence amid portents of death, it also directly addresses the spectator in an era in which mainstream cinema toyed with the boundaries of sex and violence. The personal address is emphasized by the quotation marks. Seen thematically, this injunction to *not* look also suggests an image which "looks" beyond this life at an unthinkable metaphysics, one which horror cinema, amid the growing trend towards graphic violence in mainstream cinema by the late-60s, had significantly foresworn. In this light, *Don't Look Now* positioned itself within a psychological affect-driven historical continuum arguably descending from Bauer to Lewton to *Carnival of Souls* and *The Innocents*. The cinematic and philosophical continuities which *Don't Look Now* evoked yielded one of the most explicit forerunners of modern mourning cinema.

Consonant with these tangled legacies, the difficult narrative continuities which *Don't Look Now* proposes lend themselves more readily to intuition than to rational explication. Bearing in mind traditional gender notions, perhaps this affords the film a "feminine" aura. While the rationalist in John refuses to admit his status as a fragment of fate, the female characters are open to relationships which are not so much known as intuited. The film's air of suggestion is seldom more powerfully felt than in a shot in which its searching trajectory seems to give way, its cryptic metonymic syntax resolving itself into a savage pictorial poetry. We see Laura, the bereft mother and widow, standing decorously in black on a funeral launch with the sisters Heather (Hilary Mason) and Wendy (Clelia Matania) beside her. This is the point at which we are given a hint as to where John's confused journey is leading him, while the mourning woman becomes the focus of the film's look. *Don't Look Now* has been building up to this moment, the time in which Laura is already widowed and the film realizes the implications of an understanding of experience based not on rational materialism, but on intuition and the relationship between contingency and the ideal, life and afterlife. It is a Heideggerian moment, in which we come as it were into a clearing wherein we discover the truth of our being-towards-death. Duncan writes, "All our lives are mysterious, and mysteriously going to end, but the real enigma is that we have no part, or say, or opinion or perspective on the most significant thing we ever do, after being born" (Duncan 2009: 1). Arguably, it is the moment when *Don't Look Now* states its belief in the acceptance, even the necessity of death. Unlike other moments in the film where what John, and we, see feels fleeting, virtual, slippery, the montage of red, water and glass, or when John falls from scaffolding which analogizes his perilous purchase on life, the funeral launch has a set piece quality, heralded by Pino Donnagio's joyous score. It is more redolent of a melodrama than horror, evoking a preoccupation with the pictorial, even touristy, and the public expression of interiority, that suggests a gendering of the film's aspirations. Arguably, this scene is modernist horror cinema's riposte to Annie's funeral cortege in *Imitation of Life*.

This gendering of the action also has a historical dimension. Laura's stylish widow's weeds make her the descendant of the impeccably attired heroine suffering in the classical woman's picture. Her demeanor, standing bolt upright in the boat, also recalls iconic figures of half-inhabited humanity in Lewton. In no other shot in the film does Laura look the way she does here: gaunt, ashen, other. The culmination of her burgeoning intimacy with the sisters, she even seems to look like them, echoing the police inspector's comment about how women as they age seem to converge in their appearance. (Scott 1997: 96). Mourning also makes the mourner look different. Lake's analysis seems apt: "You may have changed physically. Some people, for example, lose weight or put on weight. This may go back to before the bereavement, and

Don't Look Now. Standing erect in mourning splendor with Wendy and Heather on her husband's funeral barge in a moment of set piece splendor, Laura at last takes her place in the medium's circle.

due to the worry caused by the situation that led up to the bereavement" (Lake 1988: 51). The sisters stand behind the younger woman as if to be there if she falls. As the rapport between Heather, Wendy and Laura deepens, they begin to resemble a surrogate family, as if the bereft mother reverts to childhood in their company. This relationship is underwritten by the *mise-en-scène*: "In the bows of the launch stand three people. LAURA, looking distraught, her hair blowing in the breeze. And the two old SISTERS on either side of her. They seem to be talking earnestly to her, practically gripping her between them" (Scott 1997: 91). At this point, we recall how Heather, on first meeting Laura, claimed that she could see the child Christine between her and her husband. The reversion to childhood enacted through actor placement is symptomatic of Laura's difficult experience of grieving. It is as though losing her daughter has made Laura want to emulate Christine by reverting to girlhood. Mourning has been seen as a transitional experience, invoking memories of other transitional experiences: "The illness of mourning is a special case of a wider and more inclusive framework of disturbances that generally characterize periods of transition" (Abraham & Torok 1994: 124). If a kind of inverted introjection has led Laura to regress to childhood, we may suppose that mourning for her carries psychological reminders of other transitional disturbances. Dempsey evokes the entire film's splintering effect as he describes Laura's fragility: "Christie's face is especially delicate and touching; her subtle modulation during the film from darting pulsating little movements to calm and self-assurance expresses the change that she undergoes" (Dempsey 1974: 42). Laura's friendship with the sisters goes hand-in-hand with her growing faith in the afterlife, a kind of reversion to a fanciful language more associated with a childlike response to the fear of life's thresholds. This narrative of thwarted development resonates with Christie's other roles. Since her first major part in *Billy Liar* (John Schlesinger, 1963), in which her youthful northerner fled the smokestacks for London, the actor's 1960s image became associated with a liberated vitality then redolent of the continental influence of Jeanne Moreau, Emmanuelle Riva and others. By casting Christie as a character challenged rather than liberated by fate, *Don't Look Now* subverts the worldliness of her image while paradoxically making of Laura an increasingly liminal "actor-medium." On the launch the transition seems complete. It is due in large part to the clairvoyant Heather, another character who secures *Don't Look Now*'s seminal place in mourning cinema. In his 1926 piece *Letter to the Clairvoyant*, Artaud writes, "You come upon me, tiny, swept aside, rejected, and just as desperate as yourself; and you lift me up, you take me away from this place, this false space in which you no longer deign to make the gesture of living, since you have already attained the membrane of your repose" (Sontag 1976: 129).

Don't Look Now's significance for the cinema of mourning is due in part to the way it bridges classical representations of grief and the suggestive forms bereavement would take in modernist cinema, and in part to the access it affords the spectator to the desires and projections of grief. Like *Cries and Whispers*, *Don't Look Now* proposes a near-deserted historical space as something like a female preserve. It feels as though the film conspires with the female characters to desert the unwitting husband, the space between the Baxters uncannily growing as the film progresses. While the lovemaking scene between the couple excited much press interest in 1973 and critical interest since, any suggestion that it represents growing solidarity between John and Laura is ruled out as the film separates them with irrevocable regularity. For Duncan, "death means that our things have separated from us like objects in space no longer governed by gravity. They float indiscriminately, but inexorably, away" (Duncan 2009: 3).

The disjunction between Laura's grief and John's stoicism is graphically rehearsed from the moment of Christine's death. On occasions, they seem more like father and daughter than husband and wife. Just before Christine dies, John smiles at Laura in such a way as to hint at the potential for another sort of dynamic between them. In a church she asks him for pocket money to light candles for Christine. He later admonishes her repeatedly as if he is speaking to a child. *Don't Look Now* plots two departures; he to death, she to another carer. John is erecting a stone gargoyle when he notices Laura, left below, catching up with the sisters who are nearby. Like John, she is in some sort of denial about Christine's death. But if he has pushed the thought out of his mind, refusing even a language to communicate his grief, for her it is something that she cannot forget because it is too horrible to remember. The way Lebeau expresses this seems suggestive of the way Laura gravitates to another consciousness: "Left to its own devices, such a memory will forge associations with other ideas excluded from the conscious mind, laying the foundations for what Freud and Breuer will describe as the 'more or less organized rudiment of a second consciousness'" (Lebeau 2001: 27). John not only loses his life in Venice, but he loses his wife, too. The sense in which the film chronicles a couple drifting apart comes to its climax when John sees Laura on the launch. By this point, we have been seeing John and Laura together in the same shot less and less frequently, and when he looks now we are not sure what he is seeing. We do not see the launch and John in the same shot. Only in a medium shot of the launch do we see what caught John's eye. If John and Laura are not seen in the same shot here, they do not co-exist in the same time. *Don't Look Now* is classically Heideggerian inasmuch as, for characters to be, they must be in time. John may "see" Laura on the launch, but the way in which the editing separates them in space also separates them in time. In a Deleuzian sense, the film proposes time as consisting of "sheets" of foresight and hindsight, memory and presence, all interwoven in the editing.

The film's habitual posing of an image in which temporalities co-exist is reinforced at every turn by its setting in a decaying wintry medieval Venice. It is the perfect milieu for this sad, incipiently lachrymose story of loss. The sadness of the couple and the fluidity of time is reinforced by the water which threads through the narrative as it threads through the canals of the city. For Deleuze, writing of Jean Vigo's *L'Atalante* (1930), "a clairvoyant function is developed in water ... it is in water that the loved one who has disappeared is revealed, as if perception enjoyed a scope and interaction, a truth which it did not have on land" (Deleuze 1986: 82). Christine disappeared in the water and is revealed when John drags her up from its depths. Laura, as John had known her, also "disappears" in the water, appearing on its surface in the launch, not only in another element but in another time. If mourning films such as *Carnival of Souls* and *Interiors* propose the sea and water as a metaphor for the travail of overcoming loss, while *Three Colors: Blue* and, arguably, *Under the Sand* propose water as sanctuary, the significance of *Don't Look Now* for the mourning film consists in proposing water as the harbinger of another kind of perception of time and destiny.

Case Study: *Interiors*

> "The sea, that crystallized these,
> Creeps away, with a long hiss of distress."
> *Berck-Plage*, Sylvia Plath

The discrepancy between recollection states and contemporary subjectivity is a major theme of Woody Allen's *Interiors* (1978). The film's very title announces an essential assumption and preoccupation of this thesis. Allen's "interiors" refer to the fastidiously appointed rooms of the house in which the action takes place, and to the dislocated and damaged subjectivity of the film's characters. Little actually happens in *Interiors*, while its account of interiority is searching and of terrible consequence. One of the film's most striking aspects is the managed elegance of its visual composition. We must look back to the haunted abodes of classical horror to find such a house as a protagonist in the action. More contemporaneously, Allen's allegiance to Bergman can be felt in the similarities between this dark chamber piece, his first serious drama and consciously Bergmanesque work, and *Cries and Whispers*, which was playing the New York arthouse circuit just five years before *Interiors* opened. Both films revolve around three sisters who must come to terms with a death in the family. Both impeccably designed, in each film color is used to rigorously analogize the feelings and psychological states of the protagonists. Both films use dialogue not principally to advance narrative, but to indicate and chart inner states. Allen has paid verbal tribute to *Cries and Whispers* often enough, while his own interest in female interiority marks films as varied as *Hannah and Her Sisters* (Woody Allen, 1986), *September* (Woody Allen, 1987), *Another Woman*, and *Husbands and Wives* (Woody Allen, 1992). "I love the relationship of women to women," he told Stig Björkman (Björkman 1995: 100).

Played out in a Long Island house and its beach annex, *Interiors* charts the history of a family from Arthur's separation from his wife Eve to Arthur's remarriage to Pearl and Eve's subsequent death. These events are seen through the eyes of their three daughters—Renata, Joey and Flyn—each struggling with her own demons and the consequences of their mother's cold and controlling nature. The film's narrative trajectory seems at first obscure. It begins with Joey (Mary Beth Hurt) pacing through the house. Only later do we surmise that this scene takes place on the day of her mother's funeral. A little later Eve (Geraldine Page) visits Joey's apartment and they discuss the possibility of a reconciliation between Eve and Arthur (E.G. Marshall), but the scene in which Arthur proposes a separation is still to come. As Joey gazes out to sea from the family house, we see her and her sisters as children playing on the beach. In a session with her psychoanalyst, Renata (Diane Keaton) recalls playing as a child as we see the child Joey sitting with her father at breakfast.

Interiors. Joey, barely visible, paces through the empty house like a ghost, or like her mother did when she was alive.... Notice the thin light in this shot, and the organic progression from light to darkness.

This convoluted structure is prompted less by the film's external account of events and more by their effects on the characters and the alliances shaping the family dynamics. Immediately following a scene in Arthur's office in which he describes the decline of his marriage, Eve appears at the apartment of Joey and her partner Mike (Sam Waterston). Joey is not confident that reconciliation will take place between her parents. By putting the scene in which Arthur tells his family of his plans after that in which Joey and Eve have this discussion, the film invites us to reflect not on events, but on their emotional consequences, here Joey's ambivalent feelings about her parents' marriage. This ambivalence will become increasingly apparent as the film progresses. Later we see Eve, returning to her apartment, pottering about in the foyer. This interlude is followed by Renata's words to her psychoanalyst: "Mother paced all the time. She (sighing, then weeping). Um ... she was an insomniac. You could, um ... always hear her upstairs ... pacing in the middle of the night" (Allen 1983: 121). It is as though the scene of Arthur discussing his marriage and that of Eve in her apartment unleash more powerful, and more memorable, scenes in which the implications of this history are rehearsed by distraught others. The supposedly key events of the film's diegesis—the divorce, the suicide, the remarriage—do not remain in the memory as vividly as those scenes in which Joey and Renata reflect upon their feelings about these events. Many scenes involve characters remembering: Joey remembering her childhood, Renata remembering her childhood, Arthur remembering his marriage. The structure of Allen's film cogently exemplifies the historical evolution from classicism to modernism. Rather than delineating horizontally, here the narrative trajectory plumbs history vertically, viewing it as a series of Deleuzian temporal layers. Beginning after Eve's death, then charting the responses of her family to its possibility, and then their reactions to its reality, *Interiors* subscribes to that sense in which the mourning film is a "post-genre," a series of films which chronicle the post-life moment, anti-action in the most thorough yet most tender, profound and productive sense.

The effect of watching *Interiors* is that of witnessing a series of scenes piled on top of each other, rather than a continuous narrative driven by cause-and-effect. This impression mimics the peculiar trajectory of emotional history. We are subject to real events, and we are at the mercy of emotional histories, moments of crisis and reparation and their accompanying moods triggered by real events and "events" of memory, reflection and recollection. Evoking a palimpsest in which time and consciousness are integrally related, such hazardous moments, lacking conventional historical sense, are dispersed, random, piled one upon another like playing cards. These random atomized moods here find expression in the *mise-en-scène*, its scenes of emotional turmoil as self-contained as the beautiful rooms of Eve's house.

Amid a tradition dedicated to narrative dynamism and optimistic resolution, few American films take death as their subject and resolution quite as emphatically as does *Interiors*. Devastated at the breakdown of her marriage and clinically depressed, Eve is appropriately named as the character who throughout the film teeters on the eve of death. Drawn to walks along the seashore or to gazing through the French windows at the thrashing Atlantic surf, her daughters reinforce this precipitate metaphor. The vastness of the Atlantic, its unchanging grey presence, its unfathomable quality, is a constant in these characters' lives. Like death, the sea is always there when firm ground peters out, and the film's references to its ebb and flow foretell Eve's suicide, and hint at death's defining nature in our lives. All of the characters in this film stand at the threshold between life and what comes afterwards. We try not to think about death, but Allen here proposes characters who constantly seek to articulate its ghastly reality.

The sense of characters living precipitately between two states, life/death, interiority/exteriority, is nicely expressed by the windows in *Interiors*. Symbolizing the threshold between the individual and the outer world, windows have been an important dramatic fixture in the woman's film too: "Within the women's films as a whole, images of women looking through windows or waiting at windows abound" (Doane 1988: 138). Windows resonate with grief as a condition: "I am living behind glass or under water or whatever image suggests being at one remove from everything" (Duncan 2009: 2). *Interiors* uses this pane of glass to analogize the indiscernible distance and simultaneous proximity of the subject to the world. Standing gauntly at the window staring at the sea below, these sisters descend from those most Gothic manifestations of the woman's picture. If our view of Mrs. Danvers, seen through the window rushing from room to burning room evokes the horror of witnessing dementia from the haven of otherness, Miss Giddens's sight of Peter Quint looming in from the night evokes our own unspeakable dread of our own subjectivity. Meanwhile, taking its unearthly cue from Maya Deren, the phantom of *Carnival of Souls* peers out of the carnival house, simultaneously seeing and waiting to be seen.

In Allen's previous film, *Annie Hall* (Woody Allen, 1977), his character makes reference to Sylvia Plath's reputation: "Interesting poetess whose tragic suicide was misinterpreted as romantic, by the college girl mentality" (Allen 1983: 37). Plath's ghost echoes throughout the rooms of *Interiors*; in the sisters' experience of the sea, in Renata's vocation, and ominously in Eve's attempt to asphyxiate herself with gas. Plath grew up overlooking the Atlantic and wrote of it in a scrapbook, the atmosphere of wistful recollection descending into those moments when we see the sisters by the sea: "And so there comes a time in your senior year at high school when because you like the ocean and the wind and sand, someone grins and drives you down to the sea, and because you like poetry, someone gives you a poetry anthology for graduation" (Plath 1975: 27). Variously regarded as a symbol for the transition from the "shore" of life to the afterlife, or as a site of cleansing trauma, the sea has been associated with death since before Christianity. As the women in *Interiors* gaze out of the window, their composure seems striking, Joey observing, "The water's so calm" (Allen 1983: 175), Renata replying, "Yes (sighing). It's very peaceful" (ibid.: 175). The notion of the sea as a boundary between life and death recurs across subsequent mourning films.

Further invoking Plath, Renata is a successful poetess living in secluded Connecticut and given to panic attacks and recurring visions of her own death: "Actually it started happening last winter. Increasing thoughts about death just seemed to come over me ... a preoccupation with my own mortality. These ... feelings of futility in relation to my work ... just what am I striving to create anyway? I mean, to what end? For what purpose? What goal? I mean ... do I really care if a handful of my poems are read after I'm gone forever? Is that supposed to be some sort of compensation? ... I used to think it was. But now, for some reason ... I can't seem to shake ... the real implication of dying. It's terrifying. (sighing, crossing her arms in front of her) The intimacy of it embarrasses me" (ibid.: 124). Renata's words to her psychiatrist strike the ear as pretentious, trite and narcissistic—"Increasing thoughts about death just seemed to come over me ... a preoccupation with my own mortality"— yet this very triteness testifies to the difficulty of using language to talk about death. Allen's preoccupation with death is well known from his films and writings. The impossibility of confronting it in words is recalled in the fractured overlapping dialogue of Allen's comedies, but here he gives Renata a key speech in terms of this film and of his themes as an auteur. He describes her pessimism in more vivid terms: "That really what we're all talking about is the tragedy of perishing. Aging and perishing. It's such a horrible, horrible thing for humans to contemplate, that they don't contemplate it.... They try to block it out in every way.... But even someone like Renata ... that even though she's an artist and she has some ways of expressing these painful ideas, even the art is not going to save her. She's going to perish like everybody else. Even if her poems are read a thousand years from now" (Björkman 1995: 105).

The film is full of premonitions of death. Recalling Eve returning from hospital after her first suicide attempt, Renata describes her: "her hair looked grey ... she was a stranger" (Allen 1983: 121). Renata's words highlight that sense in which the body deteriorates when we die, that inside every human body there exists the potential for decay, of the end of that body. Renata's words to her psychiatrist—"Mother paces all the time.... You could hear her upstairs"—carry uncanny associations that this house is inhabited not by a person but by the ghost of one. Philosopher Simon Critchley writes, "The human being is death in the process of becoming.... Representations of death are misrepresentations, or rather representations of an absence" (Critchley 1997: 25–26). *Interiors* charts a death in the process of becoming, while its perfectly rendered, apparently discrete scenes contribute to the evolving consciousness of this family. The film's opening shots are a set of "dead" interiors: "almost still-life scenes" (Allen 1983: 113). As Renata and her husband Frederick (Richard Jordan) shop for a gift for Eve's birthday, he suggests a scarf. The suggestion is met with Renata's stark unequivocal "(barely glancing at the display) no" (ibid.: 126). Scarves strangle and the possibility and atmosphere of suicide is all too tangible around Eve. In one of few scenes in the film which takes place outside the house, we see no one other than Renata and Frederick at the store, while the clothes seem odd without people to wear them.

Cries and Whispers's oneiric quality is a tempting point of reference for Joey's nocturnal speech to her mother as, on the evening of Arthur's wedding to Pearl (Maureen Stapleton), Eve lurks in the shadows. "Feeling abandoned is perhaps one of the most devastating results of a suicide" (Worden 1991: 97). Even before her mother's death, in trying to speak to her, it is as though Eve has already gone. Joey's words seem to evoke the other-worldly space we enter when we look beyond life: "I feel like we're in a dream together" (Allen 1983: 172). The way the scene is shot deliberately blurs the distinction between a conversation between two people and an individual addressing herself. In this scene, Joey's interiority is other-worldly space. Eve's presence is flickering, contingent, almost absent, like a memory or an old photograph. Barthes writes of the "Winter Garden Photograph" taken of his mother as a child as if she is in it but not in it: "Sometimes I recognized a region of her face, a certain relation of nose and forehead, the movement of her arms.... I never recognized her except in fragments, which is to say that I missed her being, and that therefore I missed her altogether" (Barthes 2000: 65–66). This teetering at the edge of sight, this perpetual misrecognition, is precisely the relationship between being and presence which is so essential to the mourning film.

Cinematographer Gordon Willis shoots Joey face on in this scene. At first, it seems as though she is speaking to Allen's audience. From around 1977, Allen's work often features characters addressing the audience, whether apparently or by design. It is as if the struggle to represent difficult themes forces them to search beyond the film, almost beyond representation, for more unmediated forms of address. Typically, the model bears striking resemblances to Freudian psychoanalysis, of which Allen is famously a disciple. In the Freudian psychoanalytical method, the listener remains opaque, more mirror than respondent. As in the *mise-en-scène* of the psychiatrist's office in which the analyst is a silent witness, we never hear Eve speak and barely see her during Joey's soliloquy. Joey could be speaking to a psychoanalyst about her relationship with her mother. Standing in the shadows, Eve is elusive, almost unavailable to sight. Joey voices questions: "what happens to those of us who can't create? What do we do? What do I do ... when I'm overwhelmed with feelings about life? How do I get them out?" (Allen 1983: 172). Her words are rhetorical, questions aired rather than queries expectant of resolution, ventilation rather than solicitation. By reason of its reflections on form, Joey's speech seems key to Allen's film. She speaks of creativity, self-expression for the individual who lacks a means of communicating feelings and intuitions. If Renata's dilemma hinges on the value of her self-expression amid the frailty and finitude of existence, Joey's revolves around the means of that expression. Both women face the same dilemma; how to express their concerns before the inevitable crisis of death overcomes them. Like Joey, she struggles with language — an old poem she describes as "much too ambiguous" (ibid.: 131).

If the *mise-en-scène* of direct address to a passive listener recalls the Freudian psychoanalytical model, the analysis which it invites of the spectator is as much stylistic as moral. We are being invited to analyze Joey and Renata's problems within a structure of cinematic identification in which we empathize with a character's dilemma. But we are also aware of a context of aesthetic appreciation. Moments of direct address in *Interiors*, their earnest soul-searching couched in the exacting compositions of Kristi Zea's design coordination and Willis's cinematography, invite us to contemplate the meaning of mortality for articulate people whose dread has gone beyond language to become inscribed in the dank light and frail colors of an understated, nevertheless emphatic, look. With *Interiors*, aesthetics and its relation with death become broached by characters within the film as well as on the film's surface. This discussion is not without consequences for future mourning cinema.

While contributing to its elaboration of mourning, the film's play of *mise-en-scène* and emotion positions *Interiors* as a direct descendent of the European art aesthetic, almost a baroque glossing of the Continental model. In keeping with *Interiors*' somber theme, at the beginning five pale simple vases drained of color on a white mantel announce a lifeless *mise-en-scène*. This washed-out look is reflected in Eve's preference for "beiges and ... earth tones" (ibid.: 118); "the paler tones would make a more subtle statement" (ibid.: 116). Eve's taste sets the tone for the film's look. Arthur reflects on her fastidious construction of the family environment: "She'd created a world around us that we existed in ... where everything had its place, where there was always a kind of harmony" (ibid.: 114). An oneiric quality, the sense in which this house does not belong to an objective world, permeates *Interiors*. Allen's admiration for European art cinema informs dialogue which, for all its inadequate striving, seems overly articulate and precise rather than naturalistic and overlapping as in, for example, *Annie Hall* and the forthcoming *Manhattan* (Woody Allen, 1979). Reflecting the precision and exactitude of Eve's work as an upmarket interior designer, precision and exactitude are essential to *Interiors*' sense of design.

The visual precision also reflects the "written" quality of the dialogue. Allen himself has acknowledged this: "When I write my dialogue for certain films, I'm almost writing it in a way you would a subtitle rather than human-speak. It's an odd little problem" (Björkman 1995: 117). The literary mood is borne out as Joey closes the diary in which she has written of her mother's funeral, effectively ending the film. Worden endorses the role of writing: "Keeping a journal of one's grief experience or writing poetry can also facilitate the expression of feelings and lend personal meaning to the experience of loss" (Worden 1991: 53). Allen says that "I wanted [the film] to be in the realm of the subconscious and the unconscious" (Björkman 1995: 99). In cases of suicide, family members often retreat into themselves. In this family, the failure to talk is longstanding. Notice how self-contained Eve's speeches seem. As she speaks, the character is invariably seen in isolation rather than in a shot with another character. Compare this scheme with the representation of Pearl, earthy, outgoing, sociable, as she does card tricks with Mike and Frederick, or cavorts at the wedding reception, mingling unabashedly with her adopted

Interiors. Joey writes in her diary of her feelings following her mother's funeral. As grief therapists have observed, keeping a journal of the grief experience can memorialize the dead and be an aesthetic daily record of its convolutions.

family. Driven by her appetite for life, a bon viveur in love with fine food and good times, in spite of Eve's embodying the gravitas of his theme, Allen is generous to Pearl. It is she who gives Joey the kiss of life following the younger woman's attempt to save Eve from the waves. Pearl's presence promises to bring the family out of the "ice palace" (Allen 1983: 115) in which they have been living.

But the film belongs to Eve, who wanders through it as if waiting to cross some line to another place. Arthur describes the woman he met: "Very pale and cool in her black dress ... with never anything more than a single strand of pearls. And distant. Always poised and distant" (ibid.: 114). Arthur's words remind us of a corpse. Clinical psychologist Paul Pretzel writes of the stresses facing women which can end in suicide, "especially being or feeling abandoned by the important man" (Pretzel 1972: 39). Part of the power of *Interiors* is its account of the way people persuade themselves that the relationships that they are in at a given moment are meaningful, everlasting and irrevocable. Such fictions sustain them for years. Then, in Arthur's words, "suddenly, one day, out of nowhere ... an enormous abyss opened up beneath our feet. And I was staring into a face I didn't recognize" (Allen 1983: 115). Arthur's very choice of words — "abyss," "face I didn't recognize" — reminds us of death itself, how sudden, irrevocable, disfiguring, final it is when it comes, and of how strange, inhuman, other, Eve will become.

If Eve is presented as a set of pathological symptoms, a grey gaunt figure, when she appears at the wedding she seems wraith-like, not speaking and barely there. All we see is her face in the shadows. "The representation of death," Critchley writes, "is always a mask — a *memento mori* — behind which nothing stands" (Critchley 1997: 26). Curiously, despite actual shots of the shadowy figure, Allen's focus on Joey seems to elide Eve from sight, or perhaps conjures a vision of her, a further manifestation of the play of memory and interiority explored in earlier shots of children on the sand. As she reminisces, Joey seems to summon her mother from the night air. Eve is a link between the bereft Bauer heroine and the inconsolable Marie in *Under the Sand*, another figure who walks towards the sea at the end. Writing in cinema's inaugural year, Maxim Gorky famously observed in a passage oddly presaging *Interiors*' mute frozen quality: "Last night I was in the Kingdom of Shadows.... It is a world without sound, without colour. Everything there — the earth, the trees, the people, the water and the air — is dipped in monotonous grey. Grey rays of the sun across the grey sky, grey eyes in grey faces, and the leaves of the trees are ashen grey. It is not life but its shadow, it is not motion but its soundless spectre" (Gorky cited in Frampton 2006: 1).

Nothing is forever, Allen's film counsels. Only death is truly irrevocable. "Irrevocable" is a word the characters keep using. The prospect of Joey having a child rather than realizing her artistic ambitions is "totally irrevocable" (Allen 1983: 125). Arthur describes moving out of the house as "not an irrevocable situation" (ibid.: 123). The irrevocable informs the temporal organization of the film. We know before he has announced his desire to leave his wife that Arthur will do so because Joey and Eve have already discussed their feelings about this. We suspect that Eve is unstable enough to kill herself because Renata discusses her periodic return from a psychiatric ward before we see Eve preparing to take her life. Subsequent viewing of the opening scene also primes us to anticipate Eve's absence. By emphasizing characters' feelings about events over the events themselves, the film makes it inevitable that these events will occur. This unconventional structure makes for engrossing drama and audience participation becomes an irrevocable fait accompli.

Eve's willful nature also contributes to that sense, acknowledged by Joey, that she cannot live in this world. Eve's inability to come to terms with the end of her marriage is made obvious when Arthur announces that he is moving out. Her mood vacillates between the panic-stricken — "I'll move *out*" — to the imperious — "I don't want to discuss the details just now" (ibid.: 123–124). Throughout the film, she manipulates her daughters into bolstering her fantasy that Arthur will return and things will continue as they did in the past. Eve's fantasy adds to the other-worldly nature of the character. The film confronts Eve, her family, and the spectator, with the terrible realization that nothing lasts and the things that we lay great store by — love, work, history — are transient. When the revelation that Pearl has been married more than once is dropped into the conversation, are we to take it that her marriage to Arthur will also not last? As Freud writes, "If we are to take it as a truth that knows no exception that everything living dies for *internal* reasons — becomes inorganic once again — then we shall be compelled to say that the 'aim of all life is death'" (Freud 1920: 246).

Eve's detachment from reality — she keeps shutting out the wider world — "Would you mind closing the window? The street noises are just unnerving" (Allen 1983: 117) — and her studied management of the family scene are classic symptoms of psychosis. In his 1924 essay "The Loss of Reality in Neurosis and Psychosis," Freud writes that "psychosis is ... intended to make good the loss of reality ... in [an] autocratic manner, by the creation of a new reality which no longer raises the same objections as the old one that has been given up" (Freud 1924: 569–570). The autocratic manner is evoked in Eve's manipulative ways. Less a traditional mother, Eve is more a matriarch, a symbolic figure given less to nurturing individuals than to controlling her offspring. When she attempts suicide, the preparations are shot from Eve's perspective. As she secures the doors with masking tape, we see only a pair of hands, the tape, the door frame, lending the scene a chilling subjectivity. All we hear is the tearing of the tape, a wrenching aural metaphor for a character becoming detached from life. Allen kindly grants admission to this woman's last interior design, her final professional show, as Eve arranges the *mise-en-scène* of her demise. There is a cut to an ambulance careening along a New York street as Eve is taken to hospital, its hysterical siren as shocking as the rasping of the tape.

Unusual for an Allen film, *Interiors* does not have a music soundtrack. The absence of music carries a suggestion of "God's Silence," the metaphor perennially explored in Bergman and evoked in the conversation of many a 1970s Allen protagonist. Of Bergman's 1963 release *The Silence* (*Tystnaden*, Ingmar Bergman, 1963), Nigel Floyd wrote in *Time Out*, "Bergman's severe symbolism emphasizes both the seeming impossibility of, and the absolute necessity for, human tenderness in a Godless world" (Pym 2006: 1051). Floyd could be writing about *Interiors*. Mourning films can contain moments of tender complicity between characters. Snatched from death by Pearl's kiss of life, Joey flings her arms around Mike, with whom she has had a fretful rapport. Renata and Joey, estranged throughout the film, silently hug and comfort each other following Eve's funeral.

Interiors may at first appear to be a film about unrequited love, but it is about much more. Remonstrating amongst themselves, Joey and Renata are torn between propping Eve up and letting her down easily about Arthur's intentions. Meanwhile, the ghastly truth erupts in Eve's voice: "I have nothing to live for anymore" (Allen 1983: 128). In another of Allen's serious works, *September*, an aging physicist tells a younger man that the universe is "haphazard, morally neutral and unimaginably violent." Faced with the loss of love, the end of unions, the fear of death, life itself can seem haphazard, morally neutral and unimaginably painful. Its haphazard nature is lived out through Joey, the youngest daughter and still trying to find her vocation. A personality common in Allen's oeuvre, this rudderless figure drifts, an artist without the means to live out her art: "I feel a real need to express something, but I don't know what it is I want to express" (ibid.: 125).

Joey's wandering around the empty house at the beginning seems apposite. Earlier, she tells Renata of their mother that "my whole life I've only ever wanted to *be* her" (ibid.: 139). And so Joey makes her way, like her mother, into the sea. So unthinkable are death and suicide for individuals confronted apparently endlessly with the details, projects and contingencies of living, that they seem absurd, theatrical conceits akin to Renata's litany about death, rather than authentic, coherent and everyday occurrences. And so the impeccably dressed Eve striding sedately into the Atlantic, recalls an old melodrama in which a heroine in a mink stole gives up life rather than continue to face its implications. Of Page's performance, David Thomson writes of "exquisite self-pity" (Thomson 2002: 662). Self-pity is itself a performance designed to elicit a response from one's "audience." Yet in the face of loneliness and death, for the human subject, unable to combat despair with language, finding a way to articulate death can drive them into cliché or into a sea of eviscerating dreadful consciousness. As the screen fades to black, the sisters stand gazing wordlessly out to sea. Echoing the prospect of a life returning to the matter from which it sprang, the final image restates the opening one in which a woman looks out to sea. We are reminded of a musical symphony, in which the climactic third movement draws to a close and the opening theme returns.

The preceding case studies sought to demonstrate how the transition from classical to post-classical cinema afforded increasingly involved and nuanced accounts of grief and mourning. Departing from traditionalist sentiments of earlier eras, and the aesthetic conventions which accompanied them, modernist films in Europe and America proffered progressive uses of the medium to plumb the interiority of grief-stricken and confused protagonists. The films examined here use color, *mise-en-scène*, framing, lighting, flashbacks, convoluted time structures, dialogue, acting and editing to explore these themes. In their shaping of narrative space, these films become projections of the psychologies which inhabit them. Preoccupied with their grief, the protagonists inhabit geographies not of space and time but of the mind and the spirit. While earlier traditions evoked the consolations of a heavenly paradise to which the dead depart, modernist films of grief posit the living in some earthly limbo all the more modern for being private and unavailable to consensual interpretation and succor. These characters cannot comprehend death and are utterly alone in their feelings about the dead. What these films make manifest are the complex and painful forms grief takes for these isolated and unhappy people. The results are as elusive and difficult as the experience which they attempt to elucidate. Chapter 3 shall trace their impact, with some contemporaries and antecedents, on a series of releases appearing over the last twenty years.

Chapter 3. Acceptance

> "Nothing has been altered since that last night."
> Mrs. Danvers, in *Rebecca*

Recalling that stage of mourning theorized in therapeutic literature in which the mourner becomes reconciled to their loss, in tracing the recent flowering of a mourning cinema, Chapter 3 will describe the aesthetic attempt to integrate classical and visionary registers within the same film, and in dramatic terms to reconcile the absence of the dead with the mourner's continuing sense of presence. This theme of reconciliation is literalized, for example, in the discussion of *Three Colors: Blue* later in this chapter, in which Julie's recovery is signalled by her periodic emergence from a swimming pool. However much the intensities of grief wrack the protagonist of the mourning film, theirs is a journey which must end in acceptance, however beholden to narrative, as in *Moonlight and Valentino*, or to narrative ambivalence, as in the films discussed in this chapter. Either way, for the mourner, the world has changed forever. If mourning is about coming to terms with that change, of assimilating the varying logics of grief, the theorization of the mourning film must be an attempt to negotiate extremes of aesthetic temperament.

In this chapter, the theme of "acceptance," however cautious, reluctant, fractious, unresolved it is in the films discussed here, is read as the movement from distrait, disarray and heterogeneity to a new sense of cinema. The films examined in Chapter 3 represent mourning in new and powerful ways in an era in which, while witnessing fresh experiment in the image, the cinema reached its centenary amid talk of its own "death." As one among a range of aesthetic impulses coming to recent fruition, the mourning film answered the need for a new definition of what cinema is. These films become places in which presence and absence, continuity and difference, meet. Writing at another historical watershed for cinema in 1927 in a piece entitled "Cinema and Abstraction," Antonin Artaud could have been foreseeing the significance of the moods of mourning to the re-invigoration of cinema in the 1990s. His words catch something of the atmosphere of the films examined here: "Nothing exists except in terms of forms, volumes, light, air — but above all in terms of the sense of a detached and naked emotion that slips in between the paved roads of images and reaches a kind of heaven where it bursts into full bloom" (Sontag 1976: 149).

This variegation of form and volume in mourning cinema reflects the varying intensities of the mourning process itself. Writing in "Mourning and Melancholia" and elsewhere, Freud used the term "grief work" to characterize the tasks necessary to the fulfillment of mourning. In grief counseling it is acknowledged that, in Parkes's words, "numbness, the first phase, gives place to pining, and pining to disorganisation and despair, and it is only after the stage of disorganisation that recovery occurs" (Parkes 1996: 7). Worden outlines four tasks, corresponding roughly to the acceptance of loss, working through the pain of loss, adjustment to a fresh environment, and the emotional relocation of the loss: "It is essential that the grieving person accomplish these tasks before mourning can be completed" (Worden 1991: 10). Yet as we have seen, therapeutic literature acknowledges that grief work does not always follow prescribed patterns. Seldom as neat as Parkes's trajectory would suggest, these distinct phases often blur into one another in a process of ebb and flow. While the hope is that the malaise should heal like a physical wound does, unlike a disease: "grief is a process and not a state" (ibid.: 7). Grieving is not a self-contained experience, but one through which the individual passes in their own time, an experience bringing with it a multiplicity of feelings and states. The parallel between the indistinct phases of grief and the flows and energies of the mourning film is not difficult to see.

To adapt the processes theorized in grief therapy to discussion of the mourning film enables us to see the type as an aesthetic and affective process in which moods and effects become integrated. It is worth reiterating Parkes's evocative metaphor from Chapter 2: "Grief is not a set of symptoms which start after a loss and then gradually fade away. It involves a succession of clinical pictures which blend into and replace one another" (Parkes 1996: 7). In *Three Colors: Blue*, effects of color and light shape Julie's transition from acceptance to emotional relocation, just as the evolving heats and modulations of music chart her psychological journey. Like mourning, the mourning film is organic, its atmospheres and intents reverberating, however fitfully, across the film like the pangs and inattentions of grief. Mourning films are among the most haunting to watch, moments remaining fixed in the mind long after the film is finished. Also explored in case studies here, *Birth* and *Under the Sand* end with lingering shots of bereft women on deserted beaches. However ambivalent the character remains about her loss, it is clear that the spectator will carry this image with them out of the cinema. Resonating with therapeutic accounts of grieving which emphasize the fluidity of grief states, mourning films challenge the narrative protocols of dominant cinemas. While examples as disparate as *Secrets and Lies, Moonlight and Valentino* and *In the Bedroom* plot mainly optimistic scenarios in which protagonists apparently get over their losses, because mourning films are principally *about* feelings (emotions rather than activity are what they chart), there is always an excess, a sense in which the film cannot quite bear its account of experience, any more than a single shot or scene can contain within it everything it has to say to the film as a whole. If the narrative trajectories of *Moonlight and Valentino, Secrets and Lies* and *In the Bedroom* are, broadly speaking, horizontal, those of *Interiors, Birth* and *Under the Sand* are vertical, plunging us into the interiority of their protagonists as we watch the film. Such a contrasting motion provides a useful metaphor for gauging the aesthetic ambitions of individual mourning films. As we have seen, the modern mourning film derives aesthetic instincts from melodrama and the horror film, genres dependent for their power on excesses of emotionalism and a *mise-en-scène* infused with portent and desire. Films as scattered in time, place and genre as *After Death* (1915), *Destiny* (1921), *Portrait of Jennie* (1948), and *Carnival of Souls* (1962) have been praised primarily for what would in Anglo-American critical parlance be called set piece moments in which emotions fairly pour from the screen while light, color and camerawork wrack the image. In contrast with the part-whole analytical approach used in chapters 1 and 2 to explore relationships between particular scenes and the film as a whole, Chapter 3 takes a more holistic approach, seeking to reconcile such excessive moments with the rest of the film, showing how they inform and shape, and are themselves informed and shaped, by other scenes and sequences. Again, the filmosophical approach seems so apt: "[if] it is a matter of *Three Colors: Blue*'s defocussings … a good theory of film must be able to cope with the margins of film form, and not relegate it to an 'excess'" (Frampton 2006: 79).

The discussion of classical and modernist antecedents undertaken in chapters 1 and 2 highlighted moments and effects in which an excess of feelings pushed the film to experiment with visionary ways of exploring interiority, as a particular film's aesthetics foregrounded the image as image or hallucination, the manifestation of something imagined or dreamt. Postwar modernist films negotiate secular crises of identity and purpose through the singular experiences of their protagonists. The plenitude and ambivalence of these films' imagery could be said to invoke a modern version of religious transcendence. If the celestial appeals of classical melodrama either strongly implied or blatantly referred to a higher power, the visionary register in modernist films occasionally contains at least the "memory" of the metaphysical.

Possessed by their claims of visions and voices, Florence Carrez's and Maria Falconetti's attitudes of quiet longing in, respectively, *The Trial of Joan of Arc* (*Procés de Jeanne d'Arc*, Robert Bresson, 1962) and *The Passion of Joan of Arc* (Carl Theodor Dreyer, 1928), exemplify this memory of absence, a desire which lingers off-screen. Quiet longing is a recurrent attitude in the modern mourning film, testifying to the type's preoccupation with time and duration and marking its commitment to a modern fall from grace, or some fresh conception of the metaphysical. Deleuze writes, "The direct time-image is the phantom which has always haunted the cinema, but it took modern cinema to give a body to this phantom" (cited in Bálint Kovács 2007: 41). Because many of the antecedents already cited straddle generic boundaries and historical paradigms, they set a pattern for a mourning film which comes to seem "excessive" in relation to the usual critical categories used to discuss these films. If the purpose of this study is to find a language to talk about a newly identified category of film, this chapter will build on the exploration of similarity and difference in the attempt to enable the mourning film to come into its own.

The multiplicity of emotions experienced by the mourner will also guide this chapter's discussion of how individual mourning films work as organisms, growing as we view them until they are more than the set pieces which stood out at first, and take on distinctive identities, which while haunting our thoughts cross and violate their generic and institutional parameters. Picking up on aesthetic effects discussed earlier, the following case studies will seek to account for the play of aesthetics and psychology in mourning films of the past two decades.

Case Study: *Three Colors: Blue*

> "Reflect that when we
> Suffer, Lord, we doubt...."
> *À Villequier*, Victor Hugo

Krzysztof Kieślowski's *Three Colors: Blue* (1993) remains one of the most powerful, alluring and difficult mourning films of recent years. The spectator's first impression is of a relentlessly visual experience, an academic exercise and a immersive film which from its title onwards, demands to be contemplated and felt rather than a narrative to be followed and explained. *Blue*'s effect is cumulative. Few modern films have used color to make the spectator feel with such clarity. Many critics have explored the film's imagery, which is on first viewing a flight of pure visuality offering bold and strange access to the plight of its bereft heroine. Wilson writes of a work offering "a charged analysis of a terrorized and numbed survival, of the isolation of the trauma victim and of the gradual rediscovery of relationality" (Wilson 2003: 16).

In hindsight, the film's title seems increasingly descriptive of a numbed survival. But if the color blue represents liberty as symbolized in the French tricolor, the film's exploration of the psychological consequences of loss offers a cold, raw and devastating freedom, one characterized by loneliness, melancholy and unimaginable pain. True to its high art aspirations, *Blue* is a challenging auteur statement built around an elusive muse, in Ginette Vincendeau's words, valuing "ambivalence, mystery and anguish, especially when embodied by a beautiful "tragic" woman" (Vincendeau 2000: 249). But while *Blue* has been praised chiefly for its look, its stealthy integration of color, theme and performance is adroit and resonant, recommending it as a worthy exemplar of Deleuzian aesthetics, and the legatee of a rich heritage. *Blue* fulfills the experimental project of modernist art cinema, loosening traditional links between the image and conventional narrative and characterization to plumb daily interior travail, while soaring onto a metaphysical plane. From the isolating stillness of its shocking premise, *Three Colors: Blue* plots the odyssey of a silent interior soul as she tentatively reestablishes connection and solidarity with others.

The narrative premise is brutal. After Julie de Courcy (Juliette Binoche) loses husband and daughter in a car crash, she retreats from friends and family, and the public life of her composer husband and grieves alone. But while the film elliptically suggests the inner trauma of grief, it vividly connects interiority and environment. *Blue* interprets its theme not in the optimistic political sense of an individual's liberty from personal and social constraint, but in terms of an individual bereft of the anchors of connectivity, abroad and lonely. For Slavoj Žižek, the film is about the rediscovery of connectivity from the Hegelian "night of the world," in which all is representation and nothing belongs to the subject, the most dreadful of freedoms: "to the 'concrete' freedom of the loving acceptance of others, of experiencing oneself as free and finding full realization in relating to others" (Žižek 2001: 171). Žižek plots an emotional transition from an early close-up of the convalescing Julie's eye, its glassy surface reflecting an approaching doctor, with a panning shot appearing much later in which the camera departs from Julie's face to drift across the lives of four significant others: the boy who witnessed the car crash, Julie's elderly mother, her friend Lucille (Charlotte Véry), and Sandrine (Florence Pernel), Julie's husband's mistress. Of the earlier shot, Žižek writes that "the eye covers almost the whole screen, while the external reality ... is seen only as a reflection in the eye.... It is no longer (diegetic) reality which contains its suture-spectre; it is reality itself which is reduced to a spectre appearing *within* the eye's frame" (ibid.: 52). Deleuzian in its insistence upon reality as a spectre emanating from subjectivity, this shot literalizes that sense in which the mourning film thinks around its protagonist while reality is made a product of consciousness.

One of the consequences of Julie's plight is her urge to cross class boundaries, an experience which, while locating her irreducible and undeniable turmoil within a shapeless ambivalent phenomenal world, makes of her a seminal modern wandering heroine. Following discharge from hospital, Julie relocates from her detached country house to an apartment near the center of Paris, one liable to burglary and rodent infestation, and bringing her into close proximity with individuals from other social classes. This retreat from the comforts of the cultural elite — Julie's husband was an eminent figure — is an aspect of the fluidity which *Blue* explores. Julie's social trajectory becomes an odyssey by one cut loose from middle class convention and aspiration by a sudden ghastly reminder of the fragility of experience. Amid the odd and disfigured connections discernible in Kieślowski's universe, the multiplicity of milieux, cultures, feelings and impulses to which Julie's experience leads, is strangely conjured by a scene in a strip club in which she glimpses a television talk show in which her husband's work is being discussed.

Consonant with therapeutic accounts of grief, Julie's demeanor seems steered by invisible forces; demonic, willful and resentful. The nature of her suffering suggests what grief therapy brackets under the term "complicated" or "abnormal" grief reactions. Compared with traditional grieving responses, Julie's lack of emotion is itself a form of suffering. Hence her exchange with her housekeeper Marie (Isabelle Sadoyan): "Why are you crying?" "Because you're not...." The "natural" response to grief is to cry. In *A Short Film About Love* (*Krótki Film o Miłości*, Krzysztof Kieślowski, 1988), a young man asks his mother why people cry. She replies, "People cry for various reasons. When someone dies, when they are left alone ... when they can't stand it any longer." As Žižek recognizes, Julie's real tragedy is that she cannot mourn. First she loses her husband and daughter to death. Then she loses her idealized version of her husband when she realizes that he was unfaithful. Žižek writes, "when a person remains traumatically attached to a past relationship, idealizing it ... to a standard which all later relationships fail to meet, one can be absolutely certain that this excessive idealization is there to obfuscate the fact that there was something terribly wrong with this relationship" (Žižek 2001: 165). The perils which attend the acceptance of loss in the modern mourning film shall be borne out in *Birth* and *Under the Sand*.

Julie's lack of emotion makes it difficult for the audience to identify with her. Grief therapy refers to a wide range of causes and symptoms of maladaptive grief, yet Julie seems so opaque that, while we know she is hurt we can only imagine how it makes her feel. While in the hospital, she smashes a window. She may be attracting attention to a suicide attempt, or it may simply be a symptom of rage at her misfortune. Later, she invites her husband's colleague, Olivier (Benoît Régent), to visit her and they have sex. Then she makes him leave. Is she punishing an unfaithful husband, or identifying with him, or is this Julie's way of remaking herself in preparation for a new life? While Julie will eventually begin to plan for the future, in counseling theory a key indicator of recovery, she is for most of the film an unreadable person. Tempting as it is to interpret the episode with Olivier in Freudian terms, as Julie's melancholic acting out of her ambivalence towards an unfaithful spouse, this feels reductive. In a film as beholden to the image, to music, to other ways of speaking, rational explanations of grief seem especially impoverished. Never as compelling as the sheer artistry of Julie's personality, classical psychoanalysis offers limited orientation. Modern therapeutics too can be perplexed by modern grief. In cases of sudden bereavement, "the nature of the crisis can be of such a magnitude that it takes some time beyond the event to process and assimilate the full extent of the destruction that has occurred" (Humphrey 1996: 154). *Blue* proffers a matter-of-fact semi-engagement, a case study which we must interpret through apparently discrete behaviors and aesthetic gestures rather than through words and sentiments. Even Julie's laconic reactions — "Nothing is important," she tells a petitioner who comes to the door — become metonyms for some vaguely discerned private story.

Julie's un-readability prompts comparison with other pathologies. Her unpredictable responses connect her with the delinquent whom Binoche plays in *Les Amants du Pont-Neuf* (Léos Carax, 1991), and suggest an odd parallel with Nikita, the "difficult" protagonist, played by Anne Parillaud, in its contemporary *Nikita* (Luc Besson, 1990), a French film with as much flagship status in the multiplex as *Blue* would have in the arthouse. The comparison with *Nikita* is not as eccentric as it seems. Both films chart the trajectories of women who wander, beyond their social stations, their usual environments, and their customary demeanors. Neither actor courts her audience, holding us at bay just as their characters cannot bring themselves to trust. Wilson writes, "Binoche's face, its impassivity, its opalescent surface, is an object of fascination. Yet it remains largely inexpressive, a screen between the viewer and Julie's feelings" (Wilson 1998: 352). Its imagery determined by its wandering protagonist's mood, the camerawork in *Blue* will become progressively more handheld as Julie's rigid pose breaks down. It is a measure of the film's complicity with her subjectivity that the disciplined camerawork of earlier scenes conspires with Julie's calm and, apparently, collected demeanor. It is not that Julie's affect-less behavior is particular to the experience of grief, but that modern mourning films are inclined to muddy the traditional enactment of grief, while keeping faith with the complexities of modern therapeutic research.

Few film titles tout the experimental potential of modernist cinema like *Three Colors: Blue*, a title with all the blank descriptive character of an avant-garde film. But few mourning films since *Cries and Whispers* have experimented so tellingly with color. *Three Colors: Blue* is a film of feelings, a gift to Frampton's filmosophical approach: "much film form enacts an emotional side of "thinking": colors are mood-giving, movements are inexact in their impact, framings can be sensuous — forms that resemble human feelings more than rigid thinkings" (Frampton 2006: 96). Wilson has commented persuasively on the significance of blue in *Three Colors: Blue*. For her, the color symbolizes liminality, a key notion in mourning films. In the passage from day to night, a perennial metaphor for the passage from life to death, the sky turns from blue to black. Not darkness itself, blue is "the cousin of darkness" (Coates 1996: 20). Wilson evokes modernist painter Vassili Kandinsky's observations about the color: "Blue is the typical heavenly color. The ultimate feeling it creates is one of rest. When it sinks almost to black, it echoes a grief that is hardly human" (cited in Wilson 2003: 21). If the blue in *Blue* was touted in interviews and promotional literature as a symbolization of the Republican blue of the French status quo, use of the color evokes a less politically grounded and more spiritual mood. Charting a case of very isolated human misery, the film's title better invites a vernacular interpretation. *Three Colors: Blue* recalls human destiny as a rhapsody in blue. Its contribution to mourning cinema consists in the treatment of grief as pathology, the rigorous portrait of a distressed humanity expressed in the suggestiveness of a color.

Reinforcing the fluidity of behavior, lifestyle and milieu proposed by *Blue*'s account of Julie's grief is a series of interludes in which she takes to the water in a swimming pool. Sławomir Idziak's camera is sensitive to the flux of azure shadow and white light in these scenes. Such moments find *Blue* taking up a specific attitude towards its protagonist. Julia Dobson recalls *Blue*'s "persistent emphasis on reflection and light [presenting] Julie as icon and ultimately [repressing] her subjectivity" (Dobson 1999: 238). The swimming pool interludes become part of the way in which the film obscures its protagonist's interiority, even while its imagery, awash with the hue of melancholy, never allows us to forget how hard this film is thinking distrait. Essential to *Blue* both for their literal metaphor for the disparateness of grief's ebbs and flows, and for the film's play of mood, these amorphous watery scenes contribute to Julie's opacity, the "buried" aspect of her selfhood. They find echoes in the delicate blue filter which creates a wash across music notation, or those thin shards of blue light echoing the passages of music in Julie's head when she sits locked out of her apartment. The play of water also recalls the play of light on the blue mobile which belonged to her daughter Anna (no record), the only thing which Julie retrieves from her old life. The film's most insistent metaphors for a multifaceted and evolving destiny, the blue crystals and the lapping water permeate the film in a play of similarity and alterity which is simultaneously mournful and hopeful, everyday while sublime. For Vincent Amiel, "The glass beads on the chandelier symbolize this world of projecting facets that shed light on an infinity of unpredictable and changing traits" (Amiel 2004: 243).

Fluid, fractious and opaque, the pool water is Julie's private space and the sense of refuge which it provides for the bereft mother, a pre–Oedipal space perhaps (see footnote, Wilson 2003: 162), in which union with the dead daughter is evoked beyond the travail of Julie's misery and isolation, seems convincing. Here the water suggests solidarity with the child who was once inside Julie, and Julie's solidarity with a mother figure. At one point, we see her in the water in a fetal position. Lucille comes to the pool and Julie observes that Lucille is not wearing underwear. As Julie appears to emerge from the "womb" of her watery refuge, the positions of the women, Julie between her legs, Lucille crouching over her, recall a child emerging from its mother. Observing that she is crying — how does Lucille know this amid the drops of water on Julie's face? — Lucille hugs her. It is a moving moment, respite from Julie's disconnectedness and the film's cool academicism. Bálint Kovács writes, "All that is at stake in modern melodrama is *understanding helplessness*" (Bálint Kovács 2007: 89). From classical modes to its postwar intellectual variant, melodrama has been associated with the distressed, disenfranchised and desperate, characters whose condition makes them vectors for feelings and emotions. The melodrama, from Griffith and Bauer to Antonioni and Kieślowski, has sought to understand the private consequences of personal distrait. Julie's brief respite in the water is borne out in real-life histories of grief. Of moments after swimming, Duncan writes, "I feel as if the blur which was my life or "reality" before has achieved definition; as if I have made those minor adjustments to the telescope which sharpen the edges of Venus" (Duncan 2009: 3)

The relationship between Julie and Lucille is interesting in regard to *Blue*'s elaboration of female spaces. In the 1980s, a number of feminist film writers proposed that relationships between mothers and daughters offered spaces in which female interiority could be explored beyond the patriarchal looking relations of traditional representations. Lucille works in a strip club on the Place Pigalle and is disapproved of by her neighbors who petition to have her evicted. Julie does not sign the petition and the women tentatively strike up a friendship. Placing her beyond the realm of conventional morality, almost beyond the category of the social itself, Julie's grief has predisposed her to a friendship which contravenes normal class and social boundaries. Significantly, at the swimming pool this relationship briefly suggests a mother/daughter bond, reinforcing the sense of social, even amniotic, fluidity to which Julie becomes prone. As in the growing alliance between the grieving Laura and the sisters in *Don't Look Now*, there is something transgressive about the relationship between the women. Commenting on representations of the female as grotesque, Tania Modleski could be endorsing any transgressive or fugitive alliance between women when she writes of the "search for female figures who at the same time embody possibility, error, and risk and hence open up spaces for women (spaces in which untold stories may emerge)" (Modleski 1999: 200). Pushing her into unusual and unlikely alliances, loss can find the mourner metaphorically at sea, taking her to spaces from which untold stories *may* emerge, spaces which may amount to a rethinking of the material world. Writing of a classical melodrama protagonist who takes to an ice-borne river when ostracized from civilized society, Lucy Fischer suggests a temperament reminiscent of Julie's: "in her refusal of double standards, in her resistance to frigidity, in her heated female liquefaction of the solid masculine world" (Fischer 1996: 68). The flight into another element can seem to the mourning heroine irrevocable. When Lucille and Julie embrace at the water's edge, grief makes it difficult for Julie to leave the water on her own.

In a film which relentlessly plumbs the mourner's psychology, the swimming pool interludes serve a double function. They find the mother retreating to an intrauterine memory. They also act as a metaphor for her numbed negotiations on land, her sense of being unable to relate, by making the swirling water her own space, cut off from others by another element. In the swimming pool, Julie "acts out" her terrestrial disorientation. The mourning film proposes water as a metaphor for grief's ebbs and flows and as an imagined, dreamt, or hallucinated alternative space, perhaps the space "proper" to its wandering protagonist. For Julie, water reconciles the living and the dead in the memory of amniotic fusion with Anna, and enables her to work through her grief in preparation for another life "at land."

If the mourning film has been a saga of unremitting tears, the heroine of *Blue* is immersed in silent lachrymal passion. She takes to the water because the water makes her feel and look the way she feels and looks to herself, cocooned by her condition while her motives and intentions are fractured into a million slivers by the shimmering water. Vincendeau could have been anticipating the water when she writes of Binoche that "her distinguishing characteristic is her ability to evoke, alongside the cool exterior, the intensity of passion. One key to this success is this play on surface and depth, which has turned her into an icon of Neo-Romanticism" (Vincendeau 2000: 242). Vincendeau acknowledges that the gamine quality of early Binoche performances recalled French New Wave icons Jeanne Moreau, Delphine Seyrig and Emmanuelle Riva (as already noted, *Blue* pays tribute to the heroine of *Hiroshima mon amour* by casting her as Julie's mother), the Neo-Romantic in

Binoche, her "embodiment of sexy melancholy" (ibid.: 250), linking the modernist woman to a tradition of waiflike female heroism going back to Lillian Gish. Vincendeau evokes Vera Karalli when she writes that "the face of the Neo-Romantic woman must remain mask-like and distant, her body ethereal" (ibid.: 250). Nick James, too, evokes the modernist line of descent, writing that "Blue devotes the vast bulk of its screen time to gazing at Juliette Binoche, an actress of great talent and beauty, as she goes about doing remarkably everyday things" (James 2002: 34). This tension between extraordinary female allure amid a prosaic *mise-en-scène* was endemic in the classical woman's picture, while the disparity seems more self-consciously alluded to in such modernist works as *Cléo de 5 à 7* (Agnes Varda, 1961) and *Jeanne Dielman, 23 Quai du Commerce, 1080 Bruxelles* (Chantal Akerman, 1975). Much has been written about Binoche's beautiful visage. *Blue* begins and ends with close-ups of her. Vincendeau writes (after Jacques Aumont) that "the manipulation of proximity and distance characteristic of close-ups relies on the quality of Binoche's face, its beauty and luminosity attract the camera like a magnet, but its smoothness refracts the gaze of the spectator" (Vincendeau 2000: 249).

Refraction of personality, motive, appearance and light, is the dominant impression we get of Julie. Like the water which envelops her, the color blue haunts the film's imagery. When Julie convalesces, the screen turns blue as she sits with her unbearable memories. For Frampton, the film feels with her: "It is the power of Julie's memories that the film feels through colour, blushing blue with her as the past surges up to the present" (Frampton 2006: 120). Earlier in the hospital, Julie touches the blue screen of the television set on which she is watching the funeral of her husband and child. Because she is unable to attend the ceremony herself, Julie witnesses the public record of what has happened to her at one remove. This public record is the proof that once upon a time Patrice (Hugues Quester) and Anna actually existed and were part of Julie's world. The hand on the glass speaks an instinctual need for connection, and reconciliation: between Julie's past world and her present, between the excessive blue of the film's imagery and the film's instinct to plot narrative amid a sea of misery. In this difficult, often opaque film, we imagine that we know what Binoche's voiceless silent looks are conveying. Either this is the touch of the bereft wife and mother who longs for communion with her dead family. Or it is the perplexed touch of a muddled traumatized mind, astonished by her existential dilemma. (Recall how Renata fingers the window in *Interiors* for a precedent in the mourning film, and the way in which Juliette will touch the furnishings when she arrives at her sister's home in *I Have Loved You So Long*). The former interpretation echoes that sense in which the transparent pool to which Julie retreats, in appearance so like a television screen, is her attempt to enter some liminal space in search of the dead, some sleep in life in which she may be with them as if in reverie. The second proposes a sensual concision, the search for proof of one's purchase on things. *Blue* is a film which makes you look into the crevices of experience — a sugar lump absorbs coffee, a mouse scurries with its young — from which Julie, and we, derive a sensual piquancy. This negotiation of the sensual can have generic implications. When a fugitive from a street fight enters her building and hammers on the door and a window slams shut, we perceive the events through Julie's apprehension. The prospect of a house haunted by invisible agents finds *Blue* briefly resonating with the horror film. *The Haunting* featured a similarly fraught heroine agitated by disembodied noises. This emphasis on the contingent effect, the poignant, often disturbing detail, becomes symptomatic of a consciousness closed off from a sense of rational design, an everyday trust in the order of things. Of *Blue*, Kieślowski has observed, "We are trying to show how the heroine perceives the world. She focuses on small things, things that are close to her. She is trying to limit herself" (Kieślowski 2003). What is powerful about this scene is a use of sound so pronounced that it seems to "fill" the image, that is, what we remember about the scene is most poignantly recalled as sound. Paul Coates conflates noise with the off-screen, an often vital space in the mourning film: "Noise is the off-screen, the invisible, the danger Julie wants to shut out, the racket as a street brawl ... percolates up the staircase, with clattering feet and frenzied beating on her door ending in the swish of something (someone?) being dragged away" (Coates 1996: 20). In a mourning tradition preoccupied with feelings, the focus on sensory contingency finds *Blue* elaborating on a perennial trope of the type, one recalling the sudden frights of the parlor séance. The point, as in other mourning films, as in the séance, is not the objective status of this moment. The point is the velocity of its impact on subjectivity.

In counseling parlance, Julie's emotional relocation will come through her investment in the completion of a concerto that her husband was writing when he died. Like the blue washes that recur to externalize her pain, bursts of this music intermittently wash over the film, a sporadic chorus which invades her like the intrusive banging door. Žižek writes, "Her struggle against music is her struggle against the past; consequently, the main sign of her coming to terms with the past is that she finishes the deceased husband's composition, reinserting herself in the musical life-frame" (Žižek 2001: 165). If, increasingly, the music reminds Julie of her husband's infidelity, her completion of it lays his ghost and reasserts her identity. It is the nearest that the film comes to a goal-directed scenario. In being less about actions than feelings, *Blue* is truly modernist. Its bursts of music, then, underlie the action as classical program music did, but plot an emotional interior rather than a worldly narrative. The music is like the water: fluid, immanent, shocking: "Linearity, chronological editing, dramatic necessity all fade away, and in their wake come constant surprise and shifting significance" (Amiel 2004: 244). In a film guided by feelings and moods, there is a sense in which music becomes the script for the film, Julie's notation its strange codification. Near the end there is a close-up of her finger tracing the notes on her husband's score. Later there is another of her writing notes herself. These moments, like the sugar lump in the coffee, are beautiful to contemplate. We see them through the prism of trauma and the delicate blue aestheticization is compelling. Music is *Blue*'s aural metaphor for the hints of social interconnectedness that characterize Kieślowski's trilogy, the search for design amid the chaos of modern life. And music is an analogy for narrative. *Blue* is less interested in narrative than in what occurs before words have something to say. Philosophically, the film is phenomenological inasmuch as it reveals a protagonist who, rather than being able to stand aside, to deduce, define and decide what her life means or could mean, is already caught up in the aural, the colored, the felt. Loss is literally unspeakable, so color, light and space become its gestures.

Occasionally, the imagery in this film is so blissful that it suggests transcendence. Yellow light streams through hospital windows. Convalescing, Julie basks as the sun catches her face. The gentleness and warmth of the light in these shots, the sense in which we feel it as much as see it, the way in which it suggests an eventually beautiful world, reminds the spectator of being as a phenomenological state. At such moments, the film overcomes its academicism, seeks to recuperate the dislocated woman in the grace of everyday experience, amid occasional clearings of thinking light. Celestial beauty is common in the mourning film. If it rehearses an instance of sheer despair, *Blue* is eventually deeply affirmative. And while descending from a modernist arthouse tradition which has seemed agnostic, even atheistic, in its scepticism, there is much in Kieślowski's film to suggest that it may be "the most convincing apologia for the metaphysical since Bresson" (Armstrong 2007: 278).

Case Study: *Under the Sand*

> "That you'll be waiting for me. Through
> Forest and mountain pass I'll go.
> No longer can I keep from you."
> *Tomorrow, when the meadows grow*, Victor Hugo

If *Three Colors: Blue* bore hints of a debt to melodrama and horror, in *Under the Sand* melodrama and horror come together in the same film. Set against the staid backdrop of professional Paris, the film works out a story of adultery and familial discontent, archetypal melodramatic territory, leavened with intimations of death and putrefaction more commonly associated with a very different genre. This blend resonates with the contradiction at the film's heart. That the "adultery" consists in a widow's affair with another man suggests the sense in which, underlying this melodrama, with its naturalistic account of middle class experience, lies a poignant and shocking story of estrangement, grief and dementia. Vincendeau writes of a film that "suffuses the everyday life of the Parisian middle classes (those classic clothes, those elegant apartments) with a sense of dread" (Vincendeau 2001: 59). The generic referents of melodrama are not without precedent in French cinema. In Claude Chabrol's "Hélène" cycle of the 1970s, we find a middle class milieu disturbed by the prospect of violent death. While Chabrol was less interested in the emotional consequences of loss, *La Rupture* (Claude Chabrol, 1970) and *Juste avant la nuit* (*Just Before Nightfall*, Claude Chabrol, 1971) trace breakdowns in language and ethical assumptions which are central to *Under the Sand*. Melodrama and horror also feature to varying extents in Ozon's own oeuvre. On the one hand, there was his evocation of high Fassbinder, *Water Drops on Burning Rocks* (*Gouttes d'eau sur pierres brûlantes*, François Ozon, 1999), and the Hollywood melodrama pastiche *8 Women* (*8 Femmes*, François Ozon, 2001), of which Vincendeau wrote: "Barely hidden beneath the humour is a fantasy of beautiful but 'tragic' and faintly pathetic older women, not so far from Charlotte Rampling's glacial English lecturer in Ozon's earlier *Sous le sable*" (Vincendeau 2002: 46). On the other hand, the short *Regarde la mer* (*See the Sea*, François Ozon, 1997) generated a palpable sense of unease through the encounter between an abandoned English housewife and a mysterious interloper.

Under the Sand describes a character torn between conflicting perceptions of her experience, her condition and her history. Like *Three Colors: Blue* and *Birth*, *Under the Sand* offers scant relief from the misery of loss, but with stealth and economy delineates one of its more pathological variants, moving from a fraught study in complicated grief to question the underlying assumptions of a bourgeois marriage: "Hence a persuasive, intimate study of grief is transformed into a more general critique of romantic self-delusion in conventional marriage" (Hammond 2006: 1222). My reading seeks to show how melodrama and horror interact, pushing the portrait of a well-upholstered life to explore the epistemological and phenomenal rot which lies beneath.

Marie Drillon (Charlotte Rampling) is one of the most persuasive portraits of self-delusion in mourning cinema. Willfully denying that her husband Jean (Bruno Cremer), who disappeared in the sea while on holiday, is probably dead, Marie becomes detached from reality and from those around her.

Andrew Asibong writes of Marie's "inexplicably missing husband" (Griffiths and Evans 2009: 116), catching that sense in which, aside from the trauma and distress, loss is overwhelmingly mysterious. Going about her work as a university lecturer, shopping and socializing as if Jean is still alive, when she is alone Marie speaks to and imagines that he is in the room with her. Griffiths and Evans write, "The irruption of the spectral tears a hole in the ontology of our lives, a hole neither easily mended, ignored nor explained" (ibid.: 3). The discrepancy between exterior reality and interior delusion is patiently dramatized by the actors, and becomes reflected in the look of the film as it corroborates Marie's malaise. Diana Diamond writes, "Cinematic techniques, such as making the husband's ghostly presence real to the spectator and magnifying Marie's face in close-up in almost every scene, with the background always a bit out of focus, highlights Marie's dual mode of thinking and experiencing" (Diamond 2007: 150).

As in sightings of the dead in other mourning films, we only ever see Jean when Marie is looking, as when we see her look up at him when in bed with Vincent, or see a figure in the distance at the beach at the end of the film. But while appearing within the same naturalistic visual register as Marie, there is something chilling about this silent figure drifting from room to room at Marie's behest. Like the little boy in *Birth*, we do not quite know where Jean is coming from when he appears. And we do not know where he goes when Marie is not there. Even before Jean goes missing, the couple oddly do not seem to be together. In the holiday home to which they retreat at the start of the film, they talk too politely, there is little physical contact, they do not have sex. In the autoroute rest area where they take a break, they spend no actual time together. Indeed, the first time we see Jean he is unconscious, asleep in the passenger seat, an ominous portent of events to come. We wonder whether he has gone missing or has died. Only the silent dismay with which her friends greet Marie's ongoing investment in the relationship, in seeming to underwrite our perception that she is deluded, persuades us to believe that he is dead. By leaving Jean's fate only a likely possibility, *Under the Sand* emphasizes death as insistent absence. Demise is mysterious because it is overwhelmingly about someone not being there anymore. The film taps most emphatically into the sense in which the mourning film from Bauer onwards dramatizes the lack in the image, and the apprehension to which this gives rise in the spectator. Indeed, the anxiety which absence generates is often, paradoxically, expressed in the mourning film as presence. To illustrate a tension discussed in the introduction, these films toy with an idea with no verbal expression in English. If the most visually compelling figure in the mourning film is the bereft heroine, who is unmistakably "there," the most insistent "presence" is that of absence, so eloquently expressed in *The Innocents* as a tear on the schoolroom desk, in *After Death* as a manifestation of the dead actress, and in *Under the Sand* as an endlessly receding man on a beach.

In charting the visitations of Jean after he has departed, *Under the Sand* seems to analogize the estranged couple they were when he was alive. While we suspect that Marie is deranged, this life/afterlife mirroring has the effect of contributing to the realism of those scenes in which she impossibly communes with her absent husband. It is as though Ozon dissects this imperfect union through the prism of an afterlife, using death as a medium to explore the fractures and discontents in the living relationship. The realism of Jean's appearances, this sense of the continuation of an experience after death, is grounded in real experience. Joyce Carol Oates offers a lucid account: "— glancing into one of the ghost rooms unprepared. And stunned seeing—at Ray's end of the sofa—a shadowy figure, or the outline of a figure—what is called an 'optical illusion'—which is to say the *idea*—the *memory*—of a figure" (Oates 2011: 150). The vivid sense of presence can be "the cognitive counterpart to the experience of yearning. The grieving person may think that the deceased is somehow still in the current area of time and space. This can be especially true during the time shortly after the death" (Worden 1991: 26). Few films explore the conundrum of incommensurability that accompanies loss as perceptively as *Under the Sand*.

The film's descent from objective reality into subjectivity begins with a slow descending long shot from a bridge on the Parisian skyline to the surface of the Seine. This is a film in which the grieving protagonist is unable to reconcile life and death, and will, so to speak, wander between them. Following Jean's disappearance, Marie spends the entire film psychologically alienated from those she interacts with, psychically absent from the rooms in which she finds herself, as if hovering above the reality of everyday experience. Rampling's trademark elegance and poise assist in the illusion. In a boutique, she tries on a red dress, seeming to float above the carpet as she disports herself in the mirror. It is as though, without her mirror reflection, Marie does not exist. We are reminded of that scene in *Carnival of Souls* in which Mary tries on a black dress in a department store, admiring herself in a mirror, but cannot get anyone to take notice of her when she speaks. That Marie is unable to pay for her purchases because Jean's credit card has been frozen reinforces the sense of fantasy, of being somehow apart from everyone else. At dinner at her friend Amanda's, Marie's face takes on a mask-like quality as she negotiates a conversation in which her friends' knowledge and her delusion are increasingly at odds. When Vincent (Jacques Nolot) appears to show what Marie feels is an inappropriate interest in a married woman, conversation between them ceases and the scene, as though embarrassed by their silence, comes to an end. In conversations with Amanda (Alexandra Stewart), Marie does not seem to be listening. They endlessly talk at cross purposes about Vincent, in whom Amanda is trying to interest her friend romantically, but Marie rebuffs the suggestion, clinging to the fiction of her continuing life with Jean. The prospect of an individual "stuck" while life goes on around her is neatly analogized in the montage of fleeting landscape and a still passenger during Marie's railway journey back to Les Landes.

Under the Sand is suffused with conflicting claims to verisimilitude. Occasionally, an incident brings the truth home to Marie and the effect on her is a violation of her consciousness, an invasion of her isolated state. In a lecture theatre, she sees the young man who assisted her in the search for Jean back in Les Landes. Reading Virginia Woolf's *The Waves*, Marie stalls as she spots the young man in the sea of student faces before her. In a scene in which she looks around the house for Jean, a mirror emphasizes Marie's isolation, opening a door and catching sight of herself there. These glimpses of reality take on a dreadful patina when, looking over a new apartment, Marie collapses when she catches the view through a window. It is a cemetery. While her words to the *agent immobilier* prompt the camera to move to the window, as if the film as a film has been "directed" by its protagonist, the textured sea of cramped grey stones and sepulchers, like the rippling waters of the Seine, envisages the ghastly outcome of Marie's delusion. These are not merely the familiar pangs of recollection associated with normal cycles of grief. They serve to remind Marie that her husband is gone, but also that she is not adjusting to this in a normal way. Marie's shock at seeing the cemetery shows her what she has become, the camera pausing to stare at the tomb's objectal correlative through her window. Abraham and Torok write, "Inexpressible mourning erects a secret tomb inside the subject ... the objectal correlative of the loss is buried alive in the crypt as a full-fledged person, complete with his own topography" (Abraham and Torok 1994: 130).

In fleeing the apartment, Marie is fleeing from herself. Grief therapists acknowledge forms of acting out as a symptom of grief repressed. Marie's delusion, her insistence to friends and to herself that Jean is still alive, could be seen as an "acting out" scenario, one which is dangerously interrupted by such incidents. The fact that *Under the Sand* does not pathologize Marie, that her delusion occurs within the same realist visual and aural register as life around her, makes the acting out seem all the more alarming, a kind of quiet dementia occurring in a quotidian setting. We are reminded of the women in *The Haunting, Interiors, Birth* and other mourning films: sleepwalkers in a grey logical world for whom too much reality may trigger mental breakdown. Vacillating as it does between Marie's solipsism and moments of shocking lucidity, *Under the Sand* is Marie's film inasmuch as it represents, echoing Bauer, the psychological and aesthetic struggle for the twilight of a woman's soul. For Frampton, this consciousness teetering between logic and fantasy characterizes cinema itself: "Film disrupts principles of reason and judgement and so becomes a *truth* with its own will" (Frampton 2006: 200). This stranded consciousness is central to the mourning film, analogized no more eloquently in *Under the Sand* than in the shot of Marie stranded on the beach at the end. The sense in which the mourning heroine carries the film with her, so to speak, her deprivation and misery warping its portrait of existence, throws light on the film's insights into psychology under stress, and underwrites identification of the mourning film as a genre. In an ostensibly realistic film, the final scene in which Jean's form recedes as Marie pursues it seems all the more shocking for its sheer oddness. If the most disturbing moments in films from *The Innocents* and *The Haunting* to *The Orphanage* are those in which narrative space is slightly twisted like the surrealistic "twists" in a Magritte painting, in the final scene of *Under the Sand* the beach seems to move beneath Marie's feet, endlessly conveying her away from the man she strives to find.

Sudden incursions of reality into Marie's consciousness portend the film's investment in horror. *Under the Sand*'s descent into the Real is hinted at in its references to the soil and its inhabitants. Like mourning films from *The Innocents* to *Morvern Callar*, *Under the Sand* recognizes that death involves the return of the human to a material state. At Les Landes, Jean turns a rotting log over and we see ants milling beneath it. Marie tells her doctor that she hears humming or buzzing noises. We are reminded of insects. "The English are fascinated by things morbid," Vincent says to her at dinner. Marie must eventually examine the decayed body of a man who is supposedly her husband. It is a scene in which the horrific details of putrefaction and mutilation are spelled out in clinical detail, while the corpse itself is off-screen, a keeping from spectatorial view which figures in other mourning films, reminding us of the type's investment in psychological horror. Less interested in confronting the spectator with the visceral detail of death, *Under the Sand* is more intrigued by the effect this has on the protagonist. In a film privileging Marie's consciousness, we feel the ghastly sight of the inert, decaying and stinking body through its impact on her face. Even a clinical mask cannot protect us from the revulsion in her eyes and the realization that this sight will fleetingly force on her. Here the shock of the Real is as much the trauma of witnessing physical abomination as it is the trauma of losing a close relative. We are not sure whether Marie is registering recognition that her husband is dead, or whether she is disturbed, as the living are, by the sight of human decay. The oddness of human decay can be transcendent. Marie's shocked expression before the grisly mystery of death could be seen as a metonym for the restoration of metaphysics which Stan Brakhage discusses in connection with the defamil-

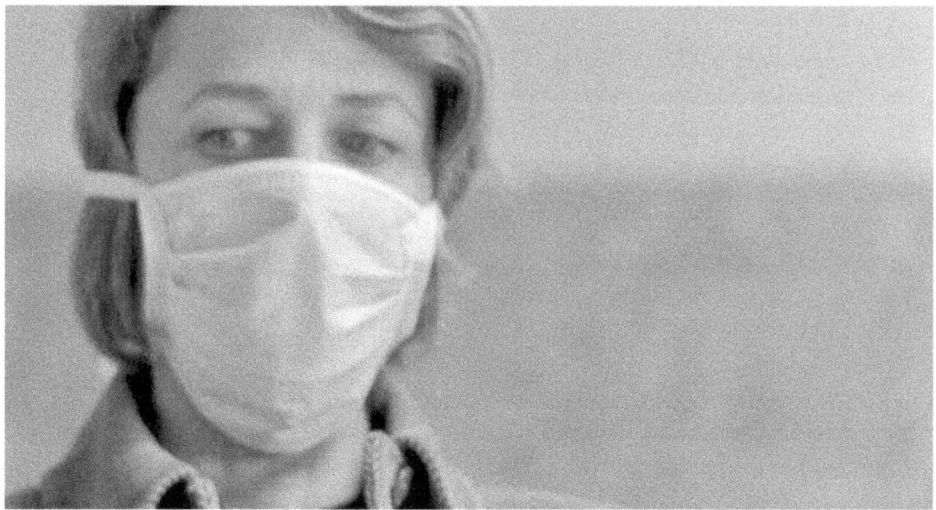

Under the Sand. The act of seeing the dead can cause such shock as to blur grief, revulsion and pity into one inscrutable but overpowering look, the congeries made all the more emphatic by the mask Marie wears here.

iarized body parts of his morgue documentary *The Act of Seeing with One's Own Eyes* (Stan Brakhage, 1972); even that title, with its implication that the "seeing" may not otherwise be authentic, may be a surrogate "seeing," weirdly foretells Marie's ambivalent odyssey into death. We do not see what Marie sees. We just watch as she looks. We do not know whether what she sees are Jean's remains, or somebody else's. For once, supposing that what she sees is her husband's corpse, when Marie looks we do not share a vision of Jean.

Charlotte Rampling's performance is a miracle of self-control. When we see her at last in tears by the spot on the seashore where she was last with Jean, it is as much a relief from denial for the spectator as we feel it must be a relief for Marie to break down. Tears are rife in the melodrama, in particular the woman's picture, normally coming after long passages of denial and misery. But in *Under the Sand* Marie's tears, while inviting us to share the heroine's misery, also invite us to share for one last time her delusion. If tears are seen in grief therapy as a healthy sign of assimilating grief, here they preface further immersion in the protagonist's condition. Are these tears shed in response to Jean's untimely death, or tears shed for a marriage that was not what it might have been? Either way, Marie cries for a very real sense of absence. Whether bereft because her lover has died, or bereft because her lover never loved her, Marie cries for something that is not there.

It is significant that we recall Les Landes as deserted, unlike the busy populated scenes of Marie's life in Paris. Returning in off-season, the film reinforces this sense of desertion, echoing *Hiroshima mon amore*, a place of the mind than a real location. Although Vincent knows the region quite well, he does not recall the exact place where Marie and Jean spent their last holiday. It is as if it does not exist. Like the sea's waves which lap over many mourning films, the moment when Marie cries on the beach will give way to another "realization" as she dashes across the sand towards the hallucinatory figure, the film's split consciousness once more deferring to its protagonist's tortured will. The sense in which *Under the Sand* takes place on different levels — mental, physical, metaphysical, contingent — played out at differing stages of consciousness and existence, is viscerally felt as Marie cries, her emotion erupting out of her as if she is going to vomit. Grief is something inside that must find its way out. Grief that so resembles revulsion may be as much a reaction to the sight and smell of the corpse as it is a delayed reaction to loss. We are relieved that Marie is finally able to emote; a case of blocked mourning seems to be coming to an end.

But as she runs towards an apparently receding figure, the consciousness of the image is once more Marie's and the film seems to return from melodrama to horror. Like the sight of human putrefaction, hallucinations may carry intimations of the transcendent. Grief therapy occasionally acknowledges the possibility that grief enables access to something more. Worden writes that "with all the recent interest in mysticism and spirituality, it is interesting to speculate on whether these are really hallucinations or possibly some other

Under the Sand. Like an illness of the body, grief wracks Marie, seeming about to burst from her being like an embodied substance.

kind of metaphysical phenomena" (Worden 1991: 26). As we see it through Marie's eyes, the film toys with the possibility of the metaphysical. And for the spectator confronted by a melodrama with a horrific undertow, the prospect of the widow running out to sea to assuage her grief, or a medium reaching out to another form of being, resonates powerfully with the mourning film's roots and ancestry. Ozon has reported that he shot the Parisian scenes, dominated by close-ups of Marie, in 26 mm, and the scenes on the beach in 35 mm. The industry standard lens in Europe and America for decades, 35 mm has become the norm for naturalism in mainstream and art cinema alike, here conferring a realist patina on Marie's viewpoint. Ozon's decision was canny, muddying the distinction between objectivity and subjectivity, an inner world of anguish, and an outer world of unremitting absence, an earthly existence of painful limitation, and a realm of magical thinking.

What are we to make of this enigmatic final scene? One of Marie's last acts is to push her hand beneath the sand as if she is scooping it up. Is she, like Renata in *Interiors*, like Julie in *Three Colors: Blue*, seeking some tactile imprint to validate that it is in fact she who is having these feelings, that she can leave a trace of this life? Or is she doing what Virginia Woolf did, preparing to fill her pockets so that she will be dragged down by the water's undertow more easily (like Jean may have been)? As in other mourning films, here the sea, with its rippling heterogeneity yet peculiar vista of endless sameness, sets the scene for this ambivalence, offering the wandering heroine release from the possibility of pain in the certainty of that which comes after pain. For Britt-Marie Schiller, "the ambiguous ending points ... to an ambivalence at the heart of mourning—a tension between a wish to live among the living ... and ... a wish to live with the dead in a timeless, eternal world" (Schiller 2005: 223).

Case Study: *Birth*

> "Useless these tears I pour!—
> When I cried out: 'The child I had just now,
> I don't have any more!'"
> *À Villequier*, Victor Hugo

There is a scene in *Birth* in which in a darkened room a woman blows the candles out on a birthday cake. When the lights come on, a child's voice is heard asking to speak to one of the guests. The suddenness of the sound fissures this scene like a memory, the emanation of another life. Indeed, this image of a group of people clustered around an elderly lady focused on an eerily glowing space in a gloomy room recalls nothing so much as a séance.

When the lights go, on the voice makes all look off-screen at where the sound came from. There seems to be a child in the room. Not present before the lights went out and the cake was brought in, the child could have materialized out of the ritual itself, perhaps even called up by unspoken thoughts. The *mise-en-scène* is uncanny. The darkness, the faces caught in the glow, the attitude of spectators all gazing off in the same direction, absence made presence. All of these characteristics are common to the séance and the cinema. In recognizing the connections between these gatherings, *Birth* recalls the very roots of cinema and the medium's feeling for the sway loss and absence hold in our lives.

Birth is an exceptional film in many ways. It is a Hollywood release with an A-list star which moves with all the grace and hauteur of a European art film. It is a recent multiplex film reliant not upon rapid cutting and a mélange of stocks, but on stealthy camera moves, lingering takes and assiduous control of its wintry palette. Charting the emotional consequences of a widow's adjustment to loss and a new life with a new husband, it is rare for a mainstream film to be *about* grief, rather than to act as a palliative for it. It is customary for a Hollywood film to revolve around romantic love, but rare for one to be so analytical about what love is, or can be. For critic Tom Charity, *Birth* seems unique: "Presenting love as an enchantment — or a curse — this modern fairy tale is an extraordinarily perverse film to come out of the mainstream" (Charity 2007: 197). And it has always been difficult to find a Hollywood film which ends so unhappily.

Marketed and critically described as a supernatural thriller, *Birth* subscribes to a very particular susceptibility in the horror genre. It is as sad as it is unsettling, as quiet as its intimations are colossal. Appearing when it did, *Birth* registered the metaphysical turn signalled in varying ways by *The Sixth Sense*, *The Blair Witch Project*, *The Devil's Backbone* (*El Espinazo del Diablo*, Guillermo del Toro, 2001), and *The Others*, all of which placed children at the heart of their explorations of the afterlife. Emerging from a generic tradition bent upon revealing the mystery, the spectre, the thing, to the audience by the end of the film, *Birth* is unusually astute in its treatment of off-screen space, what we do not see but know is present. For this reason, it hails from the psychological wing of the genre, sharing moods and longings with films as diverse as those mentioned, as well as *The Innocents*, *The Haunting* and *Carnival of Souls*. This is especially beguiling given how *Birth* begins.

The camera follows a black-clad figure as it jogs through a snowbound landscape. The take is long, pursuing the figure for some minutes though woods, beneath tunnels. We get an authentic, even Bazinian, sense of the passage of space and time, of the serendipity of their relationship. Only once does the camera change perspective, cutting to a long shot as the figure is seen clearing some trees and heading for another bridge. The cut is deliberate for, unlike the earlier shot, it does not follow but draws, and meets, the jogger beneath a tunnel. He takes a breather, collapses and dies in the snow. Much later, the widow Anna (Nicole Kidman) will stand at the mouth of this tunnel, having been drawn there all the more insistently by the camera, and it will pull back slowly to a small boy, standing to off-screen right as he was at the birthday party. The sense of characters being "pulled," so to speak, into encounters despite themselves, physically by the camera, and psychologically by a boy's compelling story and the desire it enflames, is powerful in *Birth*. The revelation is shocking because, like Anna, we do not quite see yet how this boy got there, having inveigled his way into this family to tell Anna that he is the reincarnation of her dead husband. Stopped in its tracks, it is as if the camera is momentarily jarred by what it has found. It is not the first time this happens in the film. Earlier, we saw an apartment security man idling with a handball in the lobby. Called to the intercom, he tells someone to "watch the fort," and tosses the ball. Following the ball, there is a cut to a boy standing off to the right. Again, the film is jarred by what it finds.

Elsewhere, the camera roams at liberty around Anna's apartment at night like a ghost. Startled by the presence among them of Sean (Cameron Bright), the family seems oddly transfixed, unable to do anything about it: "He is coming ... into our house." The pause in her diction suggests people perplexed by movements they cannot control. Precocious in his knowledge of the family

Birth. Subtly narrating the evolution of Anna's thoughts of Sean, this close-up is a compressed but vivid micro-history which seems barely to contain the entire film's emotional caprice within it.

and of Anna's relationship with her late husband, also called Sean, thoughts of the boy begin to dominate the widow's thoughts. In what is critically acknowledged as one of the film's most powerful moments, the camera lingers for what feels like minutes on a close-up of Anna's face at the opera. Like the traveling shot at the beginning, it is a record of space and time. With what is behind her out of focus, we contemplate Anna's face as she smiles slightly, registers guilty embarrassment as her fiancé Joseph (Danny Huston) whispers in her ear, all the time her eyes blinking in progressively longer interludes, a smile alternating with a childlike mouth ajar. This woman is imagining another world. She closes her eyes and the shot ends. Not since Julie Christie's evolution from nervy fragmentation to serenity in *Don't Look Now* has an actor so vividly charted grief's inner odyssey. Vividly inscribed with subjectivity, with this close-up the film begins to feel with its protagonist. *Birth* yields to a filmosophical reading: "The filmind understands the change in the relationships of two characters, and thinks (feels) the twist in their world" (Frampton 2006: 100–101).

Recalling witnesses of an evolving objective space at a Lumière *actualité*, or Julie's idle gaze in a park in *Three Colors: Blue*, the close-up paradoxically catches the evolutions of an intensely subjective intuition. Ira Konigsberg writes of the pragmatics of the device: "If the subject is interesting, the screenplay immediate, and the performers real, a refreshing honesty and candidness may be the result" (Konigsberg 1988: 196). For Mary Ann Doane, this utilitarian candor makes the close-up seem like the portal to "an almost irrecoverable depth behind the image. The discourse seems to exemplify a desire to stop the film, to grab hold of something that can be taken away, to transfer the relentless temporality of the narrative's unfolding to a more manageable temporality of contemplation" (cited by Mulvey, 2006: 164). Doane's implication of plumbing depths rather than charting narrative flow evokes the "vertical" narrativization which is implicit in the mourning film's saga of static sensibility, a mood of stillness which Mulvey finds in the "hidden, secret nature of film itself" (Mulvey 2006: 156). Evolved by Griffith and others in the early classical period, a close-up is used in Griffith's melodrama *Orphans of the Storm* (D.W. Griffith, 1921), in a scene not without parallels with the opera close-up here. In Griffith's film, Lillian Gish hears the voice of her long-lost sister in the street below. Kevin Brownlow writes: "Griffith holds Gish's ethereal face in close-up; her blonde hair is illuminated by a halo of light. The electricity ... is so hypnotic that the audience finds itself straining to catch the merest movement of an eyelash ... her eyes flash with wild hope, then the lustre fades as she attributes the sound to her imagination. When the voice recurs ... the tears well in her eyes" (Brownlow 1979: 62). There are a number of similarities with *Birth* here. We are (re)introduced to the sister via a disembodied voice. Griffith remains on Gish's face for some time while Harris Savides's camera registers Kidman's every blink. In both films, the prospect of a human being reunited with their equivalent, be they sibling or lover, is searchingly anticipated by the camera. In melodrama and in horror, the close-up is a salient device since both genres are concerned with troubled subjectivity, the device often embodying a film's most powerful moments. In film after film, the woman's face becomes the measure of what she sees and feels, either the mirror of the horror before her, or the window on her feelings. Looking into Gish's and Kidman's eyes, the close-up affords privileged access to the protagonist's interiority, while the anticipation embodied in these scenes recalls the anticipation of presence at the horror programmer or at the parlor séance.

It is significant that Anna is seen alone in the opera scene for *Birth* is signally about being alone, one person's feelings about that, and the way their loneliness determines how others react. Roger Clarke wrote of this moment that "the camera slowly zooms in on Kidman's face as the full horror and delight of the situation cascades silently within her: the thought of her dead husband in the body of a boy and the ensuing backwash of dementia. It's a masterpiece of spine-chilling micro-acting" (Clarke 2004: 24). Making vivid play with off-screen images, *Birth* re-reads off-screen space as mental space. The opera shot may be one of the most ambitious attempts to film thought in recent cinema. As in other mourning films, *Birth* prompts us to question the verisimilitude of what we see. Boldly delineating Anna's mental world, it invites us to read events as the narration of interiority. Notice how often Sean appears when Anna is looking. This privileging vision is a common thread in horror and mourning films alike. In *The Innocents*, Quint's ghost only appears when Miss Giddens looks. In *Carnival of Souls*, only Mary sees the dead. In *Under the Sand*, we see Jean because Marie "sees" him. Graham Fuller writes: "Young Sean is surely the creation of Anna's doubts and imaginings, someone her unconscious coughed up to sustain her illusion of Sean as a loving husband and to fend off the smugly persistent Joseph, who has an unspoken alliance with Anna's imperious mother to entrap her in her Fifth Avenue ivory tower with its airless apartments and mausoleum-like lobby" (Fuller 2004: 40). Given the film's awareness of cinema's beginnings, there is even the tantalizing thought that the boy Sean does not actually exist, other than as a projection of Anna's grief. By obliging us to reflect on images, watching films makes us question their nature. Colin Davis could have had *Birth* in mind when he wrote: "Film transforms the familiar world into a land of ghosts, between life and death, seething with dangers as yet unseen and unnameable. It exhibits haunted subjects who do not know by whom or by what they are haunted, and who find themselves touched by death before and beyond any encounter in time and space" (Davis 2007: 42). *Birth* highlights not simply the similarities between hailing the dead and hailing the image, but invites us to see cinema as a necropolis of dead souls.

That his character may not exist is a notion reinforced by Cameron Bright's performance. He is quiet and, like Sean's appearances, elliptical and terse. Glazer has said of the actor: "There's a real sobriety and austerity there ... and something very vague, which allows Anna to imbue him with what she wants" (Clarke 2004: 23). The sense in which Sean is a screen upon which Anna projects recalls his initial manifestation, its *mise-en-scène* so like the cinema. After she tells Clifford (Peter Stormare) that the boy is Sean, there is a lingering series of dissolves of Sean's face, its profiles and attitudes, effectively specularizing the character. It is not difficult to envisage another version of this film in which a boy does not appear yet the widow, and the film, becomes just as abstracted, elusive and possessed by his image. Even at her most skeptical, when they first meet Anna allows herself to speculate: "But if the timing was a little bit different, who knows? Maybe." By this light, the haunted little man may be a spectre, the everyday incubus of a mind coping with despair. It is interesting to compare Bright's sometime blissful expressions — sitting in his bedroom, for example — with Falconetti's ethereal attitude of devotion as Dreyer's Jeanne d'Arc, another film in which the world is seen to be insufficient before the longing for metaphysics.

The staging of the boy's presence and absence is cunningly played out in shots of Clara (Anne Heche) leaving the party; does she see or sense Sean? Where is he in relation to her? Clara's attitude here is like that of the family at Eleanor's birthday party, all looking off-screen at where the voice came from. For Chion, off-screen sound is "acousmatic," a sound we hear without being able to visualize its source. Granted primary identification with the camera — we saw the family from the space from which Sean's voice came — the "acousmêtre" "has the power of *seeing all*; second, the power of *omniscience*; and third, the omnipotence to act on the situation. Let us add to that in many cases there is also the gift of ubiquity — the acousmêtre seems to be able to be anywhere he or she wishes. These powers ... often have limits we do not know about, and are thereby all the more disconcerting" (Chion 1990: 129–130). By blurring the distinction between what is onscreen and what is off-screen, the acousmêtre Sean becomes the locus of the metaphysical, like a clairvoyant the very space from which the conundrum of presence and absence central to the mourning film and to cinema itself, is staged.

Meanwhile, the psychological implications of Sean's presence are vivid and compelling. When Clara sees/senses him, Sean is seen bouncing a ball on the floor. The parallel with the child's game of "fort/da" related by Freud is irresistible. There the child gains control over his feelings about his mother's perennial absences by playing a game in which he repeatedly throws a wooden reel wrapped in string into the corner, then reels it back to himself: "This then was the complete game — disappearance and return. As a rule one only witnessed its first act, which was repeated untiringly as a game in itself, though there is no doubt that the greater pleasure was attached to the second act" (Freud 1920: 225). If we interpret Sean in Freudian terms, recognizing that his status as reincarnated husband is deeply implicated in his apparent status as a pre-pubertal boy, Sean's action of bouncing the ball so that it pleasingly bounces into his hand seem increasingly redolent of this anecdote. Indeed, the boy's very vigil in the lobby becomes the long period of "*fort*" (gone) prior to the blissful return of the mother substitute embodied in "a joyful '*da*' ['there']" (ibid.: 225, Freud's italics).

We may question why *Birth* proposes a nine-year-old boy as the reincarnation of Anna's lost suitor, given its lack of a discussion of her feelings about motherhood. This seems relevant to the film's discussion of masculinity generally. True to a woman's picture in which the woman took center stage, *Birth* proposes adult male characters who seem ineffectual, even childish, compared with a fascinating heroine courted by a nine-year-old. Clifford is dumbstruck by Anna's revelations, while Joseph, his authority challenged by a child, can only throw a tantrum, whimpering, "He kicked my chair!" It was almost axiomatic that, under classicism, divas Bette Davis, Joan Crawford, Irene Dunne were courted by the likes of George Brent, John Boles, Herbert Marshall, minor players in the Hollywood firmament and relegated to second fiddle in all the best scenes. The mourning film too has its divas, a pantheon in which Kidman deserves a place. Meanwhile, *Birth*'s scorn for the male is measured here by Stormare and Huston's subservience to a child who seems not only more privileged and more insightful, but more attractively mysterious than they are.

Recalling the woman's picture protagonist articulating her longing, Anna seems as elusive as Sean. When her mother Eleanor (Lauren Bacall) asks Anna what she is going to do about the boy, Anna says that she doesn't know, but that she cannot give Sean up. Ignoring her, Eleanor tells Anna to send the boy back to his mother. The dictatorial attitude marks all of Eleanor's exchanges with Anna. In psychoanalytical terms, Eleanor could be the "Bad Mother," the willful dominatrix as opposed to the traditional nurturer. Cinema history oscillates between these paradigms. In film-historical terms, Bacall's presence in *Birth* is significant. E. Ann Kaplan writes of the mothers in 1940s Hitchcock and Lang, that they "are blatantly monstrous, deliberately victimizing their children for sadistic and narcissistic ends, and thereby producing criminals" (Kaplan 1987: 134). Referring to a recent manifestation to which *Birth* may owe some allegiance, Kaplan, after Fina Bathrick, observes that the "Monstrous Mommie" cycle in the 1980s had at least been a "comment on 40s Hollywood Mother depictions in being *about* Hollywood stars" (ibid.: 134, Kaplan's italics). If it seems inevitable that Anna's affection for Sean will find her wanting to violate a fundamental sexual taboo, the prospect seems in part due to Eleanor's coaxing.

Bacall's frosty demeanor descends from a baleful lineage. The breakdown in communication between mother and daughter in *Birth* echoes the stiff instructional regimen of *Rebecca*'s housekeeper Mrs. Danvers, and her film-historical descendent Mrs. Dudley in *The Haunting*. Responding with unrelenting pragmatism to Anna's unhappiness, as far as she is concerned Eleanor is dealing with an embarrassing social incident rather than a desperate case of complicated grief in a close relative. Eleanor might be chastising a teenager for taking up with a delinquent, an impression borne out by Anna and Sean's trysting in déclassé public spaces, such as the school yard, a park, the street at night. A taboo liaison between a woman and a child thus carries faint recollections of such postwar melodramatics in *The Innocents* and *Tea and Sympathy* (Vincente Minnelli, 1956), in which Deborah Kerr's alienated wife contemplates seducing a teenager. Eleanor's blinkered attitude is typical of the summary lay judgment of the bereaved that counseling literature cautions against. Her reluctance to address Anna's misery in a more imaginative way recalls Eve's opaque responses in *Interiors*. There, the mother's "disdain" (Allen 1982, 172) for her daughter, rather than being *about* the daughter, is as much a symptom of a refusal to listen. Meanwhile, Joey's need to express herself rematerializes in Anna's need to talk.

The atmosphere in which Anna lives seems geared towards her re-marriage; many family scenes are conducted around marital preliminaries. During such scenes, we wonder who Anna's father was. The lack of nurturing women in these scenes may be a related issue. As powerful in her way as Eleanor, rather than supportive like the bereaved mistress Sandrine in *Three Colors: Blue*, Anna's husband's mistress Clara is manipulative, even demonic. Never as mobile, or impassioned as Anna's, Clara's face is a mask. In a close-up wrestling with Sean for Anna's love letters to Anna's first husband, Clara is made to resemble a witch. Meanwhile, Anna's sister Laura (Alison Elliot) is her rationalist mother's daughter, invoking the dogma of self-evidence at a family inquisition—"You are *not* my sister's husband!" (The fact that Laura is pregnant makes us wonder what her relationship with a daughter could be like).

Made bereft by loss, language and those around her, Anna is an archetypal wandering heroine, a creature in thrall to her feelings and atmospheres, the characteristic protagonist of the mourning film. A wintry Central Park is reminiscent of *Portrait of Jennie*, another story of reincarnation played out amid an artificial "garden" in which a wandering heroine yearns to bridge the worlds of the living and the dead. What is contemporary about *Birth*'s discussion of reincarnation is that it comes with none of the visual trappings and celestial temper of classical treatments of the theme. Ostensibly, Sean is just a kid who walks in off the street sporting the clothes, the haircut, even something of the surliness of a modern child of his class and generation. His claims could be just a prank. We are thus challenged as to whether to take him seriously or not. But what *Birth* has in common with the celestial tradition is its faith in what its protagonist *believes* is happening. Throughout *Portrait of Jennie*, we and the other characters question whether the girl in the park actually exists, or whether she is a figment of the artist's imagination. Eventually, the film will incline towards what the artist believes because this is his story. In *Birth*, we must take this little reincarnation seriously, not simply because Sean is a part of the ontology of the image in Bazinian terms. We must take Sean seriously because Anna believes he is there and this is her story. It is precisely to the metaphysical dimension of Bazin's thought that *Birth* appeals. Sean's otherworldliness, his timelessness, paradoxically finds its parallel in the photograph. "The photographic image," Bazin writes, "is the object itself ... freed from the conditions of time and space that govern it" (Bazin 1970: 14). While the most unnerving, and in some odd sense the most irrefutable, moments in *Birth* are those as the camera reveals something unbidden in the image, often, significantly often when Anna is looking, the most powerful scenes are those of Anna alone with her thoughts. And in this film, the prospect of a boy on the cusp of two worlds, and a woman torn between worlds, emphasizes the fabulist properties of the image, its ability to be imaginary and real, "present" but not there.

The sense of being "present" but not really there is borne out in an unusually vivid shot of Anna on her way to the park amid a crowd yet isolated from the sea of faces around her. Paradoxically, few shots of the protagonist in public find us more involved with her private space. As at the opera, Anna's surroundings are out of focus. As at the park, the camera is "pulling" her forward. It is worth emphasizing that this is a scene of a woman going to meet her lover because this is what she *thinks* she is doing. *Birth* is a film in which the relationship between the succession of images and its protagonist are especially organic. In terms of the evolution of the modernist image, this glimpse of interiority in a crowd is a classic trope, one evoked in art cinema from Antonioni to Allen. Yet here it seems far from hackneyed, still as unsettling as the prospect of an adult woman having sex with a little boy. This is one of the few moments when we see Anna away from her family and the suffocating apartment in which they live. The sense of the clandestine, of a desire preferably contemplated in an anonymous place than in the social space of familial interiors is very poignant here. The clandestine is spelt out graphically when Anna leans over to kiss Sean in the street. With her lithe figure and short hair, looking unusually, perhaps significantly, boyish, Kidman's Anna seems peculiarly androgynous in *Birth*, making her attitude in this scene especially redolent of emotional and sexual abandon. Amid the apparently toppling nude statuary of her emotional disarray, the protagonist of *The Innocents* bends down and is kissed by a little boy. Aside from the connotations of submission implicit in this posture, the prospect of a woman bent over double suggests a fetal position, a primal way of being, as in the swimming pool in *Three Colors: Blue*. We recall how the long take at the opera ended with Anna shutting her eyes, re-entering oblivion just as Julie sought the water as a metaphor for how she felt. In charting the regression to a fetal state, this scene finds Anna moving outside the linguistic and institutional structures of patriarchy, as represented by Sean's interrogation and the rehearsal for Anna's wedding, towards a pre–Oedipal space of pure feeling and unspoken solidarity.

At the dinner table Anna is pressured into testifying to what she feels in front of her fiancé Joseph, Eleanor, Laura and Laura's husband Bob (Arliss Howard). Language becomes tautological as it strives to gain purchase on states of affairs: "He told me he's Sean. I suppose that tells me he's telling me he's Sean." Later, she tries to explain herself to Clara and her husband Clifford. As Anna struggles with the words, they look on, perplexed by this confused testimony. (Clara's glacial mien is peculiarly obvious here). As so often in the mourning film, before the inconsistencies and inattentions of grief, language stalls. And the loss of words is accompanied by the loss of agency. In her confession to Joseph, one engineered by Eleanor, what comes across is the inadequacy of the words. There is nothing concrete about what Anna's says: "What happened to me was not my fault. There's no way I could have behaved any differently." In American narrative cinema, the protagonist utterly without agency is rare. Anna's response to death, like death itself, is irrevocable, out of her control. *Interiors* was another film played out in an airless setting, an atmosphere of control paid for by the unpredictable feelings made manifest by the matriarch's condition. For characters in thrall to the sea inside, irrevocability is a condition that they must live with.

Explored in *Birth* is the dual nature of love and the irrevocability borne by those who feel it. Whether in humor or in all seriousness, in Hollywood cinema there is a long tradition of dramas proposing marriage not as a desirable outcome but as a trap. *Birth* could be read as a modern "paranoid woman's" picture, the strand identified by Doane in the 1980s as a loose context for those scenarios in which impressionable young women become trapped in marriage to weak or overbearing men, paying the price in fear and paranoia. In this regard, the complicity between the matriarch Eleanor and the persistent, sometime violent Joseph is redolent of the incarceration of the heroine in such films as *Rebecca, Notorious* (Alfred Hitchcock, 1946) and *Caught* (Max Ophüls, 1949). The actor placement at Anna's confession is chilling, her beseeching him while he coolly judges her. The mood is brooding, even medieval, Anna taking Joseph's hand like a supplicant before a Borgia. Anna's entrapment is underlined by the fadeout which lingers before her face like an archaic iris out of Griffith's day.

We last see Anna on the seashore floundering in the water, torn between land and sea, life and death. Are we witnessing a suicide attempt? Or does Anna simply seek the fluid bliss of the water after the bewildering clamor of her grief? As in *Under the Sand*, the price of acceptance may be the mourner's self-destruction. As Joseph approaches her, he holds his hand out flat as if taming an animal rather than approaching a human being. References to the otherness of animals and nature are telling in the mourning film. Earlier a cat dashed across a table as Sean is being interrogated by the perplexed Bob, seeming to sense the other-worldliness of this boy. It is as though the mourner reverts to a state recognizable only to other species. However far from our everyday thoughts, alien to everyday language, distant it may be in time and space, death is inevitable and we will share this condition with all living things. Far from the rationalism of a scientific civilization, far from the towers of Central Park West, animals think according to ancient instincts and intuitions. Anna is not looking at Joseph now, and we are left to wonder whether this creature belongs with him, whether this is truly enchantment, or a curse.

Birth. The prospect of the mourner in deep disarray, "at sea" perhaps, is vividly dramatized in Anna's extreme state of ambivalence in this scene.

Case Study: *Morvern Callar*

> "Now that I can sit here beside the sea
> And by the calm horizon feel reborn,
> Examining the furthest truths in me,
> And noticing the flowers on the lawn —"
> *À Villequier*, Victor Hugo

By turns explicit and elusive, *Morvern Callar* (2001) marshals the emotional insights of cinema to plumb the mysterious and beautiful complexities of a bereft psychology in search of the poetry of loss and longing. Like *Interiors* before it, few mourning films evoke the "image-sign" which Pasolini proposed as the modernist expression of the world of dream and memory within us like *Morvern Callar*. Appearing from a national cinema still in thrall to a realist tradition, this British film also extends aesthetics derived from Continental modernism. In France, the film was distributed with the title *Le Voyage de Morvern Callar*, and its portrait of a peripatetic young woman dislodged by loss joins a sisterhood of wandering women from Bauer to *Three Colors: Blue*. Chris Darke makes more explicit the film's modernist heritage: "There's the sense that Ramsay is experimenting with an Antonionian image-poetic in which the camera's point-of-view lends itself to interpretation as the perspective of a 'missing person'" (Darke 2003: 16). Of this often obscure film, Xan Brooks writes, "In essence ... *Morvern Callar* is a story of love and bereavement; the study of a relationship that continues its trajectory after one party has gone" (Brooks 2002: 50).

Critics have observed that the film's power and energy cannot be explained purely by reference to its scenario. While its premise is compelling, Morvern Callar (Samantha Morton) awakes on Christmas Day to find that her boyfriend has committed suicide in their dingy flat, its account of her subsequent behavior and odysseys abroad are bound to be reduced in their resonance by a synopsis. Linda Ruth Williams writes that "the divine moments of *Morvern Callar* ... are the most insistently insinuating — and the hardest to recall. They stick inside you like ... repressed thoughts that are never quite gone" (Williams 2002: 25). If *Secrets and Lies*, *Moonlight and Valentino* and *In the Bedroom* are narratives of trauma and reparation, *Morvern Callar* closes with a mysterious non-closure spelled out in a haunting blend of sound and vision. Charted here is not the optimistic outcome of works subscribing to a staged model of grief, but a sullen acknowledgement that something has happened. Like *Under the Sand* and *Birth*, *Morvern Callar* charts the consequences for a protagonist who retreats before a double loss to a place inside herself.

Comparison with *Under the Skin*, featuring Morton as a young woman mourning the death of her mother, is revealing. If that film found its protagonist "acting out" her grief in increasingly histrionic and confrontational terms, in *Morvern Callar* Morton offers a quiet, almost still performance—Darke likens her to "the great actresses of silent cinema" (Darke 2003: 18)—one which, like that of Juliette Binoche in *Three Colors: Blue*, challenges the spectator to ponder her inner life. *Under the Skin* emphatically locates Iris within its northern working class milieu, a discernible Liverpool of housing estates, working men's clubs and vandalized phone boxes. But *Morvern Callar* is less interested in physical spaces than in how she feels. While the earlier film descends from the socio-cultural verisimilitude of the postwar British New Wave, films with a stake in geographically locating their protagonists, Iris a gender riposte to that cycle's chief protagonist, the "Angry Young Man," its vivid music cues, cutting and lighting find *Morvern Callar* nearer to the British art school tendency variously typified by Nicolas Roeg, Peter Greenaway and Sally Potter.

Morvern Callar is a meditation on interiority. From the beginning, it positions the spectator inside the mind of the protagonist. The opening scene finds us alone with Morvern as she sits with the corpse of her dead lover. Rack focusing, in which the camera changes focus in the same shot, in this instance from Morvern to the surrounding flat and back again, suggests growing detachment from the world around her. We know nothing of her relationship at this point. Was she happy? Was it fraught: "Perhaps it is the very effort to separate the love and hate that incapacitates the mourner, leaving them trapped in a painful and devastating limbo that can take the form of exhaustion or panic" (Leader, 2008: 48). None of the other characters is told what has happened to Morvern. Yet however enigmatic and opaque she seems to us and to those around her, our knowledge of Morvern's circumstances continually fascinates the spectator. Occasionally, the film shifts to another character's point of view, inviting the spectator to see her in another way. While she is in Spain, Tom Boddington (Jim Wilson) and his colleague Susan (Dolly Wells), arrive from a London publishing house to discuss the book Morvern has appropriated from her author boyfriend James (Des Hamilton). We see Morvern from their perspective, tidying up the memorials in a cemetery. While we suppose that this behavior makes sense to Morvern, her own reaction to her loss, we do not really know what she is doing any more than they do. She tells them to "Shhhh" and the scene is played out in silence. The camera then pans from her over each memorial and finally, inexplicably, returns to her, moving from left to right only to arrive back at Morvern herself. It is a very unusual moment, eliding her walk past the memorials. Such an elision finds the camera effectively panning through time as well as space. From a filmosophical perspective, the film's psychology becomes the protagonist's. From the moment when Morvern says "Shhhh" until the end of the scene, the film is thinking her thoughts. By "thinking her thoughts" in this way, *Morvern Callar* evokes a character who is as much in time as in space. At such a moment, the film reads its debt to a melodramatic tradition preoccupied with women's feelings through a specifically modern philosophical prism.

Hitching a ride with a Spanish family, Morvern sings blissfully to herself, a gesture triggered by her host's enthusiastic recollection of another song and observed through the eyes of the young daughter sitting next to Morvern. The transition from the jolly collective sing-song to a solitarily recalled tune measures the extent of Morvern's distance from those around her. Few films emphasize the otherness of other people as resonantly as this one does. This is not the only moment in which the film's relentlessly personal perspective renders bereaved subjectivity as a private reverie which only we and the protagonist comprehend. When she returns to the supermarket, where she works as a cashier, a low angle shot finds Morvern making for the lockers to get changed for work. On the soundtrack, Nancy Sinatra and Lee Hazlewood sing *Some Velvet Morning*. The effect of seeing this blank-eyed enigmatic figure traipsing soporifically into work to this accompaniment is archly evocative. Oddly, the moment recalls the arrival of "The Man with No Name" in a Sergio Leone western. This comparison is not so far-fetched in this context since this young woman, who has arguably now seen it all, will be heading shortly for the dry and dusty Almeria region of Spain, where Leone actually shot many of those westerns. Not as knowing as the exchange with Morvern's publisher, more redolent perhaps of her inability to grasp what has happened, a throwaway line nevertheless makes for a moment of unpredictable levity. Asked in a club where her boyfriend is, Morvern replies, "He's at home, in the kitchen."

Because she does not tell her friend Lanna (Kathleen McDermott) that James is dead, their relationship falters, eventually making it impossible for Lanna to comprehend Morvern. The sense in which Morvern lives in her own private space is made explicit by Lanna's "What planet are you on?" The enigma of Morvern is obliquely announced from the start. In the flat, James's suicide note on the computer reads, "Read Me." There is a cut to Morvern's face, suggesting that the film will require us to "read" her. It is a challenge the film, and Morton's studied quietude, reiterates. Darke writes: "Morvern becomes as ghostly as her dead boyfriend. But she's our ghost, the spectator's own projection, and Samantha Morton — with her extraordinary satellite dish blankness — receives and projects back what the audience requires of her" (Darke 2003: 18). This blankness can make for moments of comic irony. "That's when you know you love somebody when you can sit on your own and not really say anything," says somebody at a party. She could be speaking about Morvern sitting with her lover, both silent. Listening to the music

James left her and silent for much of the film, for Brooks, she "cranks up the volume to maintain a private dialogue" (Brooks 2002: 50). A shot of Morvern on the living room floor next to the corpse makes it appear as if both are dead. James has gone "to another country," she tells Lanna. This "other country" could be interpreted as the interior realm to which the mourning individual retreats when the world around them is no longer enough. The inability to reconcile worlds, to bridge presence and absence, is a phenomenon borne out in *Under the Sand* and *Birth*. To those left only with memories and feelings about the dead, the distinction between a reality filled with objects, people and processes, and a realm in which the dead live on is akin to the coexistence of contemporaneous but temporally unaligned worlds, spatially proximal but materially other. Abraham and Torok anticipate Morvern's apparent inability to acknowledge her loss: "the refusal to reclaim as our own the part of ourselves that we placed in what we lost; incorporation is the refusal to acknowledge the full import of the loss ... that, if recognized as such, would effectively transform us" (Abraham and Torok 1994: 127). The failure to introject, to assimilate ideas, denies the possibility of a language to speak of why individuals cannot mourn. Paradoxically, this lack of explanation or emotion, the "swallowed" grief, "speaks" the insufficiency of language when confronted with death, leading to the breakdown in Morvern's rapport with Lanna, a friendship which dies as surely as James did. Yet Morvern's failure to reclaim that part of herself lost when James died, or that part of herself which she invested in Lanna, means that these people have not actually "gone." Those moments, such as that around James's corpse, and later in the cemetery, in which we find the imagery "speaking" on behalf of a mute protagonist, offer another kind of testimony, one in which the mourning film finds its raison d'être. Like Marie in *Under the Sand*, Morvern has erected a tomb inside herself. The cemetery becomes a spatial metaphor for this crypt, a silent place bounded at one end by Morvern's denial of speech, at the other by the presence of one liminal because, like the widow, she somehow embodies death. Morvern's behavior contains its own logic. For Torok and Abraham, the crypt is never completely silent: "Sometimes in the dead of night, when libidinal fulfilments have their way, the ghost of the crypt comes back to haunt the cemetery guard, giving him strange and incomprehensible signals, making him perform bizarre acts, or subjecting him to unexpected sensations" (ibid.: 130). The internal crypt echoes across the life that houses it and echoes across therapeutic literature. Of the grief that follows suicide, Lake observes, "It may be a fitting memorial that you should never be truly alive in your own right" (Lake 1988: 126).

This retreat inside is starkly analogized by the play on the "presence" and "absence" of subjectivity which characterizes the image in *Morvern Callar*.

The film begins with a series of images of Morvern separated by fades to black. It is as though the protagonist, so abstracted by her condition, cannot even be contained by the image. From the start, the film makes an issue of her identity. As the image fades, the words "MORVERN," then "CALLAR" appear on screen. If we see the character in her objective state, a woman here looking at the camera, her name, conventionally the signifier of very specific subjectivity, appears after she has gone. Throughout the film, Morvern passes herself off as "Jackie," the name on a neck chain she has found. Reliant upon words to understand the subjectivity of another, we are confronted with the ambivalence of language, the feints and displacements, the schizophrenia of speaking, the mystery of a name, effectively the uselessness of trying to understand someone who has walled up her loss.

Like subjectivity, the unyielding fact of death stares back at us like a cemetery. It is all the more vital for the bereaved, then, to adorn the fact with commemorative sentiments and gestures, and for fellow travelers to understand why. Like death, subjectivity is an invisible space on which purely nominal identity finds perilous purchase. Williams writes, "Then the credits spell out the name, first MORVERN, then CALLAR, separated by screen time into different, adjacent frames" (Williams 2002: 23). These adjacent frames are the film's metaphor for the parallel universes of objective and subjective worlds, together but incommensurable, the world and the crypt. At the end of *Morvern Callar*, this teetering between light and darkness, inner and outer worlds, is reiterated in the dark interior of a Spanish nightclub when strobe lights flash over Morvern's dimly perceived form as she wanders among the crowd, the effect making her intermittently appear and disappear. As spatially obscure as it is elusive in its delineation of character and motive, it is a Deleuzian moment. Deleuze writes of the time-image, "These are pure optical and sound situations, in which the character does not know how to respond, abandoned spaces in which he ceases to experience and to act so that he enters into flight, goes on a trip, comes and goes, vaguely indifferent to what happens to him, undecided as to what must be done" (Deleuze 1989: 261). Not knowing how to respond, abandoning herself to abandoned spaces in which she seems in flight from experience, coming and going in peripatetic fashion, Morvern Callar becomes the quintessential protagonist of mourning cinema. Analogizing her psychology in the play of light, shadow and silhouette, accompanied by the plangent strains of the Mamas and the Papas' "Dedicated to the One I Love," we can say too that the film here filmosophically "becomes" in accordance with its protagonist's interior life. This "becoming" is then offered to us. Rather than the eye following the image as in classical spectatorship, this effect seems to be being projected directly onto the retina. Deleuze writes of the "purely optical and sound situation, where the seer (*voyant*) has replaced the agent (actant): a 'description'" (ibid.: 261). So mesmerizing is the nightclub scene, recalling the apparitions of a séance, that it is an opera with one aim; to project Morvern's physical and interior movement, just as apparitions once bore credence as the projections of interior longing. Of a scene in the visually extravagant *Someone to Watch Over Me* (Ridley Scott, 1987), a film which in its day bore witness to the sophisticated hybridizing of the optical and sonic taking place in nightclubs and multiplexes when Deleuze was writing, Chion could be evoking *Morvern Callar*: "We get the feeling that this visual volubility, this luminous patterning is a transposition of sonic velocity into the order of the visible" (Chion 1990: 134).

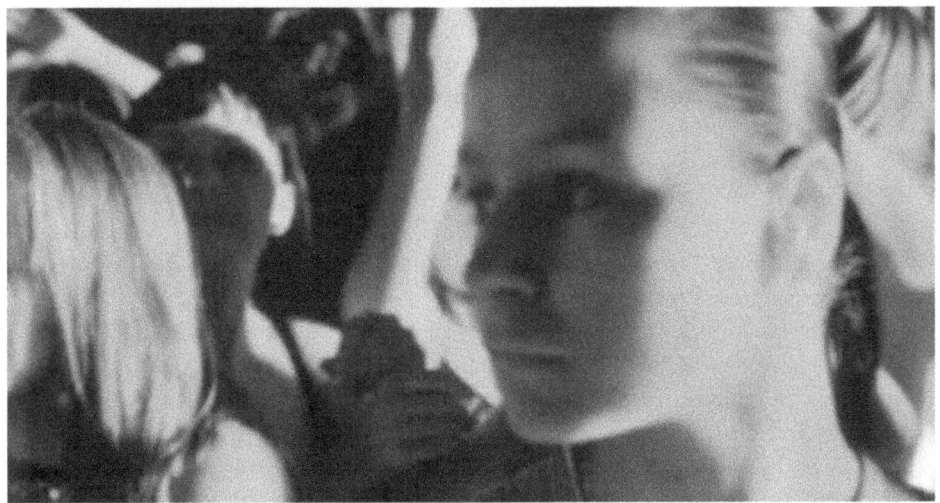

Morvern Callar. An instrument of the rage of sound and fury within her, Morvern Callar here becomes pure being on the cusp of sound and silence.

The high angle shot in the closing scene contrasts with the film's overall mode of close and intimate observation. *Morvern Callar* is full of unexplored territory, moments of grotesque existence that reside normally on the fringes of consciousness. In the spot in the Scottish Highlands at which Morvern disposes of James's remains, we see worms and wood lice in a damp crevice. Stream water flows over her hands as she washes them. In the supermarket where Morvern works, she touches a maggot writhing on a decaying carrot. "I like the ants," she tells Tom and Susan when they ask her if she is enjoying Spain. As in other mourning films, this preoccupation with the everyday grotesque is suggestive of the thematic of death and decay which the film explores. James lies dead on the floor for some time before Morvern removes him to the bathroom. His corpse will then undergo further decay. Poet John

Donne wrote of this death after burial, "Corruption and putrefaction and vermiculation" (cited in Dollimore 1998: 74). The brute facticity of the earth and its denizens, rotting flesh and degrading blood in these scenes possess a savage mystery. For Bazin, their vividness is intrinsic to the nature of the image: "Photography affects us like a phenomenon in nature, like a flower or a snowflake whose vegetable or earthly origins are an inseparable part of their beauty" (Bazin 1970: 13). Like the death of which we cannot speak, such vividness is inherently disturbing. For Kristéva, "the corpse ... that which has irremediably come a cropper, is cesspool, and death; it upsets even more violently the one who confronts it as fragile and fallacious chance ... refuse and corpses show me what I permanently thrust aside in order to live. These body fluids, this defilement, this shit are what life withstands, hardly and with difficulty, on the part of death. There ... the corpse is the most sickening of wastes, is a border that has encroached upon everything" (Kristéva 1982: 3). James will not lie in state or be buried with due Christian ceremony, nor will he be mourned. Here the mourning film comes furthest from the optimistic protocols of the past: "The corpse, seen without God and outside of science, is the utmost of abjection" (ibid.: 4).

Yet in *Morvern Callar*, abject defilement becomes a symptom of the protagonist's curiosity about death. When she discovers the corpse, Morvern lies with it, touching it. The touch may be sexual, an attempt to relive another life, for her a symptom of living between worlds. Her touch seems further from regret and closer to a sexual or morbid tactility. Leader also gestures towards identification, a strange homeopathy with the dead: "We inhabit their space, taking on aspects of their behaviour, mannerisms, and even their ways of looking at the world" (Leader 2008: 50). Of a similar ambivalence in Ramsay's *Ratcatcher*, Annette Kuhn writes, "While these scenes are darkly humorous in tone, the conjunction of play and waste, the carnivalesque and the abject, is unsettling" (Kuhn 2008: 41). Morvern wants to know what a corpse feels like. The contradiction of morbidity and longing is there when she dismembers the corpse. The camera observes her from just outside the bathroom, as if tentative about intruding on an intimacy occurring between the couple in this private space. But like the innocent touching on the kitchen floor, it could also be a space of play. Of *Ratcatcher*, a film set amid the consciousness of a child, Kuhn writes, "What *Ratcatcher* does, *through cinema*, is create a childhood world or way of being as it were from the inside, inviting the viewer to enter into that world" (ibid.: 69, Kuhn's italics). As Morvern rhythmically saws the flesh, we see the arterial blood spraying on her shoulder. Again, the moment could be sexual but is certainly tactile, a sensual experience derived from a purely material act. However potentially emetic this experience is for Morvern, it is also a new experience. Of the corpse, Kristéva writes, "Imaginary uncanniness and real threat, it beckons to us and ends up engulfing us" (Kristéva 1982: 4). What the film explores here is less the histrionic passion of grief rehearsed in other mourning films than a 21-year-old girl's passive inquisitiveness about the materiality of death. Morvern is a child innocently probing the monstrosity of nature. Because we are alone with her during this scene, like those in which she contemplates the woodlice and the ants, the film offers us no vantage point from which to question this childlike quality. Indeed, if in mourning films from *The Innocents* to *Three Colors: Blue*, the protagonist's confrontation with the grotesque is horrific, a sudden revelation of the unspeakable Real of death and decay, in *Morvern Callar* the girl herself seems to anticipate, to want these moments, taking the film with her as if she is reverting to a space before culture and society intervene in the name of taste and propriety. The sense in which Morvern's curiosity carries vestiges of the sexual becomes more compelling if *Morvern Callar* is seen in conjunction with *Kissed*, in which a young trainee mortician gains some sexual education by toying with corpses. What is most compelling about that ostensibly subversive film is its tenor, poised on the verge of the romantic gesture just as Morvern's explorations of the disgusting teeter on the verge of some kind of reparation.

Such moments become another kind of negotiation with death. It is a measure of the film's power that we never see Morvern cry. Crying occurs only by displacement. In another moment, the film "feels" for its protagonist, when Lanna confesses that James slept with her Morvern turns away and we

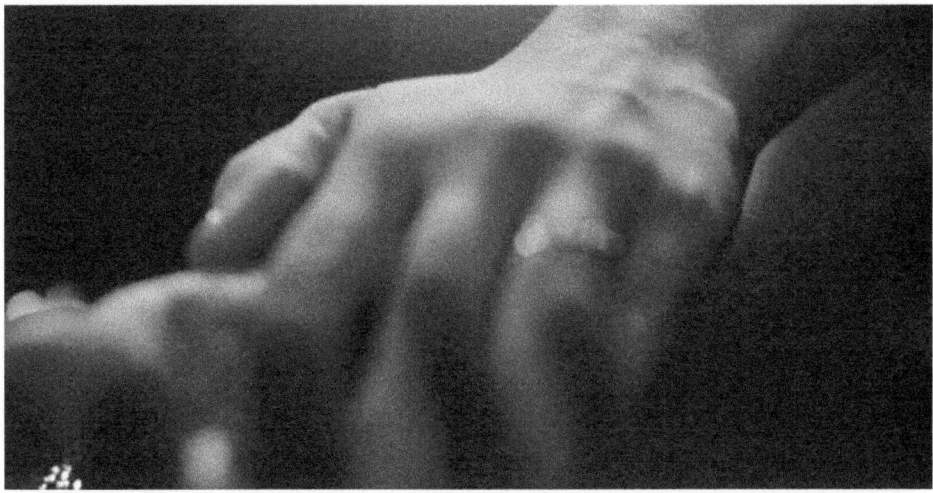

Morvern Callar. In the clammy half-light of a winter morning, life reaches out to death in childlike wonder to know the place where the light ends.

see her face through a window as raindrops streak down it. Hers is a malaise experienced either by proxy or through a defamiliarized rapport with nature, a retreat to a dank room or a hole in the ground, rather than the breakdown before society charted in other mourning films. "I like the ants" is definitely symptomatic of diminished social interaction. From what we see of Morvern Callar, we surmise that grief has driven this wandering woman away from the crowd to dwell in the hidden crevices of existence. In another metaphorical moment, she looks out to sea at the island where her foster mother is buried. If in other mourning films the prospect of the sea is a displaced impression of the churning grey grief the protagonist feels, the sea inside, here the protagonist looks out to sea at a tomb. We are reminded of Marie staring at the cemetery, or Anna standing in her wedding dress at the seashore. All of these women are survivors, but in none of them does survival lead to acceptance that the other has gone, only that their lives have changed and will never be the same again.

A Case Study: *Genova*

> "Remember me when I am gone away,
> Gone far away into the silent land;
> When you can no longer hold me by the hand,
> Nor I half turn to go yet turning stay."
> *Remember*, Christina Rossetti

Genova, Michael Winterbottom's 2008 examination of loss and mourning set in the medieval Italian port of Genoa, from which it derives its name, sets itself the difficult assignment of examining the grief of a child. Few films have attempted this task with any degree of success, and those that have, among them *The Curse of the Cat People, The Spiral Staircase, Le Petit Prince à dit, Ponette,* and *The Devil's Backbone,* tread a stealthy path between mawkishness and academicism, generic expectation and obscure experimentalism. Touted in the press as a supernatural thriller while described by Winterbottom, evoking traditional melodrama, as one family's attempt to deal with their bereavement, *Genova* seems to embody the tantalizing possibilities of generic and aesthetic melding just as it tackles the painful contradictions of living with loss.

The idea that children are especially susceptible to supernatural occurrences is one which recurs in nineteenth century Gothic literature and horror cinema alike. Henry James's short story *The Turn of the Screw* (1898), one of the most accomplished and vivid supernatural narratives in the canon, revolves around a boy and his younger sister who mediate between the ghosts of a dead couple and their lonely and paranoid governess. The film adaptation — *The Innocents* — is one of the most celebrated supernatural horror films of all time, and is also a key touchstone for the depiction of grief in modernist cinema. Even its title emphasizes a guileless, morally neutral characteristic of childhood, that quality which seems so quintessentially a part of the child that we never know. We never suspect that this individual can possess an intuition which adults have lost, perhaps be the portal to life after death, with all the joyful or baleful implications that this may entail. Meanwhile, its exploration of the "intelligence" of children is especially relevant to *Genova*'s exploration of a little girl's spiritual instincts. The presence of the child, or the childlike adult, in modern cinematic representations of mourning, whether these were marketed and critically described as horror or melodrama, indicates these films' subscription to a cultural perception that children are more receptive to the metaphysical, becoming in many literary and cinematic texts the "apports," to use the archaic spiritualist term, which bring spirits into the house. They suggest childhood as a privileged space, a "beyond" not yet apprised of scientific rationality and open to what a scientific era deems "irrational" influences. Grief theorists concur with this perspective. Atle Dyregrov writes, "Magical components are still part of their thinking; they may assume that the dead person can see or hear the living, and they may work hard to please the deceased as a consequence of this" (Dyregrov 2008: 19). Arguably, *Genova* is all about a daughter's attempt to try to "please" the dead parent, or to make amends for something they have done. Far from a post–Enlightenment dispute between reason and witchcraft which we have long outlived, these films proffer childhood as a scene of carnival, in which the post–Enlightenment, perhaps even a "post-secular," cultural moment is played out as an unsettling display of oddness, hallucination and instinctual image-creation, a space in which childish games and startling visitations, abject horror and precipitate revelation mingle in a mélange of the metaphysical and the quotidian. Examples of unearthly visitation, warped visual logic and unsettling moods abound in horror/mourning narratives involving children from *The Curse of the Cat People* to *Genova*. While for its indebtedness to both melodrama and horror, *Genova* suggests a modern mourning cinema which is becoming increasingly aware of its genealogical roots.

At the dramatic heart of the film is a young girl — Mary — whose mother has died in a car crash, leaving her wracked with sorrow for her loss, and guilt for perceiving herself as the cause of her mother's death: "Like countless ghost, horror and supernatural films before it, *Genova* uses the age-old device of a child to create tension and discomfort" (Clarke 2009). Histrionically powerful and exerting a lachrymal and disturbing influence over the film as a whole, Perla Haney-Jardine's performance as Mary also resonates with therapeutic observations about grief. If the literature on grief has regularly asserted the role guilt plays in childhood sorrow, Mary's guilt is both the representation of a universal grief symptom and a specific characteristic of her own case history. From a film-historical perspective, *Genova*'s debt to "spiritual" horror cinema and its status as a developed and intelligent modern mourning film find common cause in Haney-Jardine's articulation of sorrow. We have only to examine cinema's mourning archive to find precedent figures in the (serendipitously-named) mourner Amy searching for her lost mother in *The Curse of the Cat People* and in Ponette, the little French girl who loses her mother, also in a car crash.

This dual typological status, simultaneously finding its instincts within a traditional film-historical precinct while broaching an obscure though related generic Otherness, is a pattern which also reflects *Genova*'s look and rhythm. It is a film which inhabits liminal spaces. Throughout, the spectator gets the sense that Mary, her father Joe (Colin Firth) and her older sister Kelly (Willa Holland) are living on the edge, inhabiting the interstices of states, rather like children playing a game in which they have told themselves they must walk only in the cracks between the paving stones. The adolescent Kelly deals with her loss by drowning real experience in the soundtrack from her iPod. Having remedied the family loss by taking them all to Italy where he will teach and his daughters will "get a language," Joe remains stoic, constantly overreaching himself in order to keep tabs on his grief-stricken daughters. Joe's taciturnity, his adamant need to maintain a stable emotional atmosphere, is an understandable reaction to loss, but it also typifies the male role in the mourning saga, a genre which from its roots has appeared to revolve in many key instances around female protagonists. Consonant with its liminal mood, *Genova* makes much of daylight and darkness and the strange transition between them. At one point there is a picturesque succession of shots of Genoa as darkness falls. Elsewhere, Mary and Kelly are seen wandering the old town in semi-darkness, the tall medieval buildings illuminated only by thin strips of sky far above them. A number of scenes, like that at the girls' piano lessons, shot by cinematographer Marcel Zyskind in Winterbottom's trademark handheld fashion, elliptically concentrate our comprehension with rapid movements, cuts and snatches of dialogue. It is as though in this film meaning endlessly slips between the cracks, or between the cuts. This cinematically generated sense of "intermittence," of something appearing and then disappearing from the spectator's view, is perhaps set up in the game the girls play in the family car at the beginning in which they cover and uncover their eyes repeatedly, and it will underwrite this tale of supernatural visitation, coming to a climax near the end of the film.

There is what could be described as an "incontinent" quality to these characters, a sense in which they appear split and dislocated both from each other and from themselves, that is vividly, if disgustingly, announced at the funeral at which Kelly, trying her first marijuana cigarette, promptly vomits in the snow. Such a sense of dislocation is widely acknowledged in therapeutic writing on grief and mourning. Here it is worth recalling Tony Lake's words: "There may also be times when you feel completely disassociated from your own feelings, as if you are watching yourself from outside your body, looking down from a high position" (Lake 1988: 114). This mood of dislocation finds expression in Kelly's almost perpetually spaced-out quality, simultaneously *with* her father and sister on planes and trains and on the beach but also *apart* and in her own world. If Joe struggles to center himself in attempts to control Kelly and involve her in family life, her burgeoning adolescence, and her buried grief, increasingly distance her from the suffering Mary, adding to her sister's isolation. Kübler-Ross could be observing Kelly and Mary when she writes, "Children will react differently to the death of a parent, from silent withdrawal and isolation to a wild loud mourning which attracts attention and thus a replacement of a loved and needed object" (Kübler-Ross 2003: 158).

Genova's precipitate quality, expressed in characters' behavior and in the film's aesthetics alike, takes its stark cue from the dramatic premise in which the mother's sudden death leaves no time for goodbyes. "It is a terrible shock when a life is cut short," says the priest at Marianne's funeral, and the film concurs with a series of shocking awakenings. From the beginning of the film, Mary is the character whose actions announce this precipitate quality as it shapes the film. Paradoxically, it is precisely her isolation in her grief which makes Mary engage so unashamedly with what has befallen the family. This signal intuition could be described as a wake-up call, both figuratively and literally. The cut away from the moment of the car accident is marked by Mary in tears, distressed at the memory of her mother's death and the perception that she caused it. Significantly, the narrating of the accident and the wintry funeral takes place before the film's credits. Through this positioning comes a very strong sense in which the main action of the film, played out five months later in Italy in high summer, visually distinct in its garish colors from the sombre blacks and greys of the earlier scenes, narrates another life for these characters, one seeming to be dramatically different, yet linked to the old life by Mary's perennial insomnia and weeping. It will not be the last time Mary's crying marks the end of one shot and scene and the beginning of the next. Her wrenching sobs, as visceral as an animal in pain, are very affecting, leaving the spectator nearly overwhelmed by Mary's sorrow and regret. As Worden starkly observes, "People in pain make us feel helpless" (Worden 1991: 52), and there is perhaps no more poignant a figure for mobilizing pity in our culture than a little girl in tears. Mary's nocturnal wailing descends from a rich tradition of sorrowful Victorian spectres, while measuring the emotional depth of this film in particular.

The sense in which Mary bears *Genova*'s emotional and psychological freight is borne out more subtly in the drawings that she does, haunting charcoal sketches of a car with a spectral driver, a mysterious figure seen in a window, strange Munch-like scenes which accumulate throughout the film as though forming its unconscious: unspoken, fleeting, oneiric, mysterious but begging to be felt and heard. As always in this film, comprehension, *the* meaning (as if life's events and phenomena always only have one), is always already mobile and moving out of reach. The film's emphasis upon Mary's drawings, along with its elliptical visuals, announce the mourning film's especial investment in the image, as opposed to words—"It's hard to know what to say" (Joe)—the type's conviction that mourning is particularly inaccessible to explanation, peculiarly susceptible to literary or artistic articulation, but poignantly favored by cinema's language of presence and absence, the ontologically real and the phenomenally visual. Echoing Worden's advice to grief's witness, it is as though film already "knows" something about a theme before which verbal language flounders: "This helplessness can be acknowledged in a simple statement like, 'I don't know what to say to you'" (ibid.: 52). Film, meanwhile, addresses the space between words and experience, and that between the griever and the dead. While indicative of the primal ludic creativity of grieving children that we find in mourning films from *The Curse of the Cat People* to *Ponette* and *The Sixth Sense*, Mary's drawings also evince a theme of creativity which is perennially explored in modern mourning films from *Interiors* to *Three Colors: Blue*.

In the scene at the monastery in which Mary confesses to family friend Barbara (Catherine Keener) that she has been seeing her mother and speaking to her, Mary walks out of the door and seems literally to disappear into the sunlit glare outside. It is an apt visual metaphor for her existence, half with the living, half "beyond," half involved in normal daily activity, half deranged by desperate nocturnal instincts and perceptions. It is perhaps a mark of Mary's vindication, the sincerity of her grief, its eventual "truth" in the face of a familial unconcern which comes to seem mendacious, that, increasingly, we too will see her mother when she "sees" her. These visitations are presaged by a series of odd moments in which we see Mary from just beyond the space of the Genovese apartment, suggesting that perhaps she is being "watched" by someone who is not there. Indeed, the credits sequence unfolds over a series of aerial shots of Genoa as if seen from "Heaven." When her mother, Marianne (Hope Davis), comes to Mary at night there is a naturalism about the bedside scene which we know is as much about the memory of nocturnal mother/daughter meetings in life as it is about yearning for a mother who is no longer there. "Visitations" by the dead are commonly attested to in therapeutic literature, seeming to be an actualisation of the grieving person's ongoing conversations with the departed. It is precisely this curious blend of the uncanny and the quotidian that the scenes of Marianne's appearance evoke. Far from the billowy wraiths of Victorian literature and early cinema, manifestations of the dead in modern mourning cinema have a matter-of-fact "contemporary" quality, just as they presumably possess for the mourner who is experiencing them. The "ghost" comes with just the mien and appearance that they possessed in life, and often — *Under the Sand*, *The Sixth Sense*— they are seen from the perspective of the seer, rather than seen from a neutral perspective which would suggest objective presence. Compare early instances of Marianne's appearance with that of the ghostly Zoia in the Russian spiritual melodrama *After Death*. Rather than springing up before our eyes clad in a wispy nightgown as Zoia does to the grieving hero, as if she were visible to more than one person, Marianne "appears" in the interstice between Mary's looks to the bottom of her bed, as though sutured between shots of Mary perceiving and our looking. "She comes to me sometimes, she comes to forgive me," Mary tells Barbara. This matter-of-fact, almost nonchalant, confession has a realist patina because it is "necessary," and that is because it is what Mary experiences as a result of her grief. Through its technical facility, cinema is peculiarly able to articulate the spectral visitation. To revive Emma Wilson's vivid observation: "Film itself has proved a privileged medium for the exploration of the hesitation between life and death, of phantoms, of the living dead, of wish-fulfilling animation, visual memories and hallucinations" (Wilson 2003: 7). That the apport of the unearthly unbidden image/memory is in mourning cinema's salient works a girl/woman testifies again to the dominance of the female gaze in the mourning film.

The extent of Mary's sense of dislocation is played out in her conviction that her mother wants her to follow her, and so in the film's climax we see Mary, lost amid the busy Genovese traffic, pursuing Marianne's image. Again, we see Marianne because Mary "sees" her in a scene which is disturbing because it seems as though Marianne has "taken" Mary to this dangerous place with the purpose of causing Mary's accidental death, perhaps fulfilling some scenario, a secret mother-daughter contract, in which Mary "follows" her mother in order to be with her in death, to assuage her guilt. This seems all the more dramatically apposite when we consider that this is a film which is bookended by car crashes. It is apt that such a precipitate near-tragedy should serve as the climax of a film so precipitate in its moods and instincts. Beautifully orchestrating shots of Kelly and Joe fleeing to find Mary, the little girl hesitating, then stepping out before speeding traffic, Marianne wandering away on the far side of the thoroughfare, the film's visual music of intermittent visuality comes to a fluent crescendo here. The traffic climax also resonates with observations grief theorists have made about "searching," that urge the mourner has to try to re-find the dead person. To recall Erich Lindemann: "There is a restlessness, inability to sit still, moving about in an aimless fashion, *continually searching* for something to do" (Lindemann cited in Parkes 1998: 50). Visually, what is so striking about this scene is the sheer oddness of the prospect of a little girl pursuing a figure who seems to get further away the closer she gets to it. We are reminded of the drawings of M.C. Escher, in which some twist in perspective has been affected which makes the eye's traversal of the image yield simultaneously explicable and inexplicable outcomes. If we recall, Gem Duncan could be approaching the same scene from the perspective of the mourner: "Death means that our things have separated from us like objects in space no longer governed by gravity. They float indiscriminately, but inexorably, away"(Duncan 2009: 3).

By situating Mary at its center, *Genova* has little to say about Joe or Kelly's experience of loss. Much of the critical literature that has arisen around the film has acknowledged its debt to the *Don't Look Now,* another tale of a family fleeing a death to Italy and refusing to work through its grief adequately. There the drama revolved around the bereft mother of a little girl who has perished in a drowning accident, an incident for which her father blames himself and sustains a complicated grief in the process. But if in *Don't Look Now* the father's grief and its tragic consequences will move further into the foreground, in *Genova* Joe's loss and feelings about that remain perpetually invisible to us and to those around him. It is almost as though the film could be remade from his perspective, as if there is another film trying to emerge out of *Genova.* Acknowledging the thematic relationship perennially claimed on behalf of these films and the unique and perennial concision between the genres of horror and melodrama over the issue of grief, of *Genova*, a film which comes into its own the more you see it, one could say that few melodramas have explored the uncanny at the heart of hurt with such a sense of sorrow.

This chapter saw a modern mourning film informed by the process of dealing with absence, an experience continually explored in therapeutic literature. By drawing parallels between the phases of grief and the moods and aesthetics of these films, what emerges is the mourning film as process, the case study of an individual protagonist and an experiment in using film to chart a particular experience of interiority. Progressing from earlier examples in which "excessive" moments transcended conventional narrative contexts, these case studies assume their subjects to be indelibly marked by the excessive, systems of aesthetic relativity in which each film comes into its own as a form of energy, radiating and reverberating into the spectator's thoughts and back to mourning cinema's past. If part of the point of this book is to identify a series of aesthetic moments as the basis for a taxonomy, also important is mourning cinema's filmography, a catalog and pantheon in which each film contributes its own rareness to a cinema of mourning. What is becoming clear is that the mourning film transcends its immediate generic and institutional allegiances. Chapter 4 will spell out the taxonomy which will serve as the basis for the identification of this singular cinematic type.

Chapter 4. Release

"Yes, I did love someone very much. But he died."
Nina in *Truly, Madly, Deeply*

The last three chapters of this book attempt to identify themes and aesthetic devices in films treating the travails of grief and mourning. Chapter 4 seeks to position them within a taxonomy of effects which will constitute the first step towards the identification of a genre, or type, that I am calling the mourning film, or the *cinéma du deuil*. In keeping with the therapeutic schema informing previous chapters, this chapter embodies the recognition that a set of films thematizing a particular experience exists in a distinctive form, and that it can be theorized with hindsight much as the mourner finds release once they can recognize the transition through which they have passed. Preceding the exposition of the taxonomy, there will be a consideration of the ways in which the notion of genre has been traditionally reproduced as a context through which films are marketed, critically discussed and popularly imagined. This study has embraced a range of films drawn from a variety of national, cultural, cinematic and generic contexts. Examples hail from classical and modern Hollywood melodrama and the horror film, prewar European auteur cinema, the European "intellectual melodrama" of the postwar decades, and the contemporary independent arthouse film. After examining the ways in which genre has been conceived, this chapter will consider the conditions and impulses attending the possibility of conceiving a new genre in a new film-cultural era from a dispersed set of examples.

For western audiences and critics, the arch-exemplar of genre cinema is classical Hollywood, a historically specific model with congruent institutional and commercial aims and consequences. From the late–1910s until the 1960s, Hollywood studio output reflected particular generic classifications in its production protocols and publicity rhetoric. Such classifications have become entrenched and widespread, with implications for the attempt to propose a new genre in a different film-historical era. The mourning film is here being proposed by a spectator-cinephile rather than being recommended by an industry, with all its public relations affiliates and assumptions. This shift in the direction of the impetus behind generic definition takes something of its cue from an increasingly perceptible shift in film reception in recent decades.

The Hollywood studio era inaugurated a close relationship between the film industry and the critic. In the attempt to generate audience interest in a new release, during the classical decades studio publicity departments maintained strong links with newspaper editors and critics as well as cinema exhibitors. Over the decades, this rapport between studio/distributor and press has shaped, even policed, the definitions and rhetoric used to write about films. Yet despite the institutional circuits which have shaped received form, there is also a history of critical invention in the description and definition of film styles and movements. There is a history, too, of film studies categories emerging out of film-critical writings: "sword-and-sandal epic," "screwball comedy," "film noir," "chop-socky," "yuppie horror." These terms arose out of critical or academic writings around the films as they came to appear to constitute specific types. Film history has become a treasure trove of films and styles to be plundered by commercial and critical interests alike. The marketing and re-marketing of new and older films on DVD and as Internet downloads means that a "new film" is not necessarily new anymore; it is simply a film the spectator has not seen before. The decline of an apparently more monologic traditional network between industry, critic and audience, the perceived waning in the influence of the connoisseur film critic, and the proliferation of new writing on the Web, opens up a space for the re-evaluation and re-thinking of the audiovisual products at our disposal. This context not merely warrants, but encourages, the act of naming, classification and re-classification. Although descriptive of traditional trends, Bordwell's words seem ironically more relevant now than ever: "At all levels of the filmmaking and film-viewing processes, then, genres help assure that most members of a society share at least some general notions about the types of films that compete for our attention" (Bordwell 1985: 320). What Andrew Tudor saw in 1974 as a "common cultural consensus" (Tudor 1974: 138) of industry, press and traditional cinemagoers around what constitutes a genre can in another historical moment include the domestic cinephile.

Given the canonical terminology used to discuss genres since it became an important field in film studies in the 1970s, the extrapolation of a generic rubric from a wide field of contemporary availability is problematic, prompting the need for more careful definitions when approaching with a mind-set derived from Anglo-American film culture film-historical contexts beyond the Anglo-American. Yet the very promiscuity of film dissemination and comment today suggests a definitional field as fertile as that of contemporary music classification and definition. Chapter 4 will, therefore, review genre classification as it is traditionally conceived prior to assessing how useful the classical context is in a reception landscape marked by choice, and the contingencies of domestic spectatorship. While acknowledging the persistence of classical generic labeling, it is important to recognize that in an era of altered modes of marketing and atomized spectatorship it is possible to group and discuss films putatively according to different criteria, thereby identifying fresh connections, categories or types. The repertory double bill will be examined as a stage in the rethinking of similarity between one film and another. The influence of commercial imperatives shall be considered through the examination of DVD retailing strategies, repertory programming initiatives, and the categories employed in contemporary film guides. This investigation will lead to the formulation of the taxonomy.

The Generic Past

In the 1970s theoretical work on genre focused on classical Hollywood types such as the western and the gangster film, genres which were seen to derive their identities from a consensus between the industry, critics and audiences. Before television, the local cinema engendered a ready-made audiovisual community, encouraging the proliferation of certain categories and expectations. In the classical era studio publicity material, trade papers, film reviews, newspaper advertising and word of mouth collaborated in the generic description of a new release and the public discussion around it. Tom Ryall writes, "Films were marketed and advertised in ways which highlighted their generic specificity and, in addition to this, the trade press used generic terminology and referred to westerns, gangster pictures, melodramas, and so on in their discussion of Hollywood films" (Ryall cited in Hill 1998: 328). The interface between the studio and the public reflected the economic priorities of the industry. Economies of scale ensured the production of cycles of films dramatizing particular subject matter, exploring certain themes, re-using the same sets and props, and starring actors who became associated with a particular genre. Generic formulae emerged out of existing and purpose-built infrastructures. With its stock of contract players, perennially deployed urban street sets and writers hailing from the Eastern tabloids, the Warner Bros. gangster film of the 1930s remains a paradigmatic collusion between industry practice, journalistic discourse and audience fidelity over the issue of what constitutes a genre. The Lewton horror cycle at RKO was a self-contained sequence of films using the same actors, writers and crew members, resulting in distinctive preoccupations, characters, and a very particular visual and narrative atmosphere. Hollywood studio history is marked by collaborations resulting in generically congruent sets of films. *Magnificent Obsession* (Douglas Sirk, 1954), *All That Heaven Allows* (1954), *Written on the Wind* (Douglas Sirk, 1956) and *Imitation of Life* (1959), constitute a cycle of melodramas appearing from Universal in the mid-to-late-1950s. Yet while there is plentiful evidence that these generic categories originated in Hollywood's Fordist heyday, there was at the time recognition of generic fluidity. Janet Staiger writes, "Historically, no justification exists to assume producers, distributors, exhibitors, or audiences saw films as being "purely" one type of film" (Grant 2003: 194). As Staiger points out, whatever the main plot line, all classical genre films included a parallel romantic storyline. Hybridity persists in modern Hollywood, while the bricolage of dramatic concerns in any one film has implications for the generic re-description of individual titles.

From the 1970s, Hollywood production became increasingly hybridized. For Michael Allen, "slotting easily identifiable elements together in as smooth and efficient a manner as possible, [ensured] the regular generation of product which an audience can easily identify and assimilate into its existing knowledge base about the movies" (Allen 2003: 179). In *The Player* (Robert Altman, 1992), a Hollywood satire balanced between fiction and verisimilitude, new projects are pitched in such terms as these: "So it's a kind of psychic political thriller comedy with a heart.... And not unlike *Ghost* meets *The Manchurian Candidate*." Quality journalism in the United States and Britain colludes with the practice of artfully pairing films, many of its senior practitioners having been habitués of the postwar arthouse, proffering a kind of shorthand advising a contemporary spectator who finds herself amid an apparently heterogeneous selection of films at the cinema and on DVD. The release of *Savage Grace* (Tom Kalin, 2008) saw a *Vogue* poster quotation gushing: "Like Death in Venice meets The Great Gatsby on the Psycho lot" (Sight & Sound 2008: 98). For Graeme Turner, "[w]hat genre does is recognize that the audience watches any one film within a context of other films, both those they have personally seen and those they have heard about or seen represented in other media outlets" (Turner 1988: 119). This book emerged out of the impulse to connect one film to others, and the artful pairing plays its role in the evolution of thinking about a new genre.

Genre-as-World

Taking their cue from classical categorization, most critical studies agree on an understanding of what constitutes a film genre. For Hayward, it "can be identified by the iconography and conventions operating within it" (Hayward 2006: 191). For Ryall, generic classification consists in "the compilation of inventories of their characteristic subject-matter, themes, iconography, narrative syntax, and visual style" (Hill 1998: 335). For Konigsberg, genre is "a group of films having recognizably similar plots, character types, settings, filmic techniques, and themes" (Konigsberg 1988: 143). For Rick Altman, "genres are thought to reside in a particular topic and structure or in a corpus of films that share a specific topic and structure" (Altman 1999: 23). Whether defined as "subject matter," "character types," "settings" or "specific topic," insofar as a film's world and that world's accoutrements bear upon the task of defining its genre, the film's topic and the imagery to which it gives rise seems a common thread in academic and industry definitions of genre. The Western, traditionally conceived, invokes a specific milieu and its historical accoutrements. The musical, in its 1930s "backstage" manifestation, unfolds in a specific environment, one associated with a particular cultural activity and the practices and discourses which revolve around it. Film noir too has been saliently associated with the images and practices of urban experience. Edward Dimendberg identifies the American urban scene around the mid–twentieth century as a defining ground with which to substantiate film noir's claim to generic status: "[u]ntil recently, film noir scholarship remained trapped in a quagmire of attempts to define its object of study ... scholars argued whether film noir was a genre, a tone, a mood, a style, or a moment in film history. Yet space cannot be comfortably assimilated to any of these categories and suggests ... the possibility of a new optic through which to approach film noir" (Dimendberg 2004: 11). To the extent that a particular milieu and the activities associated with it have seemed such a useful impetus for the identification of classical genres, we might argue that *Three Colors: Blue*, *Moonlight and Valentino*, *Morvern Callar*, *Birth* and *I've Loved You So Long* together constitute a distinct category for sharing a preoccupation not simply with mourning, but with the specific environments of domesticity, and activities and rituals associated with mourning and domesticity.

Identification of a film's world and its associated activities has also been mobilized in the comprehension of film language and aesthetics and the expectations which they engender. Jean Mitry's now-classic definition of the Western ("situated in the American West ... consistent with the atmosphere, the values, and the conditions of existence in the Far West between 1840 and 1900" [Mitry 1963: 276]) neatly slots together milieu and thematic concerns. This semantic approach to the Western is opposed to the syntactic approach utilized by Jim Kitses in which a set of antinomies distinguishing civilization and the wilderness — culture/nature, community/individual, garden/desert and so forth — cut across individual films with implications for their specific syntax and rhythms (Kitses 1969: 10–14). In advocating a combination of these approaches, Altman catches the sense in which a genre may play out in a realm associated with certain accoutrements and effects, while individual films relate in stylistically specific ways to the genre's articulation of this realm. For the purposes of theorizing a genre in a context of fragmented spectatorship, Altman's emphasis is important: "Spectator response ... is heavily conditioned by the choice of semantic elements and atmosphere, because a given semantics used in a specific cultural situation will recall to an actual interpretive community the particular syntax with which that semantics has traditionally been associated in other texts" (Grant 1995: 38). One can envisage a semantic/syntactic approach being applied to the mourning film, with its perennial return to the moment of death and the paraphernalia associated with loss, its assertion of a world followed by the re-assertion of that world altered, coupled with highly mobile narrative effects and procedures. "We need to recognize," Altman writes, "that not all genre films relate to their genre in the same way or to the same extent" (Altman 1995: 33). Individual films evince individual levels of "genericity" (ibid.: 33), while inter-generic relationships abound. Thus, if we can envisage such widely dispersed titles as *Pursued* (Raoul Walsh, 1947), *Butch Cassidy and the Sundance Kid* (George Roy Hill, 1969), and *Western* (Manuel Poirier, 1997) beneath the generic label "Western," it becomes easier to envisage how *Three Colors: Blue*, *Birth* and *Morvern Callar* fall under a common definition, despite their international, institutional and inter-generic allegiances. A fundamental question of genre theory is the circular one of how to decide which films constitute a genre while bearing in mind which films one envisages belonging to the genre. Andrew Tudor writes: "To take a genre such as the 'western,' analyse it, and list its principal characteristics, is to beg the question that we must first isolate the body of films which are 'westerns.' But they can only be isolated on the basis of the 'principal characteristics' which can only be discovered from the films themselves after they have been isolated" (Tudor 1974: 135). The advantage, and perhaps a luxury, of deducing such a specie as a "mourning film" from a set of themes and characteristics is its empirical premise. One watches a set of albeit disparate films evincing similar themes and characteristics such that one can identify within them a world of experience and ritual paraphernalia. Thus, one classifies them according to the experience and rituals to which they overwhelmingly refer.

World-as-Ritual

The identification of an approach combining the generically fixed with the contingently mobile recognizes how genres offer boundaries of comprehension, while individual exemplars enable singular experiences. We are reminded of other experiences which are similarly bounded, yet different on every occasion, such as birthdays, weddings, funerals, and game-playing. If every ritual is a structure, we refill the structure every time we attend to the ritual. Ritual is another notion useful to the theorization of a new genre out of a range of old films. Genre theorists have seen in its very genericity the sating of human needs. Thomas Sobchack could be writing of the mourning film itself: "The cathartic potentials of the genre film can be seen in the way in which the tensions of cultural and social paradoxes inherent in human experience can be resolved" (Grant 2003: 94). We have noted the ritual nature of *Schindler's List*, *Titanic* and *Saving Private Ryan* as vehicles prompting mass commemoration of community loss. And as we have seen, as apparatus the cinema intrinsically lends itself to the fulfillment of ritual needs. Writers have seen genre as a process; on the historical level as the progression from a classical to a baroque stage, on the level of the individual text as the resolution of a specific relationship to the genre. The notion of genre as a ritual also resonates with intellectual currents informing this study. We are reminded that Freud and grief therapy, each in their way, offer accounts of mourning-as-process. The mourning film is about this process. Williams offers an argument which is both true of the way genre films work generally, but compellingly so of the mourning film: "Genres thrive ... on the persistence of the problems they address" (cited in Grant 2003: 155).

Intertextuality

Titanic's ritual status was acknowledged in critical responses to the film, yet while some bore reminders of Hollywood's generic past, others emphasized its knowing intertextuality. For Laura Miller, James Cameron's allegiance to genre was an impediment, unwittingly invoking the hoariest of archaic categories. Of Billy Zane's villain Cal, she writes, "Who lacks only a handlebar moustache to twirl" (Miller 1998: 52). Yet for our purposes Miller's criticism is double-edged. The reference to a stock archetype of Victorian melodrama may work against the film's credibility for a knowing audience, but by invoking melodrama, one of the cinema's founding genres, Miller acknowledges the film's investment in a form central to the identification of the mourning genre. That this hugely successful melodrama revolved around a mourning woman is further evidence of the central importance of a woman's grief to cinema as industry, institution, apparatus and history. Such a preoccupation enables *Titanic* to be discussed beyond the obviousness of its epic "disaster movie" status, and rethought in terms of its account of interiority and loss, whatever the success or limitations of this latter mission. Despite the rhetoric of the big release, Hayward acknowledges the role the knowing spectator plays in reading "[b]ecause genres are simultaneously bound by certain conventions and expectations and are intertextual we carry a wealth of knowledge ourselves which means that we too, in a parodic and iconoclastic fashion, can make readings of the films against the grain" (Hayward 2006: 188).

Increasingly fluid tendencies of modern genre definition reflect evolving historical circumstances in reception contexts such as the Internet chat-room and DVD retailer rhetoric. And as the breakdown of the traditional "family audience" for Hollywood product showed in the 1960s and 1970s, such fluidity encourages a "re-purposing" of genres. Intertextuality is a useful term in connection with this play, or re-use, of films, and the term has specific relevance to new ways of thinking about old films. Denoting a relationship between two or more texts, intertextuality shapes the reading of a text: "an intertext in whose presence other texts reside" (ibid.: 226). *Thriller* (Sally Potter, 1979) and *Dressed to Kill* (Brian de Palma, 1980) both allude consciously to *Psycho* (Alfred Hitchcock, 1960) to the extent that we can say that *Psycho* "resides" within them. *Genova* evinces such points of common interest with *Don't Look Now* as to court knowing complicity on the part of filmmaker, critic and spectator. The presence of Emmanuelle Riva in *Hiroshima mon amour* and *Three Colors: Blue* makes for a quietly knowing intertextual relationship. Intertextuality can also be a matter of degree. The Oxford English Dictionary definition stipulates only "the relationship" between texts (OED 1996: 713). By interpreting the term "text" according to its widest definition, we can see how particular film texts may come together because they are inhabited by a text of another kind. Classical psychoanalysis and grief therapy both theorize mourning as a form of "text" consisting of stages with distinctive mental states, procedures and practices associated with them. It becomes possible, then, to see films that narrativize grief and mourning as "inhabited" by the text of mourning. Given the spectator's propensity to make conscious or unconscious connections between a particular film and a similar other, this looser understanding of intertextuality affords a more suggestive relationship between films. Seen in close proximity, titles far flung in their cultural and institutional origins come together by the light of shared themes and atmospheres. For example, however disparate in form and style, *Three Colors: Blue* and *Carnival of Souls* share a preoccupation with mourning as "unfinished business," the role of art as a register of subjectivity, and the place of water as a cleansing and originary zone. This redefinition of texts can result in re-usage for other purposes. *Three Colors: Blue* and *Carnival of Souls* can now be read for their conciliatory qualities as texts of reparation and atonement. Such subterranean association between films seems a happy coincidence. The very idea that one text can suggest, inhabit or haunt another seems provocative and curiously appropriate to the project of theorizing a mourning genre. Of the horror film,

Carol Clover writes of "its engagement of repressed fears and desires and its re-enactment of the residual conflict surrounding those feelings" (Clover 1992: 11). She could be writing about *Three Colors: Blue* or *Carnival of Souls*. Given the shared semantic and syntactic preoccupations between films explored in this study, many of which are indicative of buried subjectivity, paraphrasing Clover's observation that horror seems to be cinema's "repressed" (ibid.: 20), it may be even truer to say that the mourning film is the lost genre of cinema.

By viewing mourning films in the light of shared preoccupations, we can see them afresh. As earlier case studies implied, genre identities which have seemed uncontested for decades may thereby be re-purposed for a new era. For example, rereading *The Innocents* and *The Haunting*, or even *Titanic*, as films about loss, releases them from a canonicity which seems limiting in an era of unbridled access and re-evaluation. It also releases the spectator from the presumptions and obligations that canonicity brings. We subscribe to the notion that *The Curse of the Cat People* is a horror classic to the extent that its critical reputation remains encrusted with the generic discourse current at the time of its release. But what does this story of a child's coming to terms with loss become when seen in a double bill alongside another exploration of the same topic; the French auteur film *Ponette*? If for Altman, "[o]ne of the founding principles of genre study is the importance of reading texts in the context of other similar texts" (Altman 2003: 81), using fresh generic terms to identify old films is an attempt "to capture jurisdiction over the right to redefine the texts in question" (ibid.: 82), and to see the film anew.

From the Double Bill...

So bringing together two disparate films can encourage fresh critical associations to be made between them. David Thomson writes, "My favourite double bills are secret, thematic pairings, films where deep below the surface one picture is speaking to another" (Giles 2008: 39). Compared with the institutionalized genres of the past, such juxtapositions enable us to rethink genre itself, perhaps in ways more sensitive to the categories that exist within categories, so to speak. The "Old Dark House" strand of the classical horror film, for example, those French "intimiste" films which deal with family dynamics, or mourning films which explore mother-daughter relationships. Such a playful attitude towards generic categories invites a more nuanced account of this important area of film studies.

Coming into its own during the high days of arthouse exhibition in the 1960s and 1970s, the double bill could be thought of as a stage in the progression from the classical genre cycle to the contemporary cinephile's domestic DVD juxtaposition. This progression seems historical and organic. Doubling bears the cultural memory of a classical era program where the main feature would be "supported" by another "second" feature at the downtown cinema, giving way to a single feature norm by the 1960s, concurrent with the rise of repertory double bills in Anglo-American metropolitan arthouses. The rise of the double bill was crucially related to postwar cinephilia. Gerwin van der Pol sees the artful pairing as fundamental to the cinephile's project: "So the 'Holy Grail' of knowledge for the cinephile is finding a novel connection" (de Valck 2005: 216). Jane Giles was a former programmer at London's Scala cinema. Her testimony reinforces the perception that the inspired double was the special province of postwar cinephilia: "Despite the obvious emphases on director, genre or star, there were no hard and fast programming rules to what made a good double bill [it was] in the hands of enthusiasts, fired up by audiences who crammed the suggestion box with their dream double bills" (ibid.: 28). As an exhibition initiative, the double bill was classically a pairing around a common director or star, occasionally the cinematographer. But such pairings can gesture towards unexpected relationships. Recalling the intertextual possibilities afforded by film history, we might envisage coupling *The Sheltering Sky* and *Shadowlands*, both of which feature Debra Winger in starring roles and both of which revolve around loss. Juliette Binoche, too, has enough mourning films to her credit, *The English Patient* (Anthony Minghella, 1996), *Damage* (Louis Malle, 1992), *Paris* (Cédric Klapisch, 2008), as well at *Three Colors: Blue*, to suggest that generic classification derives something of its impetus from an actor's conscious career decisions.

While in the 1960s and 1970s the metropolitan arthouse became a key site for the propagation of the double bill culture, a generation of television programmers excavated film history with extensive director- and star-led seasons, and the weekend double bill came into its own. By the 1980s the television double bill took on a new sophistication in the BBC's *Moviedrome* slot. In the 1990s and 2000s, the rise of Internet sites dedicated to film analysis provides another context for the search for fresh critical holy grails. The Australian site *Rouge* ran a translation of a 1972 piece by Thierry Kuntzel on *Freaks*, long regarded as a canonical horror film, but in Kuntzel's words "the narrative's organization is here inscribed in a certain sub-genre of cinema known as the *fantastique*.... Freaks perpetually de-classifies itself: a film of the transgression of biological genre, it itself transgresses cinematic genre" (Kuntzel 2005). At the British site *Talking Pictures*, Jamie Garwood muses on *Black Book* (*Zwartboek*, Paul Verhoeven, 2006): "On some levels noir, war picture and feminist flick" (Garwood 2006). In a piece on *Double Indemnity* (Billy Wilder, 1944) at the American site *The Film Journal*, I re-read the canonical film noir for its allegiance to the woman's picture (Armstrong 2002).

The project of extrapolating a mourning genre from across the annals of film history seems increasingly apt in an era of Internet DVD retailing. The British sites *Lovefilm* and *Moviemail* employ marketing strategies encouraging links to be surmised between ostensibly different films. *Lovefilm* cross-references a title with other subscriber favorites in a "Similar Collections" slot. Thus a search for *Moonlight and Valentino* "evoked" *My Life without Me* (Isabel Coixet, 2002), *Breaking the Waves* (Lars von Trier, 1996), and *Terms of Endearment* (James L. Brooks, 1983). A search for *Three Colors: Blue* evoked *Lost in Translation* (Sofia Coppola, 2003), *A Woman Under the Influence* (John Cassavetes, 1974), and *The Seventh Seal* (*Det sjunde inseglet*, Ingmar Bergman, 1957). *Carnival of Souls* evoked *Don't Look Now*, *The Innocents* and *Dead of Night* (Alberto Cavalcanti, Charles Crichton, Basil Dearden and Robert Hamer, 1945). In a curious, and for our purposes serendipitous, parallel with the séance invocation, while *The Innocents* "called up" *The Haunting* (1963), *Ponette* "called up" *Rebecca*. If a number of traditional generic and institutional boundaries are being crossed in this sample, the sense in which individual films are being watched by clients which share particular themes — loss, death, alienation, child-women, the afterlife — and perhaps the recurrence of certain images — isolation, tears, water, the sea — seems quite obvious. *Moviemail* employ a "See Alsos" slot consisting of handpicked recommendations of related films. A search under *The Innocents* evoked *The Others* and *The Haunting* (1963). A search under *Hiroshima mon amour* evoked *Vertigo*, while *Don't Look Now* evoked *Rebecca*. While the *Moviemail* linkages seem more obviously attuned to sources (Daphne du Maurier brings *Don't Look Now* and *Rebecca* together), and stars — Samantha Morton in *Morvern Callar* evokes *Under the Skin*—the occasionally artful relationship is also possible. Under the "Customers who liked this also liked" slot, *Morvern Callar* is brought together with *Lost in Translation*, another film in which a "lost" woman is found wandering in a strange environment. Despite the vicissitudes of availability, domestic delivery systems enable a potpourri of world cinema to be sampled according to personal whim, affording new kinds of association and classification, and in time perhaps prompting an enriched film literature.

When films are brought together because they share similar themes or imagery, this invites other ways of talking about them. Lucy Fischer criticizes film studies' traditional reduction of genres to charts of thematic similarity: "While we recognize the validity of [Thomas] Schatz's assertions ... his neat classification, so easily reduced to a chart, tends to calcify forms, and to mask their potential interrelations. Hence, the schema may encourage the critic to ignore the role of the mother in the crime film, or to miss a maternal subtext in the masculine 'thriller'" (Fischer 1996: 7). The task of looking anew liberates some films and complicates others. Aside from criticizing Schatz's insistence on applying gender labels to particular genres, Fischer points out that films traditionally belonging to established genres by virtue of those themes which have been seen as dominant, can also contain plots and discourses which link a film to other films hailing from other genres. Thus motherhood, traditionally a preserve of melodrama, can be re-imagined through the prism of the policier or the horror film as they are in *Psycho* or in *M*. Other thematic studies recognize how a fresh optic sets up fresh allegiances. Wilson suggests that films which treat a particular experience have the potential not only to breach generic, auteurist and institutional boundaries, but offer the possibility of changing what cinema can be: "They ... make of that encounter with the child as missing or endangered a tear or fissure in their film-making art such that new ways of seeing may briefly be glimpsed" (Wilson 2003: 10). *Universal Horror*, Kevin Brownlow's television documentary on classical American horror, returns more than once to the idea that the monsters of 1930s Hollywood horror films evoked the public spectre of post–World War I disabled and mutilated servicemen, a metaphorical depiction which might usefully inform the study of disability in the cinema. Dimendberg acknowledges a perennial theme in film noir which beckons towards even the mourning film: "traumas of unrecoverable time and space, the inability to dwell comfortably either in the present or the past" (Dimendberg 2004: 1). The thematic study of cinema has much to offer film studies in the era of domestic spectatorship.

It is worth emphasizing that motherhood, disability, or mourning can assume such importance as to complicate, even destabilize, a film's received generic reputation. Titles ranging from *Titanic* to *Under the Sand*, *Interiors* and *The Son's Room* (*La stanza del figlio*, Nanni Moretti, 2001) come together over a preoccupation with the sea at the level of theme and imagery, for example, a set of recurring ideas and images which finds the films, whatever labels have been applied to them, in allegiance to the very distinctive and insistent theme of mourning and its visual accoutrements. Other films, ranging from *Morvern Callar* to *Three Colors: Blue* and *Under the Skin*, share a preoccupation with personal testimony which is specific to the thematic of coping with grief, a preoccupation which also resonates with the films mentioned above. In short, the theme of mourning and the cultural ideas which accompanies it not only seems as coherent, time-honored, and "natural" as the iconography and preoccupations of the Western, but too grave in its insistence on shaping the aesthetics of these films to be overlooked in the language we use to talk about them.

... To the Genre.

Double bills have been prompted by a plethora of instincts and logics, but to the degree that this exhibition convention highlights undiscovered similarities between dispersed films, as method and tradition it lends itself to the task of formulating a new generic conceptualization. The contemporary precedents and habits informing this project are for the modern spectator easy-to-hand. Modern spectatorship encourages a "bottom up" model of generic identification and debate whereby a rubric is discerned and extrapolated at the level of informed spectatorship. The contemporary film guide also encourages this instinct in its indexing terminology. The subject orientation of the 2007 edition of the *Time Out Film Guide* stipulated the categorizations "Death," "Bereavement," and "Few-months-to-live stories" (Pym 2006: 1497, 1488 & 1502). Along with "Death," *Videohound's Golden Movie Retriever* stipulated "Death and the Afterlife," "Funerals," and "Reincarnation" (Craddock 2006: 1506).

While repertory exhibition has tended to adhere to the rationales of director, star, studio and national cinemas, occasionally films have been brought together according to other determinations. In November and December 2000, London's National Film Theatre (NFT) ran a major season of films dealing with sexual relations. One of its programmers, Geoff Andrew, distinguished between films around eroticism and those which treated sex as their motivating theme: "For this season is not really about pornography or eroticism; it gathers together not sexy films as such, but films about sex" (Andrew 2000: 12). Among a widely dispersed roster appeared *Queen Kelly* (Erich von Stroheim, 1929), *L'Atalante* (Jean Vigo, 1934), *Tom Jones* (Tony Richardson, 1963), *Woman of the Dunes* (*Suna no onna*, Hiroshi Teshigahara, 1964), *Written on the Wind*, and *The Law of Desire* (*La ley del deseo*, Pedro Almodóvar, 1987); in other words, this was a season drawing upon the arthouse, the mainstream, America, Europe and Asia, and spanning a century of cinema from the Edison studio's *The Kiss* (1895) to *Romance* (Catherine Breillat, 1998).

Andrew's distinction between sex and eroticism is relevant to the identification of a mourning genre. Sex and death are key aspects of the human condition, prompting the association of titles beneath these headings. However, if a film which features eroticism (Andrew suggests *Double Indemnity* and *Don't Look Now*), was not necessarily a film *about* sex, many films, *Les Diaboliques* (Henri-Georges Clouzot, 1955), *Reservoir Dogs* (Quentin Tarantino, 1992), *Ossessione* (Luchino Visconti, 1943), *A Short Film about Killing* (*Krótki film o zabijaniu*, Krzysztof Kieślowski, 1988), to cite just four very disparate examples, have been about deaths but less about loss. Many films deal with human demise in terms of its physical execution and its legal and psychological consequences for the perpetrator. Murder mysteries, thrillers, crime films and Westerns feature death as essential moves in their narratives. And if death, in whatever form it takes, is central to the narrative, the death scene is more than usually foregrounded, even specularized, in these films. To draw upon Andrew's description of eroticism, the moment of seeing death is a "come-on" (ibid.: 12).

If we see the foregrounding of death in these films as analogous to the foregrounding of sex in screen eroticism, it may be possible to see the contrast between films that foreground death and films which explore loss. Films which emphasize the death scene in all its sound and fury do not necessarily focus on the consequences of loss. This is not to say that murder mysteries, thrillers and westerns do not contain scenes in which characters grieve over their losses. But few are *about* loss in the prosaic round in the insistent way in which *Moonlight and Valentino, Three Colors: Blue, The Son's Room* and *Under the Skin* are. The distinction can be summed up by stipulating that films in which death is accorded set piece significance assume that death is a sight far from the spectator's quotidian experience, seldom if ever to be actually witnessed, thus eligible for the big aesthetic build-up. By contrast, films about loss assume that death is inevitable, immanent and, for the grieving protagonist, a quotidian experience with peaks and troughs of an entirely different order. In many mourning films — *Three Colors: Blue, Under the Sand, Moonlight and Valentino, The Son's Room, Interiors, Ponette*—we do not see the death which motivates the mourning, a fact which recalls death's invisibility from public life; meanwhile emphasizing the work of reparation. As we have seen, the move from the experience of loss to the daily living with loss becomes reflected in the mourning film's work of reconciling the visually excessive with the visually transparent. The mourning film involves the displacement of the visually excessive register from the dangerous world outside to the dangerous world inside, or rather, in this cinema of feelings the inside becomes the outside. And before the cinema's copious histories of gunfire, so to speak, the mourning film posits subterranean histories of grief, drawing on its own lexicon of spectacle. The rubric for the NFT season assumed that sex, too, could be a way of life in cinema. In recounting its myriad characteristics and outcomes, Andrew introduces a range of feelings: "that sex is liberating, healthy, dangerous, subversive, uncontrollable, mysterious; that it is a source of joy, love, fulfilment, fear, frustration, misery, ambition, jealousy, deceit, violence, lunacy, conflict, obsession; in short, what [the films] all say is sex ... is a prime defining and motivating factor in our lives" (ibid.: 13). He could be writing about loss, for the mourning film draws upon interior states and feelings, and an inner history of cinema, which is just as rich.

Taxonomy of the Mourning Film

Elaborating on observations developed in earlier case studies, and drawing on films mentioned but little discussed so far, the following taxonomy seeks to show how ideas of genre discussed in this chapter can be applied to the identification of a new genre. Using categories derived from theoretical writings on genre, the taxonomy will identify the mourning film through a comparative analysis of its common features. Examples shall be drawn from those titles which have provided precedents for the mourning film, more detailed examples from films studied in Chapter 3, plus a number of other releases of the 1990s and 2000s which share the preoccupation with loss and grief. If Pasolini asks, "How is the "language of poetry" theoretically explicable and practically possible in cinema?" (cited in Orr 2000: 44), the following observations seek to provide an answer.

Ponette. As Ponette "re-finds" her mother, she seeks tactile communication with that life she once knew, even the color here deepening as Ponette's desire itself seems to enrich the surface of the imagery.

Characteristic Themes

A recurring theme in the mourning film is the self-delusion which follows loss. *Under the Sand*, *Ponette*, *Truly, Madly, Deeply* and *Birth* all explore this theme, while *The Curse of the Cat People* provides a classical precedent. In *Under the Sand*, the measure of Marie's inability to acknowledge her loss manifests itself in scenes in which we see her with her dead husband as if he is still alive. At the end of *Ponette*, the child's mother appears to her, an event which inscribes itself on the form of the film in an enriching of the color, as if privileging her perspective. In *Truly, Madly, Deeply*, Nina's partner appears to her, while the film's color becomes increasingly grey and washed-out. In *Birth*, the displacement of Anna's affection for her fiancé onto someone she thinks is her reincarnated first husband is the film's way of literalizing her self-delusion. Thematizing self-delusion by representing a world in which the dead appear to live on, these films posit an objective metaphor for a subjective lack. Manifestations of the dead make for a striking cinematic trick, playing on absence and presence and using the image to explore the mourner's yearning for the impossible. To examine self-delusion in the mourning film is to acknowledge how the experience of "presence" evoked in therapeutic literature can be cast as a Bazinian solidity all the more unsettling for seeming so impossibly but incontrovertibly there. Challenging the originating dichotomy between fantasy and realism which traditionally structures film history and criticism, such moments also exhibit a penchant for the macabre which the mourning film shares with its horror forebears. Taking another mourning film — *The Orphanage* — and comparing it with a modern horror film — *The Sixth Sense* — one sees how recent horror cinema realizes a relationship with melodrama which brings the mourning film into sharper focus. In *The Orphanage*, a frantic mother searches for her son at a garden party and sees a child in a strange mask approaching her. In *The Sixth Sense*, a boy sees cadavers hanging in a school corridor. In their ineffable but matter-of-fact way, these images are chilling, positing visual evidence of supernatural visitation imbued with an emotionalism which reinforces their credibility. The peculiar chemistry of loss and supernatural imagery in classical horror is increasingly acknowledged in modern examples. This progression can also be felt in the evolution of the image of the departed. In a number of horror titles informing the mourning film, the ghost appears as the wraith-like spectre, diaphanous and briefly seen, familiar from descriptions of "abominations" in Victorian supernatural literature and the "apparitions" of nineteenth century trick photography. *After Death* and *The Innocents* see this legacy worked through in classical cinema. One of the most distinctive characteristics of the modern horror film, however, is the way in which the wraith of supernatural tradition has become an apparently flesh and blood figure. In *The Sixth Sense*, the twist in the tale was that the character we took to be alive was actually dead. Only at the very end of *The Others* do we realize that the mother and children with whom we have identified are also already dead. By inviting us to identify with characters already dead, these horror titles broach the question of whether the dead *know* that they are dead, making the loss of these characters all the more poignant for other characters on screen. This modern horror scenario reaches out to the world of mourning cinema, one in which the sheer solidity of the dead is the measure of the place they occupy in the psychology of the survivors. In the mourning film, the "others" are those who live on.

The issue of whether or not the character onscreen is alive or dead can also be read as a film's dramatization of the inevitability, or narrative predictability, of demise, a theme often explored in mourning cinema. The drama of the mourning film is the drama of the transition from existence to non-existence, a dilemma which it explores in different ways. Mourning cinema's antecedents were aware of this fine line; witness the scene in *The Haunting* in which Abigail Crain (Janet Mansell/Amy Dalby) ages from girl to old woman. If we interpret Mary's trajectory in *Carnival of Souls* as a being-towards-death, her peripatetic progress bringing her nearer to her demise with each passing scene, we may position this film as a harbinger of the always already dead protagonists of the recent horror trend. Just as her visions and sensations are intrinsic to her being, Mary's death is an inevitable part of her experience. In *The Haunting*, Eleanor appears in a white nightgown or raveled in a lace curtain. Such "ghostly" appearances suggest her frail purchase on life and her eventual fate. In a film permeated with death, we learn of the first two Mrs. Crains' deaths before Eleanor unwittingly speaks her own demise: "At last I'm going someplace where I am expected ... and I shall never have to come back." Like *Don't Look Now* and *Interiors*, each in its way, *The Haunting* and *Carnival of Souls* are both propelled by the notion that, without knowing what form it will take, a character is hurtling towards their end. While John sees his own funeral barge in *Don't Look Now* and Joey sees a shadowy Eve in *Interiors*, Mary sees her equivalent among the dead at the carnival pavilion. *Cries and Whispers*, *Interiors*, *The Sheltering Sky*, *La Reine Margot*, *Under the Skin*, *The Barbarian Invasions* and *Yes* (Sally Potter, 2004) are chronicles of waiting for death in which the inevitability of loss is the point of the narrative. A vigil structure is particularly emphatic in "bedside" narratives in which characters watch as death bears their loved ones away. Like the sisters in *Don't Look Now*, in *The Sheltering Sky* two English eccentrics giggle in a restaurant, inviting us to speculate whether they can foresee death. Reiterating this premonitory mood, Port (John Malkovich) observes, "Did you know that we're standing in a cemetery?" In *Yes*, camera movement inscribes the inevitability of death in a shot from Auntie's perspective in which her corpse is borne away from the grieving She (Joan Allen). If in *Under the Skin*, we are told that Iris's mother is going to die, in *La Reine Margot* Charles (Jean-Hugues Anglade) is slowly being poisoned, his sister Margot (Isabelle Adjani) observing, "Paris is a cemetery." At the bedside of Rémy (Rémy Girard), in *The Barbarian Invasions*, Diane (Louise Portal) cites the fate of the typical mourning protagonist when she muses in terms reminiscent of Virginia Woolf: "...alone, abandoned, the fate of womanhood." In some films, the line between the living and the dead and the suddenness of the transition from life to death is itself emphasized. This preoccupation manifests itself in scenes in which the living and the dead become visually indiscernible, taking the form of apparent communion with a corpse: *Hiroshima mon amour*, *The Sheltering Sky*, *Kissed* and *Morvern Callar*.

Films which revolve around suicides thematize the delusion that characters are coping, or that nothing untoward has happened. *Festen* must plumb a family's history of sexual abuse before the daughter's suicide can be mourned. In *Short Cuts*, Zoe Trainer (Lori Singer) is found dead of carbon monoxide poisoning by her neglectful mother, who then retreats further into herself. In *Jude*, Jude (Christopher Ecclestone) and Sue (Kate Winslet) discover that their son has murdered his siblings and committed suicide, Sue reacting by turning to religion and blaming herself. A peculiarly difficult experience for families to negotiate, suicide and self-delusion become crucially entwined. In these films, the inability to talk about what has happened results in a conspiracy of silence, conflicting feelings of sorrow and guilt, and increasing alienation and isolation, creating a kind of ghost which haunts the dialogue just as in other films self-delusion becomes materialized in actual images of the dead.

Out of self-delusion, or out of plain sorrow, comes isolation, another theme explored in the mourning film. *In the Bedroom, Under the Sand, Morvern Callar, Birth, Three Colors: Blue*, and *I've Loved You So Long* all feature protagonists who retreat from social interaction. *In the Bedroom* dramatizes a husband and wife drifting into separate mental worlds following the death of their son. Marie's condition isolates her from her friends in *Under the Sand*. Morvern Callar's quietness makes it difficult to know whether she is coping or not. Julie's departure to Paris physically underwrites her condition; living alone means living the way she feels. "You don't say anything! Talk to me!" is the plea of Juliette's sister (Kristin Scott Thomas/Elsa Zylberstein) in *I've Loved You So Long*. The journey into loneliness and silence is the proper territory of the mourning film, an inner quest which makes talking redundant, challenging the film to articulate through images. The final scene of *Birth*, in which the bride flees from her wedding to the beach, the waves crashing on the seashore, the film score's declining notes parodying the optimistic pealing of church bells, reiterates the mourning protagonist's compulsion to be alone and not speak and the pure energies this invokes.

The limitations of language are consciously explored in the dialogue of *Birth, Morvern Callar, Moonlight and Valentino, Under the Sand* and *I've Loved You So Long*. The mourning film's raison d'être is its protagonist's condition, the mistresses of the mourning genre coming to seem like fabulists bearing accounts of themselves which other characters must take on trust. Hence, compelling dinner scenes in *Under the Sand* and *I've Loved You So Long* in which, respectively, Marie and Juliette speak as though they exist on the cusp of two lives. In *Moonlight and Valentino*, Rebecca voices the obfuscations of language when she indulges in a word game — "the W word" — to come to terms with her widowhood. The shortcomings of language force the issue of grief's unpredictability, a recurring characteristic in *Cries and Whispers, Three Colors: Blue*,

Morvern Callar, *Interiors* and *Birth*, while finding an antecedent in the mysterious instincts of *Portrait of Jennie*, *The Innocents* and *The Haunting*. In *Moonlight and Valentino*, Rebecca's petulant words: "Don't assume that *anything* about me is sane!" sets a mood of disorientation, emphasizing that the complexity of grief highlights the difficulty of getting to know someone. Much is made in *Moonlight and Valentino* of how Rebecca's behavior is unpredictable, but while in that film unpredictability becomes expressed, albeit clumsily, in dialogue, aesthetically bolder works like *Under the Skin*, *Under the Sand* and *Morvern Callar* make the film's imagery the palette on which mysterious interiority is played out. If the appearance of the dead in other mourning films exploits cinema's conundrum of presence and absence, in these films the obscure actions and reactions of the mourner liberate the films' instinct for aesthetic experiment.

The prospect of a genre inhabiting uncertain seas of temperament is nicely analogized by the recurrence of sea and water in its imagery. *Interiors*, *Birth*, *Under the Sand*, *Under the Skin*, *The Orphanage*: it is striking how frequently the seashore is used to stage isolation in mourning cinema. The sea and water is a recurring theme from the type's prehistory, whether symbolizing death and decay (*I Walked with a Zombie*, *Portrait of Jennie*) or the possibility of self-knowledge (*Rebecca*, *I Walked with a Zombie*, *Vertigo*). In *Portrait of Jennie*, *Rebecca*, *Under the Sand*, *Interiors* and *Birth* characters drown, or may have drowned, at sea. In *Three Colors: Blue*, and metaphorically in the "sea" of sand in *The Sheltering Sky*, water is replenishing, offering the possibility of rebirth. The sea as the traditional boundary between life and death is explored in *Under the Sand*, *Titanic*, *Interiors* and *The Sheltering Sky*. With its fluidity and lack of definition, the sea in the mourning film is a metaphor for the failure of language to map grief.

Descending from explorations of the theme in *The Innocents* and *The Curse of the Cat People*, and elaborating a perennial preoccupation of the woman's film, in mourning films revolving around female protagonists, mother/daughter relationships, real or surrogate, recur in *Cries and Whispers*, *Interiors*, *Terms of Endearment*, *Three Colors: Blue*, *Birth*, *Under the Sand* and *Secrets and Lies*. It seems significant that the mourning film should stage such relationships, since in a genre so committed to interiority the real or surrogate nature of these relationships emphasizes less the conventional rapport of mother/daughter relationships as an institution, and more the feelings which give rise to it. In its surrogate form, the mother/daughter bond in mourning cinema may be prompted by the same desire for comfort as motivates the continuing "presence" of the dead. Actual mother/daughter relationships frequently work less well than those of a surrogate form. This is exemplified in *Secrets and Lies*, which dramatizes the growing friendship between the lonely Cynthia (Brenda Blethyn) and a younger woman who has recently lost her adoptive mother. That Cynthia turns out to be the woman's birth mother emphasizes the play of friendship in mother/daughter relationships much as *The Curse of the Cat People* dramatizes the rapport between Amy and her adoptive mother, and in *The Innocents* Miss Giddens compensates for being childless by befriending Flora. Other surrogate relationships such as that between Amanda and Marie in *Under the Sand*, Anna and Agnes in *Cries and Whispers*, and Julie and Lucille in *Three Colors: Blue* offer their protagonists respite from the problematic relationships these women have with their birth mothers.

The materiality of death and the abject is directly confronted in *Kissed*, *Under the Sand* and *Morvern Callar*, constituting a link with the mourning film's forebear the horror movie, for examples the abject detail of *The Innocents* and *I Walked with a Zombie*. If the mourning film's prime project is the exploration of consciousness, the form affords the "excessive" image an often equal significance. Hence that prolonged shot in *Jude* in which dead crows hang from a wooden cross, or as Morvern Callar watches a beetle scuttling across tiles in her hotel. *Kissed* provides a literary analogy for this visual contemplation. It features an embalming session which, while we do not see the corpse, its disgusting suggestion is spelt out in the mortician's briefing. This scene affords an interesting parallel with the scene at the mortuary in *Under the Sand*. If both women are in denial about the nature of what they see, for Sandra (Molly Parker) death is not horrific but a stillness which is blissful, while for Marie death is not horrific because it is not real. In veiling the image with words, a system which in other mourning films is problematic, the mortuary scenes in *Kissed* and *Under the Sand* emphasize a purely forensic discourse which for these women need have nothing to do with loss. In less coy moments, *Kissed* makes the link between death's materiality and the naturally abject more obvious, for example in scenes in which the young Sandra and her childhood friend take nocturnal trips to the woods to bury dead animals. But in this tale of a young woman's sexual education, what is emphasized in those scenes in which she has sex with corpses are her responses, her bliss, rather than the abject materiality of what she touches. The image of her bliss becomes all the more emphatic, and tragic, when she makes love to the boyfriend whom she loved before he died. At this point, we sense a celestial register in Parker's performance going back to Falconetti's Jeanne d'Arc. In *Kissed*, the grisly materiality of death becomes the almost visceral dissection of interiority. What is significant about the preoccupation with the abject in the mourning film is the way in which these women rove beyond conventional taste in search of an affinity with natural worlds. Ponette (Victoire Thivisol) scrabbles in the dirt in the attempt to uncover her mother's grave. Morvern Callar toys with ants. In *The Orphanage*, Laura (Belén Rueda) discovers human bones in an oven. *The Blair Witch Project* is teeming with natural detritus and decay, while filmmaker Heather (Heather Donohue) wants to "get it all on

16." In *Birth*, Clara's decision to bury Anna's love letters in common ground by night suggests a perverse, even occult, disposition. Because these films refrain from judging these women, we are left with an impression of aesthetic lawlessness or amorality which generations of patriarchy has tried to suppress. While Sandra is told not to wear black at work, one of her most striking features is her jet black hair; lawlessness becomes inscribed on the transgressor's body.

Another theme of mourning cinema is the mourner's attempt to express her experience in art or another exacting endeavor. Characters create in order to articulate their sorrow. Creativity has implications for the film as a construct and ultimately for mourning cinema as a category. Renata in *Interiors* is skeptical about whether it is enough that a few poems survive her death, but in other films creating lends purpose to the survivor. It informs Iris's trying out as a nightclub singer in *Under the Skin*. It is an interesting choice of vocation. The troubled chanteuse has a resonant cultural and cinematic heritage. Yet by making Iris's ambition seem eventually abortive, *Under the Skin* suggests an endeavor which is less high-minded than a form of negotiating a transitional experience. In *Three Colors: Blue* Julie completes the music her husband was composing when he died. The piece she brings into the world inevitably becomes something "owned" as much by her as by him. To read this appropriation as the fulfillment of Julie's aesthetic sensibility is less urgent a matter than to hear the music as the soundtrack of her evolving feelings about her husband, herself and their marriage. In scenes revolving around Julie's subjectivity, bursts of the music shape the sound and look of the film. Here the "art" of mourning becomes the art of the film. Music becomes a channel of solace for the mourner, one which can bring back the past. A recurrent image in the mourning film is that in which the mourner plays an instrument or sings, providing the cue for the return of the dead. The protagonist as spiritual "apport" dictates the film on the level of sound and image. In *The Innocents* Flora hums a song and the ghost of Miss Jessel appears on the lake. In *Carnival of Souls*, Mary plays the organ and the dead return. In *Truly, Madly, Deeply*, Nina (Juliet Stevenson) plays the piano and a panning camera reveals her dead lover Jamie (Alan Rickman) playing the cello.

In view of the "unspeakability" of death and loss, it is significant that wordplay facilitates a more elliptical means of release for the mourner. This elliptical quality informs Rebecca's word game in *Moonlight and Valentino*, while writing may provide tentative release for Joey in *Interiors*. While we surmise that Morvern Callar is an unlikely author, we interpret her appropriation of her boyfriend's novel as the attempt to compensate for her loss by replacing him with a part of him, however "unspeakable" it may be to her. And because she says little, even this interpretation becomes academic. In *Hiroshima mon amour*, the woman speaks of her dead French lover through a heritage of nuclear devastation, a personal tragedy elliptically plotted in language. "Art" can also arise in the form of a personal project. In *A Very Long Engagement*, the investigation of Mathilde (Audrey Tautou) into her soldier fiancé's whereabouts, lends the film a quest structure, dramatizing mourning as the mourner's characteristic "searching" identified in grief therapy. Sometimes art is an act of emotional and aesthetic devotion, such as when Sandra makes love to Matt's corpse at the end of *Kissed*. Such instances see mourning defining the project of the film, becoming vehicles for the mourning process, and metaphors for the possibility of creating a film around that process.

Characteristic Settings

The characteristic dramatic setting of the mourning film is the response to loss. The type is so-called because its dramatic motor is the process of mourning. The characteristic physical setting of the type is a domestic space, a home or a setting that stands in for "home." Mourning cinema shares this predilection for the domestic setting with melodrama, in which private space becomes the stage for private and personal problems and emotions. Another recurring space in the mourning film is the séance, a setting which, by invoking recollections, emotions and apparitions of the dead, could be said to mediate between the dramatic and physical habitations of the genre. These settings, dramatic, psychological, physical, or metaphysical, are accompanied by the characteristic accoutrements of grief and mourning.

The mourning film revolves around characters negotiating loss, whether that of another or the prospect of their own mortality. This condition is rendered as the struggle to reconcile fragile interiority with an uncomprehending or indifferent world, one from which the character is psychologically and physically isolated. Many films concerned with grief and mourning proclaim a preoccupation with interiority in their titles. *The Haunting*, *Cries and Whispers*, *Interiors*, *Truly, Madly, Deeply*, *Secrets and Lies*, *Kissed*, *Under the Skin* and *I Have Loved You So Long*, even *In the Bedroom*: all are accounts of how individuals feel, and the way this shapes the way they interact with others. These films subscribe to a tradition of "psychological," or chamber cinema more concerned with plumbing a morass of emotions than in delineating plot, less interested in narrative action than in the shapelessness of inner distrait. The material settings of mourning films become projections of interiority, the seen indissolubly linked to the seer, a condition with consequences for film form.

The mourning film's interior drama is frequently played out in a domestic, or pseudo-domestic, setting. While *Cries and Whispers, Interiors, Truly, Madly, Deeply, Three Colors: Blue, Moonlight and Valentino, Jude, Secrets and Lies, Under the Skin, Under the Sand, Morvern Callar, In the Bedroom, Birth* and *The Orphanage* find the mourner at home, other films find them suffering in a place which substitutes for home. In a hotel room, bars and an apartment in Hiroshima, the woman from Nevers grieves over the loss she suffered years before. That many of these spaces are public rather than private is less important than what goes on there, the woman's reflections becoming a mobile narrative over the miscellany of urban milieux. Private space in the mourning film takes its cue from the charged "homes" of classical and post-classical horror. In *Carnival of Souls*, Mary moves into an apartment where she begins to have visions of her lost friends. In *The Haunting*, Eleanor visits a haunted mansion where she experiences conflicting feelings about her mother's death. *Don't Look Now* finds its bereft mother decamping to a Venetian pensione where she experiences intimations of her dead daughter's presence. After her mother dies, Ponette is sent to stay with her aunt and cousins. While on its maiden voyage, a woman loses her lover on the *Titanic*, a sort of temporary floating home the state rooms of which resemble the Georgian drawing rooms of her world. While she lives in her permanent home in Paris, where she acts as though everything is as normal between her and her husband, in *Under the Sand* Marie can only properly grieve by returning to the holiday home where he went missing. "No place I go feels right," says Rebecca in *Moonlight and Valentino*, voicing a sense of displacement widely experienced in the mourning film. While the domestic setting and its substitutes are characteristic of the type, part of the labor of mourning is the failure to inhabit the "home" these characters find themselves in. Indeed, the very move from home to its surrogates following bereavement becomes a

Interiors. The mourning woman often feels herself to be pure presence, living in, but not inhabiting, the domestic space. Here Renata tentatively seeks purchase on the world around her.

metaphor for the transition from one world to another experienced in mourning. The preoccupation with self—*Cries and Whispers, Interiors, Three Colors: Blue*— the reluctance to alter their surroundings —*Secrets and Lies, Truly, Madly, Deeply, Morvern Callar*— abstracted or obsessive touching —*Interiors, Moonlight and Valentino, I've Loved You So Long*— characterize this paradox of living in but not inhabiting the domestic space.

Consonant with the characteristic setting of loss and its psychological consequences, funerals figure in *Don't Look Now, Interiors, Three Colors: Blue, Moonlight and Valentino, Secrets and Lies, Jude, Under the Skin,* and *In the Bedroom*. In *Don't Look Now, Interiors* and *Under the Skin* the ceremony is presaged in various ways; in *Don't Look Now*, as John's premonition of his own funeral; in *Interiors*, in the opening scene following Eve's funeral; in *Under the Skin*, Iris is told that her mother has only months to live. Many mourning films explore human finitude as inevitability, eventually symbolized by the looming imagery of the casket and figures in black. Yet curiously enough, given their essential dramatic preoccupation, few mourning films detail the processes which take place between death and the funeral. To varying extents, *Under the Sand, Kissed* and *Morvern Callar* focus on the conventionally hidden detail of corpse preparation and disposal. But funeral scenes in mourning films are rare. They tend to be static records of the event, in more than one sense a transition of narrative significance rather than scenes with dynamics of their own. The characteristic funeral scene is a group shot at middle distance before the camera moves closer and the scene is edited to isolate significant characters. The credit sequence of *Secrets and Lies* takes this form. That the funeral plays out behind the opening credits here suggests the formal status of a ceremony that most mourning films imply, rather than explore, in this instance setting the spectator up for the drama of mourning to come. That we are introduced to Hortense (Marianne Jean-Baptiste) and her family at a very private moment generates a sense of voyeurism. Embarrassment at witnessing the grief of others is an idea explored in *Harold and Maude* (Hal Ashby, 1971), a black comedy which presages the modern mourning film in a number of ways. Revolving around a young man who is so obsessed with death that he attends other people's funerals, *Harold and Maude* not only thematizes the inevitability of death, but in focusing on the anonymously attended funeral it draws attention to interment as a ritual bereft in the modern era of wider significance. And in both *Harold and Maude* and *Secrets and Lies* the funeral assumes narrative significance beyond its conventional status as ritual, being the site for the staging of Harold's meeting Maude, arguably the moral centre of the film just as Hortense will become the moral center of *Secrets and Lies*. Wearing black throughout the film, Hortense seems defined by loss and the humility which it confers. Not merely is she the harbinger of demise foreseen in the credit sequence, in which the actors' names appear over a series of headstones, but her awareness of life's transience makes her the conduit bringing other characters together. In *Moonlight and Valentino*, Ben's funeral provides the excuse for satirizing the platitudes of the conventional burial ceremony. Yet here the ceremony will be upstaged, even overwritten, by a ritual of black garb and painted faces in a nocturnal graveyard. Rebecca's peculiar status of being at her husband's funeral but simultaneously not inhabiting it is curiously literalized in *Three Colors: Blue*, as Julie watches a documentary of the funeral from her hospital bed. The sense of being with others yet alone at a funeral is borne out in *Interiors* as each sister is separately framed over her mother's coffin and in the ceremonies of *Secrets and Lies* and *In the Bedroom* by cutting from mourner to mourner.

With its talk of painting skulls and the hidden energies of the tarot pack, *Moonlight and Valentino* renews the ceremonials of death by looking back, however ambivalently, to a more pagan notion of finitude. Taking its cue from horror, this ancient conception of death's symbolism recurs in other mourning films. In *Jude*, a film riven with premonitions of death, there is an eerie knock at the door as Jude chisels a headstone. Such moments not only resonate with a preoccupation with magic borne from such influences as *I Walked with a Zombie* and *The Blair Witch Project*, but reiterate the mourning film's proper territory of human finitude and the process which it triggers. The mourning film codifies such moments as a kind of excess, the camera lingering over dead crows in rapt curiosity in *Jude*, peering at ants in *Under the Sand*, studying natural detritus in *Morvern Callar*. The film goes out of its way to show these moments, to remind characters that life is fleeting but death is ancient. By "stopping" in contemplation, the film reiterates an emotional and physical stasis which is proper to the genre.

Consonant with its interest in chronicling interiority, the settings of memory recur in mourning films. In *Hiroshima mon amour*, *Cries and Whispers*, *Interiors* and *Birth*, memory provides parallel temporalities for these films to explore. In *Hiroshima mon amour*, recollections motivate the film's journey through time and space. As in the flashbacks of other mourning films, memory generates set pieces. The scenes are self-contained, linked not to the rest of the filmic world nor part of the geographical space of Nevers, but confined by the temporal and spatial settings of memory like tableaux. The sense in which an inner history is being related is emphasized by cross-cutting to the woman whose history this is. That all we see is delineated by the testimony we hear is perhaps analogized by the scene of the collaborator in prison, her world limited to her memories and literally limited by the walls which enclose her. Like *Hiroshima mon amour*, *Cries and Whispers* and *Interiors* are films which emphasize personal testimony and contain scenes of recalled experience which make sense because of the recollections which prompt them. When it is not generating the film's imagery, memory generates scenes in the mind. In *Birth*, Sean's sure knowledge of the family invites them to recall, and us to imagine, a past history much as the revelations of Christian (Ulrich Thomsen) prompt the exhumation of family history in *Festen*. Yet while these histories are not dramatized, as in *Hiroshima mon amour*, *Cries and Whispers* and *Interiors*, recollections generate a subterranean space, extending the films' characteristic domestic *mise-en-scène* into consciousness like a window or a mirror extends the space of a painting. That these films owe their being to memory reinforces that sense in which the mourning film, like the woman's melodramas of the past, revolves around and is a product of the singular settings of consciousness.

Memories are not the only things of the past on which the mourning film dwells. A recurring scene is that in which survivors peruse the belongings of the dead. In *Three Colors: Blue*, the film lapses into visionary expression when Julie comes across Anna's blue crystal mobile. Significantly, it is the only thing she takes with her to her new home. The over-determined quality of the mobile is felt in its color, which gives its name to the film, and in the blissful cinematography which invests it with vitality unforeseen during Anna's lifetime. As a conduit for light, it holds Julie's somber gaze. We are reminded of the words of Saint Paul to the Corinthians in the dedication to love celebrated in the concerto she will complete. But if Julie seems to look through a glass darkly at the beginning of the film, we later see her basking in the Parisian sun, herself becoming a conduit for the light. Other scenes of reminiscence lack the studied divinity of *Three Colors: Blue*, but carry powerful freights nevertheless. In *Secrets and Lies*, Cynthia's attic is like a reliquary in which she stores her dead mother's belongings. Following Jamie's death, in *Truly, Madly, Deeply*, Nina's flat becomes a shrine to their relationship. In *Moonlight and Valentino*, Rebecca is invited to Ben's office to peruse his belongings but leaves everything as it was. What is at stake in these scenes is precisely what is at stake in the genre. In a modern culture which encourages endless renewal and replacement, the perusal of old belongings emphasizes how invisible history has become. Foretelling this setting, in *The Innocents* and *The Haunting* nurseries become powerful sites of memory and loss, in Markway's words "pressure cookers" in which the things of the past — a music box, a child's desk — will become baleful reminders. While all corridors seem to lead to it, in *The Haunting* the interior of the nursery is never shown. Hill House is a Victorian folly, its spaces cluttered and obfuscated by layers of baroque Grand Tour spoils. Insistently signifying the past in the present, such spaces actualize that Deleuzian sense in which time exists on varying levels of comprehension and interpretation. Shut away, the things of the past embody the contradictions of presence and absence, retention and repression which are essential to mourning and its narratives, becoming elliptical reminders of histories which these films suggest or imply. Suggestion, inference and implication are modes of telling appropriate to a genre which tells from the inside out. *The Innocents* and *The Haunting* bequeath an urge to investigate the "inside" of the past, a project which in mourning films from *Don't Look Now* to *The Orphanage* will chart the tensions of loss as narratives of damaged interiority negotiating spaces of reminiscence and projections of desire. Charged spaces at the confluence of reminiscence and desire mark mourning cinema from the rhizome behind the credits of *Hiroshima mon amour* to the tunnel where Sean died in *Birth*, itself a "room" in which reminiscence and desire meet.

In the mourning film's chronicle of consciousness, the space of the séance could be read as an archaic ritual not without similarities with the cluttered rooms of reminiscence. Staging the prospect of mourners waiting for emanations of a space beyond visible space, what could be described as the film's own interiority, the séance delineates the characteristic narrative and emotional bearing of the mourning film. *Don't Look Now* provides a seminal example. While the sisters' quarters are cluttered with a veritably Barthesian array of old photographs, Heather's visions link the present and the past, provide solace for Laura, and assist in the process whereby John becomes aware of his second sight, which will eventually crack open the film's baleful metaphysic. *Moonlight and Valentino* and *The Orphanage* see the séance offering entrance into the characteristically psychological space of the mourning film. In the

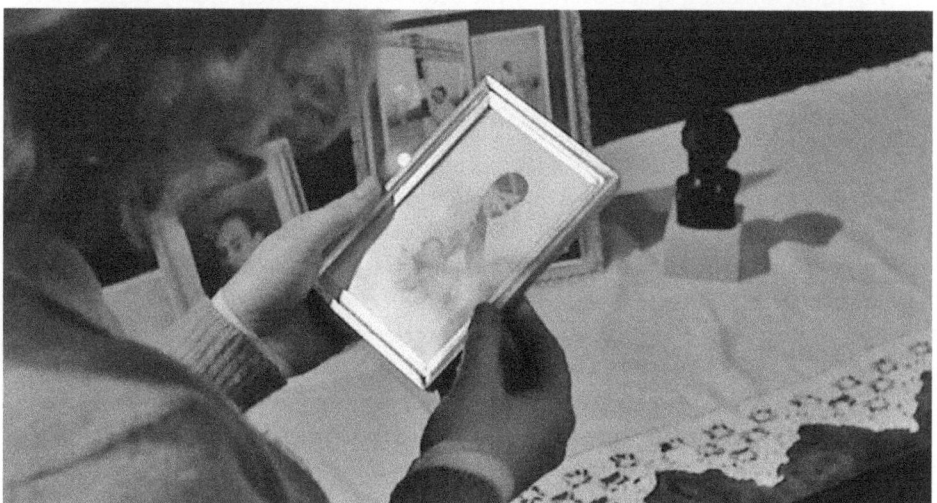

Don't Look Now. Like permanent visitations at a perpetual séance, the photographs which Laura peruses in *Don't Look Now* add another layer of temporality to the sisters' damp Venetian apartment.

former, the graveyard ritual is a kind of séance in which Rebecca is reconciled with Ben's death. In the latter, the séance seems like another element, a parallel universe which Laura observes via a closed circuit television monitor, the medium Aurora (Geraldine Chaplin) looking on screen as though she is under water, or not on the same temporal plane as Laura. The fact that we see Aurora in a high-collared black dress, a flickering figure in a film, here proposes the séance as a kind of occult heritage site, a mood foretold by the somewhat "theme park" didacticism of *The Haunting*. Like *The Haunting* and *Don't Look Now*, *The Orphanage* indulges skepticism about the séance. But skepticism has the effect of reinforcing the credibility of a beleaguered pitiful psychology which yearns to believe. While rehearsing doubts, by its very nature the mourning film inclines towards the mourner and the emotional context which accompanies them. Séances in mourning films owe their power to ambivalence to the extent that ambivalence portends emotional energies and a suggestiveness which are unique to the genre. Thus in *Don't Look Now* the faintly sexualized tone of Heather's experiences and her infatuated response to John is played off against the fact that Laura needs the succor Heather provides. In *The Orphanage* the air of charlatanism is in part dispelled by Aurora's vaguely Deleuzian talk of parallel timelines causing events in the past to effect the present. As in the epistemology of the locked room, the mourning film derives its power from its refusal to let history be. By exhibiting skepticism towards the institution of the séance even as they exploit its dramatic potential, mourning films inhabit a space between the dead and the living, one of suggestion, inference and implication which the mourner must inhabit every day.

Characteristic Narrative Syntax

In a type preoccupied with telling stories from a specific perspective, narrative organization in the mourning film is saliently involved with how the mourner addresses the world. To varying extents, a confessional narrative register animates *Hiroshima mon amour, Cries and Whispers, Interiors, Truly, Madly, Deeply, Ponette, Kissed, Under the Skin, Birth, The Barbarian Invasions*, and *A Very Long Engagement*. This register manifests itself as voiceover narration in *Hiroshima mon amour, Cries and Whispers, Interiors, Truly, Madly, Deeply, Kissed, Under the Skin*, and *A Very Long Engagement*. Testimonies take various forms: narrative-as-confession (*Hiroshima mon amour, Interiors, Truly, Madly, Deeply, Kissed, Under the Skin, A Very Long Engagement, Tatie Danielle* [Etienne Chatilez, 1990]); narrative-as-recollection (*Cries and Whispers, Interiors, Kissed, Under the Skin, Birth*); narrative-as-diary (*Interiors*); or narrative-as-audiovisual-accompaniment, as in the skype transmission in *The Barbarian Invasions*. The voiceover has a distinguished mourning forebear in

The Haunting in which Eleanor charts her disintegration in a tone the melancholy of which reinforces her growing detachment from others and presages her death. The voiceover as a commentary on the present and as a premonition of demise is rare in the modern mourning film, yet by its very nature this disembodiment of sound from image facilitates the film's journey through space and time, the transcendent voice suggesting that there are spaces where the character is no more and, by implication, a time when they are no more. Transcendence makes the voiceover peculiarly suited to the mourning narrative. The confessional register can also cue the visual narrative. Prompted by the narration, flashbacks associated with memories punctuate the action in *Hiroshima mon amour, Cries and Whispers, Interiors* and *Kissed*, literalizing the mourner's attempt to traverse and master time, perhaps to reclaim life from death.

While narrative devices reminiscent of literature betray the influence of melodrama on the mourning film, there is a visual narrative legacy the roots of which go back to Méliès and spiritualism. If the odd and eerie influence of horror can be felt in this legacy, it also enables the mourning film to realize vertical, rather than horizontal, narrative ambitions consonant with its exploration of subjectivity. Hallucinations extend the film's ability to realize this project while tracing the influence of horror and the modernist avant-garde on the genre. Hallucinatory visions and sounds occur in *After Death, Un chien andalou, The Curse of the Cat People, The Innocents, Carnival of Souls, The Haunting*, bequeathing an uneasy patina to imagery in *Cries and Whispers, Interiors, Under the Skin, Under the Sand, Birth* and *Truly, Madly, Deeply*. Almost as shocking are sudden appearances of living characters in *Interiors, Birth* and *The Orphanage*, a device envisaged in *Rebecca*. The sudden precipitate appearance is another way in which the type evokes the emotions associated with hallucination, since in these films visual style makes no distinction between hallucination and sudden appearances. The relationship between what is seen and what is imagined which is so seminal to the mourning film was foreseen by Hitchcock. In *Rebecca*, the camera pans across a room to the voiceover account of a woman's movements on the night of her death. The effect is so vivid that we could be watching her moving across the room. That the seen Other of the mourning film can be either real or supernatural, spectral or mental, suggests the extent to which the hallucinatory register is a narration of subjectivity to complement the type's tortured confessionals. In the mourning film, the hallucinated object is as much the symptom of a straitened pathology as it appears to be its cause, since by its very nature the mourning film is a dramatization of presence. This irrevocable relationship is borne out in charged narrative spaces which seem to call presence into being. With its row upon row of mislaid objects, the lost property office in *Under the Skin* contains such energies as to invoke the ghost of Iris's mother (Rita Tushingham). In *Truly, Madly, Deeply*, the camera pans across Nina's flat to alight upon a ghost. In *Birth*, a little boy appears at a birthday celebration. Is this what they see or is this what they feel? It is the contestability of narrative space in the mourning film which makes it so alluring, enchanting, and always cinematically resonant.

Off-screen and indeterminate space and sound is another way in which the mourning film dramatizes the relationship between subjectivity and the objective world. In its involvement in subjectivity, the mourning film is defined by the obscure play of the seen, the withheld and the opaque. Horror cinema bequeaths a powerful narrative device. *The Curse of the Cat People*, *The Spiral Staircase*, and *The Haunting* exploit the possibilities of the space which cannot be seen. *Three Colors: Blue*, *Birth*, *The Sheltering Sky*, *Interiors* and *Under the Sand* are marked by the excessive energies of spaces off-screen or never entered. In *Three Colors: Blue*, the moment when the young man beats on Julie's door following a street fracas evokes thundering doors in *The Haunting*, disembodied noise in *The Others* and *The Orphanage*. The schematic emphasis on sound and color in *Three Colors: Blue* also reiterates that which cannot be seen, bursts of music, tungsten halogen lamps glimpsed through a car window, an efflorescence of blue, veil narrative space yet metonymically suggest how exterior space affects the character. The blue shows as much as it hides. In *The Sheltering Sky*, characters are led away into spaces they do not recognize, the film proposing what is off-screen as a precipitate space teetering on the brink of knowledge and something unbearable. We are reminded of those moments in *The Haunting* as Eleanor strays, or seems to be taken, away from the others. In *Birth*, we become aware that the *mise-en-scène* is more extensive, but more mysterious, than it first appears. What is at stake in the use of off-screen space in the mourning film is its premonition of death, the prospect of a world in which the subject does not exist, the idea that demise is a place to which we are going but cannot know what it looks like. Describing civil existence as she envisaged it in prison, Juliette in *I've Loved You So Long* evokes the perfect metaphor for subjectivity faced with its own end, yet constrained by the bars of language, and a space made terrible by its absence: "A world without me."

By its very nature, editing cuts one image from another, and in the cut there is a space which, like offscreen space, can conceal as much as the cut reveals. If what we recall is camera movement and long takes contributing to that contemplative and melancholy atmosphere which the genre has made its own, editing's revelatory capacity lends itself in striking ways to the theme of mourning. Torn between the world of the living and that of the dead, editing is a way of intercutting between spaces of present and past, such as between Hiroshima and Nevers, or between adulthood and childhood in *Cries and Whispers* and *Interiors*. Cutting for shock value is rare, primarily acknowledging the mourning film's debt to horror. Cuts to the boy at the birthday party, and as Clara looks in *Birth*, recall Miss Giddens's look followed by the cut to the ghost in *The Innocents*. In *Under the Sand*, Marie looks down the beach and there is a cut to Jean standing looking out to sea. Bridging the gap between images, these ellipses, that which is "present" because so obviously absent, speak the anxiety of characters longing to see beyond absence. Sometimes the protagonist's look is followed by a cut to some shocking natural object; swarming ants, a maggot, a mouse, bridging that space between subjectivity and the abject over which the mourning film frets. Like the genre's characteristically lingering take, cutting can be contemplative too. In *Interiors*, Joey looks through a window and there is a cut to what she recalls; she and her sisters on the beach as children. It is as though the film is "looking" in a certain way, "knowing" something the protagonist does not any longer know. Occasionally, demise is characterized objectively as an immanent reality. In *Hiroshima mon amour* there is a series of edits between images of Hiroshima citizenry following the atomic blast as it is narrated by the woman. By classical standards, it is an irrational sequence. The images do not follow one another but are added to one another, a series of atrocity photographs each de-framed in relation to the next, placed one on top of the last. It is a catalog of horror, a mood echoed in the woman's voice as she speaks as though uttering a litany. The didactic quality of this sequence reminds the spectator of how like a documentary *Hiroshima mon amour* often is, its melancholy marriage of public horror and private agony true to its pessimistic modernist provenance. Used to establish a certain context and certain ideas in the spectator's mind, documentary's "public" mode of address, its patina of "official" history, seems far from the private account which *Hiroshima mon amour* becomes, and the catalog of micro-histories which the mourning genre is. Apparently objective montages occur as establishing sequences in *Cries and Whispers* and *Interiors*, taking the form of a series of edits from room to room, a leisurely ontology all the more noticeable for presaging narratives of sensibility and subjectivity. The montage can also be used to signify the character's mania, their stasis and detachment. In *The Innocents* the film seems to tease the protagonist as she tries to sleep, and an extraordinary sequence of dancing figures assails her consciousness. In Marie's journey in *Under the Sand*, scenes of the French countryside are seen through the train window while she is still in the foreground.

Fades, dissolves and slow motion envisage the passage of time and the inevitability of endings, or, as in the ellipsis, some unbidden state of consciousness. Their use in the mourning film is foreseen in *The Innocents* in which almost every scene ends with a dissolve, suggesting Miss Giddens's neurosis. *Cries and Whispers* suggests mortal paranoia by fades to red. The mournful tone of *Jude* and *The Barbarian Invasions* is reiterated at the end of many scenes by slow fades to black, while the fade to black following the car crash in *Three Colors: Blue* announces the film's preoccupation with its protagonist's retreat from the world. Fades at the beginning of *Morvern Callar* evoke the film's preoccupation with mortality, but as with the blue frame washes in *Three Colors: Blue* they also suggest the character's soporific demeanor. The blissful series of dissolves of Sean in *Birth* has been noted, but the passage of everything and everyone into the past is neatly expressed in that fade of Sean in the tree, leaving the spectator with a darkening photograph of the boy. We are reminded of the way in which, in *Jules et Jim*, a freeze frame "memorializes" Catherine (Jeanne Moreau). In *Moonlight and Valentino*, the combined use of slow motion and the dissolve when Rebecca is told that Ben has died evokes the effect of water or tears running over the lens. Music reiterates the theme of subjectivity becoming "smeared" across the scene, a fugue in which the initial theme is disseminated to other parts of the orchestra. This scene recalls that oddly fluid shot in *Don't Look Now* in which Laura collapses in slow motion, upsetting a restaurant table, providing a model for the film's cinematographic conflation of swirling fluids and deranged interiority. The flickering elliptical scene in the nightclub at the end of *Morvern Callar* finds an embryonic precedent at the moment in which we see Iris dancing in slow motion in a nightclub in *Under the Skin*. The mourning film's heritage in melodrama is evoked in *Birth* in the fade at the end of that scene in which Anna apologizes to Joseph, the device, as noted, seeming reminiscent of the iris in Griffith's work. The final shot of *Interiors*, in which the sisters look out of the window before the image slowly fades out, is one of the film's most striking effects. In an odd reversal of the fade's usual function, in *After Death* the recollection of a meeting in a park with a woman who is now dead is evoked as stark black figures fading in like a photographic negative passing into positive.

Characteristic Visual Style

In a genre committed to narrating subjectivity, the already problematic distinction between the syntax which propels a film's narrative and the issue of visual style becomes pronounced. But it may be possible to discern a particular look with which mourning cinema comes into its own. These are slow contemplative works that are dedicated to a narrative progression tied not to active agendas but to a passive process of psychological healing. Such dedication to the mourner's rehabilitation makes for a leisurely pace, one that encourages the spectator to notice the look of the film, an issue reinforced from within the narrative by moments in which the mourner emphasizes the tactility of the film's surfaces. Given the measured quality of narrative and the emphasis on surfaces and textures, the plaudits for cinematography habitually mobilized by Anglo-American critics writing of art cinema seem most relevant to the mourning film. By this light, even a conventional work like *Moonlight and Valentino* encourages a scrutiny more likely to register balmy woods and ochre sunrises, a project underwritten by a narrative preoccupation with painting, while *Three Colors: Blue* often seems to be *about* color and reflectivity.

In *Cries and Whispers*, *Three Colors: Blue* and *Ponette*, color underwrites a deliberate attempt to put interiority on screen. Historical precedents for this play can be found in *After Death* and *Portrait of Jennie*. Tinting enhances scenes in which the dead Zoia appears to the sleeping Andrei (Vitol'd Polonskii), and in the climactic storm sequence in *Portrait of Jennie*. What is interesting about these films is the way in which the idealism suggested by tinting is that of adults who are in many respects still children. When her mother reappears to Ponette, the color, naturalistic until now, becomes deeper, less realistic but more resonant for the child's realization that her mourning is hers and must be negotiated on her terms. The mourning film is no less visually noticeable than when it de-emphasizes color. Whether as a means of anchoring the drama in a verisimilitudinous space, according to a notion widespread in critical writing and popular perception alike that monochrome codifies the past, or whether expressing the "grey" world of the mourner, black-and-white cinematography or washed-out color appears in *The Sheltering Sky* and *Jude*, and in *Interiors* and *Truly, Madly, Deeply*. These varying symbolic orders coalesce in big commemorative works such as *Schindler's List* and *Saving Private Ryan*, which on the one hand seek to mark historical disasters, thus aspire to the monochrome convention, while chromatically suggesting the emotional consequences of loss. This "grey" look in the modern mourning film is also not without precedent. There is a tradition of films in which monochrome cinematography signifies the realm of the dead, in films as disparate as *A Matter of Life and Death* and *Alice*. Subtly insinuating narrative continuity, color in the mourning film should not be seen simply as a matter of decorative effect. It is a matter of visual style underwriting a style of life, a malaise which for some drains experience of light and radiance, while for others, as if some inner prism has been broken, tints everything with one glaring hue.

If color is a primary symptom of the mourning film's commitment to a vertical rather than a horizontal narrative, the vertical trend is sometimes punctuated by effects which seem entirely decorative. There are moments in mourning films which draw upon popular beliefs and imagery concerning the afterlife, seeming to exceed the films' narrative momentum. In emulation of traditional preconceptions about celestial and heavenly space, at such moments the films "stop" in contemplation of the natural sublime. Classical melodrama, whether secular—Bauer, Borzage—or religious—Dreyer, *The Song of Bernadette*—foresee this tendency. Glinski (Andrei Gromov) in Bauer's *The Dying Swan* utters the Romantic theology informing the link between demise and the celestial: "the most sublime peace is in death." Ultimate human destiny is sometimes expressed as a memory. At the end of *Cries and Whispers*, the sisters are recalled playing by a swing on a spring afternoon, and in *Interiors* the sisters' recollections are typically cast as happy moments by the seashore on a day now long gone. In other films, destiny is suggested by the everyday sublime. In *Truly, Madly, Deeply*, an establishing shot of a London park shows the grass and a huge sky arching overhead in a moment during which the film takes respite from a rather talky claustrophobic intensity. In an interesting contrast with those shots in *Birth*, which seem to "pull" Anna away from life and towards the prospect of an afterlife, in *Moonlight and Valentino* the opening shot is a picturesque slow pan through spring woods to Rebecca calling for Ben. Later, the film's uncomplicated belief in respite from grief is suggested by a connecting shot of the sun rising over a lake. As Rémy dies by the lakeside in *The Barbarian Invasions*, the camera tilts up at the pines swaying in the wind. If we read an allusion to the popular imaginary into that scene in *A Very Long Engagement* in which Mathilde is reconciled with her husband in a sunlit glade — "In the sweetness of the air, in the light of the garden" — the scene overturns this supposedly life-affirming resolution, especially in the light of an earlier moment in which Mathilde stands alone amid what appears to be a heavenly meadow of crosses. Finally, in *Titanic* and in *Kissed*, celestially-lit close-ups of grieving women suggest the bliss of having loved and lost in a manner which bears the heritage of mourning cinema's commitment to heavenly solace.

Characteristic Performance Style

The characteristic performance style of the mourning film has evolved out of a complex negotiation of the type's historical forebears. The protagonists of high modernist works like *Hiroshima mon amour*, *Cries and Whispers*, *Don't Look Now* and *Interiors* remain resonant models for modern mourning heroines, although the emphasis on dialogue and stylized performances in those films tends to foreground verbal reflection as explanations of their protagonists' actions and looks, whereas recent mourning films tend to play the vicissitudes of grief off physical instances of gesture and demeanor tailored astutely to the mourner's situation. If speaking of the dead is too difficult, the face of the modern mourning heroine is as likely to bear meaning as what she says. This emphasis on appearances resonates with the mourning film's historical roots but also has consequences for the type's institutional status.

The preoccupation with death and finitude in high modernism is combined with ambitious individual performances in recent mourning films. *Three Colors: Blue, Morvern Callar Under the Sand, Ponette, Birth* and *I've loved You So Long* showcase searching and emotional acting turns from accomplished

The Barbarian Invasions. Such sylvan imagery sees the mourning film take brief respite from its mission of human distress, suggesting perhaps the ancient consolations of a natural cycle in which death is merely one stage.

and charismatic stars. While resonating with modernism's experimental rigor, these films descend from a rich tradition of melodramas designed around the performances of individual personalities. Revolving around some of the most beautiful and charismatic actors of their generation, recent mourning films offer opportunities for the elaboration of nuanced and emotional performances. *Hiroshima mon amour* and *Interiors* were seminal because they mapped cinema's serious interest in mourning in an era during which art cinema tested the parameters for representing taboo subjects. These films could be said to have proposed themselves as Freudian "talking cures." But recent mourning films have seen the genre evolving from academicism into a classical phase wherein the preoccupation with mourning embodies a more integrated facility with theme and histrionic attitude, responding more fluidly to currents in film history. In contrast with dramas that stage death as a high-minded conundrum of the human condition, recent mourning films are more able to get inside the lives of specific individuals as they negotiate extreme situations. In an era during which the institutional distinctions between high art cinema and mainstream currents became increasingly blurred, it is a sign of the maturing of the mourning film that the aspirations of experimental modernism are tempered by responsiveness to popular cinematic aesthetics. It is worth recalling that such contemporary divas of mourning cinema as Charlotte Rampling, Juliette Binoche, and Kristin Scott Thomas have all successfully made the passage from French cinema to the Anglo arthouse, blurring the distinction between art cinema and the multiplex and reinforcing the mourning film's international profile. The allure of an emerging pantheon of actors is as crucial to the modern mourning film as the ambitions of its auteur. As in the heyday of classical melodrama, mourning films revolve around female stars and their histrionics. If in *Interiors*, Geraldine Page strides sedately into the sea, a diva till the very end, in a tragic moment Rampling's Marie stares balefully at a ringing phone, her down-turned mouth evoking every bit a revenant Bette Davis. For precursors of mourning performativity, we should look to the increasingly histrionic and physical countenances of Deborah Kerr, Candace Hilligoss and Julie Harris. Here are suggestive templates for Julie and Iris's delinquent behavior, for Juliette and Ponette's frustrated outbursts, for Marie and Morvern's automaton behavior, and for the perplexity which Julie, Morvern, Juliette and Ponette arouse in the communities in which they find themselves. Catherine Deneuve, star of Ozon's *8 Women*, could have foreseen the flowering of the modern mourning film when she told *Libération*, "I am not sure Ozon likes women, but he likes actresses" (cited in Vincendeau 2002: 46).

In the modern mourning film, mourning is as much physiological as psychological, with all the implications for unseemly realism that this suggests. While one of the sisters weeps vociferously in *Cries and Whispers*, the modern mourner is made deliberately unglamorous by her travails. If Eleanor and Miss Giddens are driven to the brink of tears, the scene in *Truly, Madly, Deeply* in which Nina breaks down before her counselor sees the star of the mourning film testing the limits of modern melodrama in a sustained and messy moment in which grief is overwhelmingly visceral, smearing the beautiful face with tears and mucus. As Port dies in *The Sheltering Sky*, Debra Winger emotes with disheveled and unselfconscious candor. For some performers of mourning histrionics even the prospect of facing the camera is too much, so they take their performance to another place, as when Isabelle Blais as Sylvaine in *The Barbarian Invasions*, overcome with emotion, turns away from the skype camera, or when Marie looks down and wretches up her grief in *Under the Sand*. In a type which has emphasized cinema's commitment to presence and absence, tears become the ghastly "hidden" of the genre, in Žižekian terms its "fright," the equivalent of the sight of the ghost in horror. If the mourning film revolves around the presence of the mourning actor just as the horror film revolved around the "presence" of the ghost, the sight of the actor breaking down is a moment of excess the extremity of which was inconceivable in a classical woman's picture. With this more physiological style of performance, the mourning film announces its maturity. While classical melodrama reserved its choicest moments for the beautiful visage, the impeccable star "suffering in mink," visceral climaxing in the mourning film acknowledges grief's physiological dimensions, extending melodrama's remit. Implicit in the breakdown in lovely composure is a more comprehensive acknowledgment of interiority, one which recognizes the congruence between looks and feelings, glamour and subjectivity, public and private spaces, the star's charisma and the obligation to "live" the role. Aside from extending cinema's capacity to represent, such visceral moments extend the mourning film's preoccupation with the abject. In passing from the immaculate to the abject, indeed in "dressing" the dead as if for a date in *Kissed*, Sandra lives out this space between the beautiful and the disgusting which so many mourning heroines broach.

Quiet contemplation is also central to the mourning mien. This pensive or preoccupied look back at or past the spectator, illustrated on numerous Region 2 DVD cases — *Three Colors: Blue*, *Birth*, *Morvern Callar*, *I've Loved You So Long*, *Ponette*, *Under the Sand*, *Interiors*— announces the genre's preoccupation with opaque and unpredictable subjectivity. The mourning protagonist is depicted as a traumatized figure startled, or abstracted, by grief. By exceeding salutary conventions of screen glamour, this pathological appearance proposes another kind of beauty. Here is not the glamour of the conventional cinematic icon/object, but the allure of a woman marked by history, a being in a certain time and place: weathered, singular and transcendent.

The "woman of mystery" is one of cinema's enduring icons. The mourning heroine may be her most compelling contemporary exemplar. The protagonists of *Three Colors: Blue*, *Under the Skin*, *Under the Sand*, *Kissed*, *Morvern Callar* and *I've Loved You So Long* bear an enigmatic legacy into modern cinema. Late classical horror bequeaths incongruity. We wonder why Mary studies her hands as she plays in *Carnival of Souls*. We wonder why Eleanor is so mercurial. We could cite Mrs. Danvers in *Rebecca*, or the basilisk women of Lewton's horror films for a look emphasizing the pathological potentialities of grief. With her sunken eyes, Scott Thomas even recalls the monstrous vampiric woman of horror cinema. Menace and melancholy are the twin poles of

Genova. There one moment, gone the next, Marianne appears and disappears to the grieving Mary with chilling ingenuity, here like an angel in a medieval alley. The debt which *Genova* owes to *Don't Look Now* resides in these dank spaces of the mind.

I've Loved You So Long. Sullen, unreadable, the face of the mourning is an unknown landscape, so many roads once, now so many culs-de-sac.

this enigma. Falconetti and Carrez's performances as Jeanne d'Arc, or Jennifer Jones's in *The Song of Bernadette* and *Portrait of Jennie*, are models for modern mourning heroines, emphasizing mourning's devotional aspect, a kind of beautiful melancholy which came to define Binoche's star image just as it did Jones's. The look is inherently impacted, with pain or bliss, simultaneously at the film's center and at a remove, both protagonist and effigy. While Julie suggests the unemotional, the shut down, and Sandra the blissful, "kissed" by metaphysics, Juliette seems agonized and soporific, as sullen as Eleanor, as blank as Julie, yet occasionally overtaken by a contentment which is nearly ethereal.

The mourning film's emphasis on interiority renders the relationship between its heroine's characteristic mien and her inner states obscure, just as it alienates subjectivity from the material world. Yet occasionally the type's dramatic charge consists in the light this haggard visage occasionally throws on subjectivity. Hence the scene in *I've Loved You So Long* in which Juliette is reminded of prison life, her face registering each memory with a wince. Or those scenes in which Morvern's smile suggests devastating ambivalence. For a merciful moment, Julie's look seems to reconnect her to the world around her, and all too briefly, us to her. If the mourning heroine appears "difficult" to the spectator, the necessity of articulating in words how she feels turns either to rage, as for Juliette, to a cryptic facial code, as for Anna, to a breezy negotiation, as for Marie, or back into silence before a history which resists being spelled out.

Conclusion

"I do think there's a need within us ... to believe that those who have gone and whom we dearly loved ... are constantly within us or around us."

Krzysztof Kieślowski

As discussed in detail elsewhere, there is a scene in a Spanish cemetery in *Morvern Callar* that is signally effective because it is completely silent. From beginning to end, we hear no dialogue and scarcely any sound. Other moments in *Three Colors: Blue*, *Birth* and *Don't Look Now* derive their power from their silence, or more precisely their lack of language. While the mourning film's forebears in horror featured the rapt negotiation of an utterly non-linguistic unearthly space beyond words, and melodrama aspired to a realm of pure feeling represented as music and color, mourning films too regard silence not as a gap in coherence but as another kind of coherence, an aesthetic resource expressive of the intensities of grief and contemplation. This book set out from the assumption that verbal language is inadequate to the expression of finitude and how we feel about the end of life. As we have seen, this essential conundrum of death's inexpressibility is played out in the silent nocturnal restlessness of *Cries and Whispers*, John's long odyssey through echoing Venetian alleyways in *Don't Look Now*, and scenes at the end of *Interiors* and *Under the Sand* as the protagonists look out to sea and words desert them. Just as the missing moments of off-screen space and the ellipses of editing testify to its investment in absence, and incipient presence, the mourning film incorporates silence into its aesthetic. The film, like the mourner, cannot verbally acknowledge the import of what has been lost and so the retreat into silence becomes its form of expression. If absence takes on presence in the mourning film, silence finds something like a voice of its own. Significantly, many mourning protagonists, such as Mrs. Danvers, Julie Vignon, Morvern Callar, Juliette Fontaine, are identified by their silence, inscrutability, the lack of speech as the condition of being. If the screenplays of high modernist mourning forebears *Hiroshima mon amour* and *Interiors* rigorously attempted to verbally articulate and testify to loss, modern mourning cinema is characterized by attempts to articulate loss as precisely the void between words, the gap which separates grief from its enunciation, the loss from its performance, and modern mourning from the comforts and platitudes of the past.

This "return to silence" is appropriate to the expression of an experience which in its tendency to overwhelm, typically undermines the attempt to articulate and rationalize. Hence we are confronted with the plethora of psychological shades and behaviors through which the mourner expresses herself, a repertoire with, as we have seen, implications for the recent performance of grief and the emergence of a mourning star. The taking refuge in silence affords cinema a broader expressive potential, a renewed emphasis on the image which reiterates and tests a film's potential for invention and ambivalence. We have only to compare the conventional expressions of grief in melodramas such as *Millions Like Us* or *Since You Went Away* with grief's expression in *After Death*, *Cries and Whispers* or *Birth* to recognize the baleful limitations classical continuity has wrought over an experience so convoluted and unpredictable. Death has proved a gift to the cinema's most experimental instincts. Indeed, one might argue that the modern mourning film looks back across several decades and speaks to cinema's earliest manifestations. As a theme, mourning broaches the issue of absence and presence that is so fundamental to cinema. Mourning cinema's return to silence, then, re-enacts the medium's earliest silences. Each in its way, *After Death*, *The Dying Swan*, *Destiny* and *7th Heaven* were meditations on absence, so that from the start, we see how the performance of mourning in cinema released unusual and vivid energies in the image. Perhaps mourning cinema's use of silence as a resource recalls the convention of silence as commemorative tribute in the wider world. The deployment of silence in the mourning film adds to its claim to expressive individuality while simultaneously acknowledging that the real experience of grief may be an uncelebrated form of art.

This study set out to explore the possibility that films which thematize mourning might constitute a genre in their own right. Its emphasis has been on advocacy; of an analytical optic based on theme, of a fresh film-historical perspective, of individual and variously under-examined films, of a new aesthetics, a new terminology, a new approach to conceiving genre, and a particular gender bias. This wide-ranging exploratory mission has, of necessity, resulted in certain ellipses. In the mourning film there are invariably two stories. While *Rebecca* has been fêted by feminists for its emphasis on networks of female desire, it remains crucially a film about male grief. There is an essay to be written around Ruth Fowler's grief in *In the Bedroom* and the way Sissy Spacek rehearses it, but the film's narrative motor is her husband's own coming to terms with the tragedy. John Baxter's fate is inextricably bound up with his grief. It seems obvious, therefore, that future work on the representation of mourning attends to male mourning and its impact on cinema's well established repertoire of masculine images.

Another area little attended to here has been the examination of types of death and the play of specific relationships after death occurs. By taking matters into their own hands, the suicidal individual overcomes the conundrum by which demise is simultaneously inevitable yet a mystery. Suicides lie at the heart of *Interiors* and *Morvern Callar*, raising the issue of the specific scars it leaves, and the degree of agency and perspective involved in the decision to envisage or cause one's own death. No distinction either has been acknowledged in this study between the death of adults and the death of children. *Don't Look Now*, *Three Colors: Blue* and *I've Loved You So Long* revolve crucially around the death of a child. *Ponette* revolves around a child's responses to death. While wives and lovers become bereft in five of the films studied here, in *Don't Look Now*, *Interiors* and *Cries and Whispers* mothers, daughters and sisters mourn. In *Festen*, a mother, a sister and her brothers mourn the passing of a sibling by suicide. Attention could usefully turn to the specific sense of loss experienced by different family members given various scenarios of loss, and the impact this has on specific familial dynamics.

This study touched briefly upon the social and psychiatric role films of mourning can play in the reparation of loss. Having theorized the possibility of a genre around grief, it seems important that it be seen not simply as another academic and critical category, but envisaged as a resource to be drawn upon by the therapeutic community, what Catherine Grant, introducing a roster of articles on the representation of mental illness in cinema, has referred to as "the increasingly 'film-curious' field of mental-health care" (Grant 2009). In this regard, it is worth recalling that in her preparations to play Marie Drillon, Charlotte Rampling drew on the experience of being in denial for thirty years following the loss of her sister to suicide. Mourning films are about something other than cinema. Consonant with an increasingly interdisciplinary tenor in higher education, this marriage between the aesthetic and the therapeutic could serve a much-needed purpose. If art can provide real people with a means of working through real problems, the mourning film can in its quiet way hold a mirror up to each individual's impending absence. This study, therefore, charts a history and a terrain which future research could usefully explore.

Bibliography

Aaron, M. 2011. http://www.wellbeingindying.org.uk/pdf/guidebook.pdf (accessed 13 June 2011).
Abraham, N., and Maria Torok. 1994. *The Shell and the Kernel: Renewals of Psychoanalysis.* 2 vols. Ed. and trans. Nicholas T. Rand. Chicago: Chicago University Press.
Addley, E. 2006. "Meet Mr. Rites." *The Guardian*, 3 June, 29.
Aitkenhead, D. 2005. "Our Mother Told Us Everything about Her Dying, Except That It Would Break Our Hearts." *The Guardian*, 29 October, 17–27.
Allen, M. 2003. *Contemporary US Cinema.* London: Pearson.
Allen, W. 1983. *Four Films of Woody Allen: Annie Hall, Interiors, Manhattan, Stardust Memories*, 2d ed. London: Faber & Faber.
Allende, I. 2005. *Paula.* London: Harper Perennial.
Altman, R. 2003. *Film/Genre*, 4th ed. London: British Film Institute.
Amiel, V. 1994. "Immersed in Passion: Three Colours: Blue, White, Red." In *Positif 50 Years: Selections from the French Film Journal.* Ed. Michel Ciment and Laurence Kardish. New York: Museum of Modern Art, 2004, pp. 243–245.
Andrew, G. 2000. "Sex." *National Film Theatre* program, November–December, 10–21.
Anthony El Saffar, R. 1994. *Rapture Engaged: The Suppression of the Feminine in Western Culture.* London: Routledge.
Ariès, P. 1983. *The Hour of Our Death.* Trans. Helen Weaver, 3d ed. London: Penguin.
Armstrong, R. 2002. "Lady in the Dark" http://www.thefilmjournal.com/Issue1/armstrongwilder.html (accessed 7 April 2009).
Armstrong, R., T. Charity, L. Hughes, and J. Winter. 2007. *The Rough Guide to Film.* London: Penguin/Rough Guides.
Artaud, A. 1976. *Selected Writings.* Ed. Susan Sontag, 2d ed. Berkeley: University of California Press.
Bálint Kovacs, A. 2007. *Screening Modernism: European Art Cinema, 1950–1980.* Chicago: University of Chicago Press.
Barthes, R. 2000. *Camera Lucida: Reflections on Photography*, 4th ed. London: Vintage Press.
Baxter, J. 1968. *Hollywood in the Thirties.* London: Tantivy Press/Zwemmer.
Bazin, A. 1970. *What Is Cinema?* 3d ed. Ed. Hugh Gray. 2 vols. Berkeley: University of California Press.
Belton, J. 1974. *The Hollywood Professionals: Howard Hawks, Frank Borzage & Edgar G. Ulmer.* 5 vols. London: Tantivy Press.
Benjamin, W. 1992. *Illuminations.* Ed. Hannah Arendt, trans. Harry Zohn. London: Fontana.
Beugnet, M. 2007. *Cinema and Sensation: French Film and the Art of Transgression.* Edinburgh: Edinburgh University Press.

Björkman, S. 1995. *Woody Allen on Woody Allen*, 2d ed. London: Faber and Faber.
Blackmore, E.H., and A.M. Blackmore, eds. 2000. *Six French Poets of the Nineteenth-Century*. Oxford: Oxford University Press.
Blanchot, M., and J. Derrida. 2000. *The Instant of My Death & Demeure: Fiction and Testimony*. Eds. Werner Hamacher and David E. Welbery, trans. Elizabeth Rottenberg. Stanford: Stanford University Press.
Bordwell, D. 1985. *Narration in the Fiction Film*. London: Methuen.
Bordwell, D., J. Staiger and K. Thompson. 1988. *The Classical Hollywood Cinema: Film Style and Mode of Production to 1960* 2d ed. London: Routledge.
Bordwell, D., and K. Thompson. 2008. *Film Art: An Introduction*, 4th ed. New York: McGraw-Hill.
Bowie, M. 1991. *Lacan*. London: Fontana.
Boycott, R. 2005. "A Crying Shame." *The Guardian*, 13 August, 5.
Bronfen, E. 1992. *Over Her Dead Body: Death, Femininity and the Aesthetic*. Manchester: Manchester University Press.
Brooks, X. 2002. "Morvern Callar." *Sight and Sound*, November, 50.
_____. 2006. "For One Moment It Was Possible to Dream That the Ending Would Be Different." *The Guardian*, 27 May, 29–33.
Brownlow, K., and J. Kobal, 1979. *Hollywood: The Pioneers*. London: Collins/Thames Television.
Brownlow, K., dir. 1998. *Universal Horror*. Turner Classic Movies.
Burns, P. 1999. "The History of the Discovery of Cinematography" http://www.precinemahistory.net/1830.html (accessed 10 July 2009).
Carney, R., and L. Quart. 2000. *The Films of Mike Leigh: Embracing the World*. Cambridge: Cambridge University Press.
Caruth, C., ed. 1995. *Trauma: Explorations in Memory*. Baltimore: Johns Hopkins University Press.
_____. 1996. *Unclaimed Experience: Trauma, Narrative and History*. Baltimore: Johns Hopkins University Press.
Castell, D. 1978. "Interiors." *Films Illustrated*, December, 142.
Chion, M. 1990. *Audio-Vision: Sound on Screen*. New York: Columbia University Press.
Clarke, R. 2004. "Grief Encounter." *Sight and Sound*, November, 22–24.
Clewell, T. 2000. "The Shades of Modern Mourning in *Three Colours* Trilogy." *Literature and Film Quarterly*, 28, 203–209.
Clover, C. J. 1992. *Men, Women and Chainsaws: Gender in the Modern Horror Film*. Princeton: Princeton University Press.
Coates, P. 1996. "The Sense of an Ending: Reflections on Kieślowski's Trilogy." *Film Quarterly*, 50, Winter, 96–97.
_____. 2002. "Kieślowski and the Antipolitics of Color: A Reading of the 'Three Colors' Trilogy." *Cinema Journal*, 41, Winter, 41–66.
Combs, R. 2007. "Living Rooms." *Sight and Sound*, August, 42–43.
Cook, P., and M. Bernink, eds. 1997. *The Cinema Book* 2d ed. London: British Film Institute.
Craddock, J. 2006. *Videohound's Golden Movie Retriever*. Detroit: Thomson Gale.
Craig, S.S. 2005. "Tu n'as rien vu à Hiroshima: Desire, Spectatorship and the vaporized subject in Hiroshima Mon Amour." *Quarterly Review of Film and Video*, 22, 25–35.
Critchley, S. 1997. *Very Little ... Almost Nothing: Death, Philosophy, Literature*. London: Routledge.
Darke, C. 2003. "Has Anyone Seen This Girl? Lynne Ramsay and Morvern Callar: The Chronicle of a Disappearance." *Vertigo* 2, 16–17.
Davis, C. 2007. *Haunted Subjects: Deconstruction, Psychoanalysis and the Return of the Dead*. London: Palgrave/Macmillan.

Deleuze, G. 2005 [1986]. *Cinema I: The Movement-Image*, 8th ed. Trans. Hugh Tomlinson, and Barbara Habberjam. London: Continuum.
_____. 2005 [1989]. *Cinema II: The Time-Image,* 8th ed. London: Continuum.
_____. 1995. *Negotiations, 1972–1990.* Trans. Martin Joughin. New York: Columbia University Press.
Dempsey, M. 1974. "Don't Look Now." *Film Quarterly,* Spring, 27, 39–43.
Diamond, D. 2007. "Loss, Mourning and Desire in Midlife: François Ozon's Under the Sand and Swimming Pool." In *Projected Shadows: Psychoanalytic Reflections on the Representation of Loss in European Cinema.* Ed. Andrea Sabbadini. London: Routledge, pp. 145–159.
Didion, J. 2005. *The Year of Magical Thinking.* New York: Fourth Estate.
_____. 2005. "In Another World." *The Guardian,* 1 October, 21.
_____. 2005. "The Year of Magical Thinking." *The Guardian,* 24 September, 4–5.
Dimendberg, E. 2004. *Film Noir and the Spaces of Modernity.* Cambridge: Harvard University Press.
Doane, M.A. 1988. *The Desire to Desire: The Woman's Picture of the 1940s,* 2d ed. (London: Palgrave/Macmillan.
Dobson, J. 1999. "Kieślowski's *Trois Couleurs: Bleu* (1993), *Blanc* (1993), *Rouge* (1994)." In *French Cinema in the 1990s: Continuity and Difference.* Ed. Phil Powrie. Oxford: Oxford University Press, pp. 234–245.
Dollimore, J. 1991. *Sexual Dissidence: Augustine to Wilde, Freud to Foucault.* Oxford: Clarendon Press.
_____. 1998. *Death, Desire and Loss in Western Culture.* London: Allen Lane.
Duncan, G. 2009. *Grief and Grieving—A Personal Testimonial.* unpublished.
Dyregrov, A. 2008. *Grief in Children: A Handbook for Adults.* London: Jessica Kingsley.
Dyson, J. 2006. "Fog and rain and long winter nights." In *The Innocents.* London: British Film Institute, DVD-ROM BFIVD675.
Elsaesser, T., and Warren Buckland, eds. 2002. *Studying Contemporary American Film: A Guide to Movie Analysis.* London: Arnold.
Erens, P., ed. 1990. *Issues in Feminist Film Criticism.* Bloomington: Indiana University Press.
Farrell, K. 1998. *Post-Traumatic Culture: Injury and Interpretation in the Nineties.* Baltimore: Johns Hopkins University Press.
Fischer, L. 1996. *Cinematernity: Film, Motherhood, Genre.* Princeton: Princeton University Press.
Frampton, D. 2006. *Filmosophy.* London: Wallflower.
Freeman, J. 2005. "A Painfully Poignant Study of Unimaginable Loss." *The Independent,* 27 October, 24.
Freud, S. 1991 [1907]. "Childhood Memories and Screen Memories." In the *Penguin Freud Library,* 6th ed., vol. 5. Ed. James Strachey. London: Penguin, pp. 83–93.
_____. 1991 [1915]. "Our Attitude Towards Death." In the *Penguin Freud Library,* vol. 12, pp. 77–89.
_____. 1991 [1917]. "Mourning and Melancholia." In the *Penguin Freud Library,* vol. 17. London: Penguin), pp. 243–258.
_____. 1991 [1919]. "The Uncanny." in the *Penguin Freud Library* vol. 14, pp. 336–376.
_____. 1991 [1926]. "Anxiety, Pain and Mourning." In the *Penguin Freud Library,* vol. 20, pp. 329–334.
_____. 1991 [1920]. "Beyond the Pleasure Principle." In *The Essentials of Psycho-Analysis* ed. by Anna Freud. London: Penguin), pp. 218–268.
_____. 1991 [1924]. "The Loss of Reality in Neurosis and Psychosis." In *The Essentials of Psycho-Analysis,* pp. 568–572.
Freud, S. 2005. *On Murder, Mourning and Melancholia.* London: Penguin.

Fuller, G. 2004. "Birth." *Sight and Sound*, December, 40.
Garland, C., ed. 1998. *Understanding Trauma: A Psychoanalytical Approach*. London: Duckworth.
Garwood, J. 2006. "Zwartboek." http://www.talkingpix.co.uk/ReviewsZwartboek.html (accessed 7 April 2009).
Gilbert, S. 2006. *Death's Door: Modern Dying and the Ways We Grieve*. New York: W.W. Norton.
Giles, J. 2008. "Dream Tickets." *Sight and Sound*, August, 28–40.
Gledhill, C. 1987. *Home Is Where the Heart Is: Studies in Melodrama and the Woman's Film*. London: British Film Institute.
Gorer, G. 1965. *Death, Grief and Mourning in Contemporary Britain*. London: Cresset Press.
Grant, B.K., ed. 1995. *Film Genre Reader II*. Austin: University of Texas Press.
_____, ed. 2003. *Film Genre Reader III*. Austin: University of Texas Press.
Grant, C. 2009. http://filmstudiesforfree.blogspot.com (accessed 13 September 2009).
Greene, N. 1999. *Landscapes of Loss: The National Past in Postwar French Cinema*. Princeton: Princeton University Press.
Griffiths, K., and D. Evans. 2009. *Haunting Presences: Ghosts in French Literature and Culture*. Cardiff: University of Wales Press.
Hallam, E., and J. Hockey. 2001. *Death, Memory and Material Culture*. Oxford: Berg.
Harding, L. 2005, "The Long Goodbye." *The Times Magazine*, 12 November, 57–64.
Harvey, J. 2002. *Movie Love in the Fifties*. Cambridge, MA: Da Capo.
Haskell, M. 1979. *From Reverence to Rape: The Treatment of Women at the Movies*. London: Penguin.
Hayward, S. 2006. *Cinema Studies: The Key Concepts*, 3d ed. London: Routledge.
Herman, J. 1994. *Trauma and Recovery*. London: Pandora.
Higham, C., and Greenberg, J. 1968. *Hollywood in the Forties*. London: Zwemmer.
Hill, J., and P. Church Gibson, eds. 1998. *The Oxford Guide to Film Studies*. Oxford: Oxford University Press.
Houston, P. 1960. "Hiroshima, Mon Amour." *Monthly Film Bulletin*, 27, 19–20.
Hughes, A., and J.S. Williams, eds. 2001. *Gender and French Cinema*. Oxford: Berg.
Humphrey, G.M., and D.G. Zimpfer 1996. *Counselling for Grief and Bereavement*. London: Sage.
Inwood, M. 1997. *Heidegger: A Very Short Introduction*. Oxford: Oxford University Press.
James, N. 2002. "Kind of Blue." *Sight and Sound*, April, 34–36.
Johnson, T.H., ed. 1975. *Emily Dickinson: The Complete Poems*. London: Faber.
Katz, E. 1998. *The Macmillan International Film Encyclopedia*, 3d ed. Rev. Fred Klein and Ronald Dean Nolen. London: Macmillan.
Kawin, B. 1978. *Mindscreen: Bergman, Godard and First-Person Film*. Princeton: Princeton University Press.
Kay, S. 2003. *Žižek: A Critical Introduction*. Cambridge: Polity.
Kemp, P. 2009. "Genova." *Sight and Sound*, April, 60.
Kieślowski, K. 2003. *Three Colours: Blue*. London: Artificial Eye, ART085DVD, DVD-ROM.
King, G., ed. 2005. *The Spectacle of the Real: From Hollywood to Reality TV and Beyond*. Bristol: Intellect.
Kitses, J. 1969. *Horizons West*. Bloomington: Indiana University Press.
Kolker, R.P. 1977. "The Open Texts of Nicolas Roeg." *Sight and Sound*, Spring, 82–84 and 113.
Konigsberg, I. 1988. *The Complete Film Dictionary*. London: Bloomsbury.
Kristéva, J. 1982. *Powers of Horror: An Essay on Abjection*. Trans. Leon S. Roudiez. New York: Columbia University Press.

Kübler-Ross, E. 2003. *On Death and Dying*. New York: Scribner.
Kuhn, A. 2008. *Ratcatcher*. London: British Film Institute.
Kuntzel, T. 2005. "Freaks Show." http://www.rouge.com.au/7/freaks.html (accessed 7 April 2009).
Lacan, J. 2004. *The Four Fundamental Concepts of Psycho-Analysis* 3d ed. Ed. Jacques-Alain Miller, trans. Alan Sheridan. London: Karnac.
Lake, T. 1988. *Living with Grief,* 3d ed. London: Sheldon.
Lant, A., and I. Periz, eds. 2006. *Red Velvet Seat: Women's Writing on the First Fifty Years of Cinema*. London: Verso.
Largier, L. 2004. *Hiroshima le temps d'un retour. Hiroshima, mon amour*. London: Nouveau Pictures, NPD1026 DVD-ROM.
Lawlor, L., and V. Moulard, 2004. "Henri Bergson." In *The Stanford Encyclopedia of Philosophy* www.plato.stanford.edu/entries/bergson (accessed 16 August 2009).
Lazaroff Alpi, D. 1998. *Robert Siodmak: A Biography, with Critical Analyses of His Films Noirs and a Filmography of All His Works*. Jefferson: McFarland.
Leader, D. 2009. *The New Black: Mourning, Melancholia and Depression*. London: Penguin.
Lebeau, V. 2001. *Psychoanalysis and Cinema: The Play of Shadows*. London: Wallflower.
Lewis, C.S. 1966. *A Grief Observed,* 2d ed. London: Faber.
Light, A. 1996. "Rebecca." *Sight and Sound*, May, 28–31. www.lovefilm.com 2009. [accessed 4 March 2009]
Marks, L.U. 2002. *Touch: Sensuous Theory and Multisensory Media*. Minneapolis: University of Minnesota Press.
Martin, A. 2006. Review of Mulvey, *Death 24x a Second: Stillness and the Moving Image*. *Cineaste*, Winter, 75–76.
Matheou, D. 2009. "The Family Way." *Sight and Sound*, April, 8.
Mayne, J. 1990. *The Woman at the Keyhole: Feminism and Women's Cinema*. Bloomington: Indiana University Press.
McHugh, K. 2007. *Jane Campion*. Urbana: University of Illinois Press.
Mellen, J. 1973. "Bergman and Women: Cries and Whispers." *Film Quarterly*, 26 Fall, 2–11.
Mendik, X., and S.J. Schneider, eds. 2002. *Underground USA: Filmmaking Beyond the Hollywood Canon*. London: Wallflower.
Mercken-Spaas, G. 1980. "Destruction and Reconstruction in Hiroshima, Mon Amour.'" *Literature and Film Quarterly* 8, 244–250.
Miller, L. 1998. "Titanic." *Sight and Sound*, February, 50–52.
Milne, T., and P. Houston. 1973. "Don't Look Now: Nicolas Roeg interviewed by Tom Milne and Penelope Houston." *Sight and Sound*, Winter, 2–8.
Mitry, J. 1963. *Dictionnnaire du cinéma*. Paris: Larousse.
Modleski, T. 1988. *The Women Who Knew Too Much: Hitchcock and Feminist Theory*. London: Routledge.
_____. 1999. *Old Wives' Tales: Feminist Re-Visions of Film and Other Fictions*. London: I.B. Tauris.
Moriarty, M. 1991. *Roland Barthes*. Cambridge: Polity. www.moviemail-online.co.uk. 2009. (accessed 4 March 2009).
Mulvey, L. 2006. *Death 24x Second: Stillness and the Moving Image*. London: Reaktion.
Nemerov, A. 2005. *Icons of Grief: Val Lewton's Home Front Pictures*. Berkeley: University of California Press.
Oates, J.C. 2011. *A Widow's Story: A Memoir*. London: Fourth Estate.
O'Connell, V. 1996. "The Human Heart." *Sight and Sound*, March, 59.
Oppenheim, J. 1988. *The Other World: Spiritualism and Psychical Research in England, 1850–1914*. Cambridge: Cambridge University Press.

Orpen, V. 2003. *Film Editing: The Art of the Expressive.* London: Wallflower.
Orr, J. 1993. *Cinema and Modernity.* Cambridge: Polity.
_____, and O. Taxidou. 2000. *Postwar Cinema and Modernity: A Film Reader.* Edinburgh: Edinburgh University Press.
Ostrowska, D. 2007. "Reading the Modern: Narratives in Cinema and Literature." *Vertigo,* Autumn, 3, 58–59.
Parkes, C.M. 1996. *Bereavement: Studies of Grief in Adult Life,* 3d ed. London: Routledge.
Pidduck, J. 2005. *La Reine Margot.* London: I.B. Tauris.
Plath, A.S., ed. 1975. *Letters Home by Sylvia Plath: Correspondence 1950–1963,* 3d ed. London: Faber & Faber.
Popple, S., and J. Kember. 2004. *Early Cinema: From Factory Gate to Dream Factory.* London: Wallflower.
Pretzel, P.W. 1972. *Understanding and Counselling the Suicidal Person.* New York: Abingdon.
Pulleine, T. 1978. "Interiors." *Sight and Sound,* Winter, 60–61.
Pym, J. 1978. "Interiors." *Monthly Film Bulletin,* December, 241.
_____, ed. 2006. *Time Out Film Guide 2007.* London: Time Out Guides.
Raitt, S., and T. Tate. 1997. *Women's Fiction and the Great War.* Oxford: Clarendon.
Riley, M., and J. Palmer. 1995. "Seeing, Believing, and 'Knowing' in Narrative Film: *Don't Look Now* Revisited." *Literature and Film Quarterly* 23, 14–25.
Robinson, D. 1973. *The History of World Cinema.* New York: Stein and Day.
Robson, K. 2004. *Writing Wounds: The Inscription of Trauma in Post–1968 French Women's Life-Writing.* Amsterdam: Rodopi.
Romney, J. 2003. *Atom Egoyan.* London: British Film Institute.
Sanderson, M. 1996. *Don't Look Now.* London: British Film Institute.
Santner, E.L. 1990. *Stranded Objects: Mourning, Memory and Film in Postwar Germany.* Ithaca: Cornell University Press.
Saxton, L. 2004. "Anamnesis and Bearing Witness: Godard/Lanzmann." In *For Ever Godard.* Ed. Michael Temple, James S. Williams and Michael Witt. London: Black Dog, 2004, pp. 364–379.
Scarry, E. 1985. *The Body in Pain: The Making and Unmaking of the World.* Oxford: Oxford University Press.
Schiller, B-M. 2005. "A Memorial to Mourning: Under the Sand." *Literature and Film Quarterly,* 33, 217–223.
Scott, A., and Bryant, C. 1997. *Don't Look Now.* London: British Film Institute/Sight and Sound.
Sight and Sound. 2008. August, 98.
Solomon, M. 2010. *Disappearing Tricks: Silent Film, Houdini, and the New Magic of the Twentieth Century.* Urbana: Illinois University Press.
"Soul Finders." 2006. Advertisement for ITV1 series *Afterlife. The Guardian,* 16 September, 44.
Sterritt, D. 2005. "Representing Atrocity: From the Holocaust to September 11." In *Guiltless Pleasures: A David Sterritt Film Reader.* Jackson: University Press of Mississippi, pp. 161–174.
Stok, D., ed. 1993. *Kieślowski on Kieślowski,* 2d ed. London: Faber & Faber.
Strick, Philip. 1973. "Cries and Whispers." *Sight and Sound,* Spring, 110.
Thompson, D. 1996. *The Concise Oxford Dictionary of Current English,* 9th ed. London: Book Club Associates/Oxford University Press.
Thomson, D. 2002. *The New Biographical Dictionary of Film,* 4th ed. London: Little, Brown.
Turner, G. 1988. *Film as Social Practice.* London: Routledge.
Valck, M. De, and Hagener, M., eds. 2005. *Cinephilia: Movies, Love and Memory.* Amsterdam: Amsterdam University Press.

Van Wert, W.F. 1977. "Point-Counter-Point in Hiroshima, Mon Amour." *Wide Angle*, 2 31–38.
Vincendeau, G., ed. 1995. *Encyclopedia of European Cinema.* London: Cassell/British Film Institute.
_____. 2000. *Stars and Stardom in French Cinema.* London: Continuum.
_____. 2001. "Under the Sand." *Sight and Sound*, April, 59.
_____. 2002. "8 Women." *Sight and Sound*, December, 46.
Vogel, A. 2005. *Film as a Subversive Art.* New York: DAP/CT.
Watson, G. 2004. *The Cinema of Mike Leigh: A Sense of the Real.* London: Wallflower.
Wees, W.C. 1992. *Light Moving in Time: Studies in the Visual Aesthetics of Avant-Garde Film.* Berkeley: University of California Press.
Wells, P. 2000. *The Horror Genre: From Beelzebub to Blair Witch.* London: Wallflower.
Williams, L. R. 2002. "Escape Artist." *Sight and Sound*, October, 22–25.
Williams, R. 2006 "True Colours." *The Guardian*, 11 March, 12–13.
Wilson, E. 1998. "Three Colors: Blue: Kieślowski, Colour and the Postmodern Subject." *Screen*, 39, Winter, 349–362.
_____. 1999. *French Cinema Since 1950.* London: Routledge.
_____. 2000. *Memory and Survival: The French Cinema of Krzysztof Kieślowski.* Oxford: Legenda.
_____. 2003. *Cinema's Missing Children.* London: Wallflower.
Winston Dixon, W. 2003. *Visions of the Apocalypse: Spectacles of Destruction in American Cinema.* London: Wallflower.
Winter, J. 1995. *Sites of Memory, Sites of Mourning.* Cambridge: Cambridge University Press.
Woolf, V. 1976. *Moments of Being*, 3d ed. Ed. Jeanne Schulkind. London: Chatto & Windus/Sussex University Press.
_____. 2002. *To the Lighthouse*, 3d ed. Ed. Sandra Kemp. London: Penguin.
Worden, J.W. 1991. *Grief Counselling and Grief Therapy: A Handbook for the Mental Health Practitioner*, 2d ed. London: Routledge.
Žižek, S., ed. 1992. *Everything You Always Wanted to Know about Lacan ... But Were Afraid to Ask Hitchcock.* London: Verso.
_____. 2001. *The Fright of Real Tears: Krzysztof Kieślowski Between Theory and Post-*Theory. London: British Film Institute.
_____. 2002. *Welcome to the Desert of the Real.* London: Verso.
_____. 2004. *An Ethical Plea for Lies and Masochism.* In *Lacan and Contemporary Film.* Eds. Todd McGowan and Sheila Kunkle. New York: Other.

Index

Numbers in ***bold italics*** indicate pages with photographs.

À une passante 7
À Villequier 111, 128, 139; *see also* Hugo, Victor
Aaron, Michele 8
Abraham, Nicolas 80, 89, 90, 124, 142
Adjani, Isabelle 17, 171
Adler, Carine 25
After Death (*Posle smerti*) 46, 110, 123, 152, 170, 183, 186, 187, 194; *see also* Bauer, Evgenii
Akerman, Chantal 118
Alice 16, 187; *see also* Allen, Woody
All That Heaven Allows 58, 158; *see also* Sirk, Douglas
Allen, Joan 171
Allen, Michael 158
Allen, Woody 16, 17, 26, 35, 96, ***97***, 98, 99, 101, ***103***, 104, 106, 136; *see also Alice*; *Annie Hall*; *Another Woman*; *Hannah and Her Sisters*; *Interiors*; *Manhattan*
Allende, Isabel 73
Almodóvar, Pedro 167
Altman, Rick 159, 160
Altman, Robert 35; *see also The Player*; *Short Cuts*
Les Amants du Pont-Neuf 114
Amenábar, Alejandro 24
Amiel, Vincent 116
Anderson, Judith 53
Andersson, Bibi 86
Andersson, Harriet 84, 85, 86
Andrew, Dudley 69
Andrew, Geoff 167, 168
Anglade, Jean-Hugues 171
Annie Hall 99; *see also* Allen, Woody
Another Woman 16, ***97***; *see also* Allen, Woody
Anspaugh, David 7
Anthony El Saffar, Ruth 21
Antonioni, Michelangelo 26, 31, 33, 34, 65, 72, 84, 116, 136, 139; *see also L'Avventura*; *The Red Desert*
Anxiety, Pain and Mourning 13; *see also* Freud, Sigmund
The Apartment 70; *see also* Wilder, Billy
The Art of Seeing with One's Own Eyes ***126***
Artaud, Antonin 27, 29, 88, 108
Ashby, Hal 178

Asibong, Andrew 122
At Land 66; *see also* Deren, Maya, Hammid, Alexander
L'Atalante 96, 167
Attenborough, Richard 24
Aumont, Jacques 118
L'Avventura 26, 72, 73; *see also* Antonioni, Michelangelo

Bacall, Lauren 134, 135
Back Street 52
Badreux, Jean 42
Bálint Kovács, András 26, 29, 116
The Barbarian Invasions 171, 182, 185, 188, ***189***, 190
Barthes, Roland 16, 101, ***181***
Bathrick, Fina 134
Baudelaire, Charles 7
Bauer, Evgenii 25, 35, 45, 46, 52, 53, 54, 69, 80, 84, 92, 104, 116, 122, 124, 139, 187; *see also After Death*; *The Dying Swan*
Baxter, John 47
Bayona, Juan Antonio 24
Bazin, André 16, ***62***, 91, 129, 136, 145, 170
Being and Time 27
Berck-Plage 96; *see also* Plath, Sylvia
Bereavement Care 2
Bergman, Ingmar 18, 26, 31, 84, 85, 86, 88, 96, 106, 165; *see also Cries and Whispers*; *Persona*; *The Silence*; *The Seventh Seal*
Bergman, Ingrid 69
Bergson, Henri 71
Bernadette of Lourdes 21
Bertolucci, Bernardo 25
Besson, Luc 114
Beugnet, Martine 73
Beyond the Pleasure Principle 13; *see also* Freud, Sigmund
Bid Me to Live 38
Billy Liar 94
Billy Wilder, American Film Realist 2
Binoche, Juliette 82, 112, 117, 118, 140, 164, ***189***, 191
Birth 15, 16, 17, 25, 27, 58, 109, 110, 113, 121, 122, 124, 128–138, 139, 142, 159, 160, ***169***, 172, 173,

175, 179, 180, *181*, 182, 183, 184, 185, 186, 187, 191, 193, 194; Bright performance 133; close-ups 130–132; language 137; mother-daughter relationships 134–135; off-screen sound 133; perverse sexuality 136–137; "presence" 136; the sea 138, 139; spiritualism 128–129
Bissette, Stephen R. 66
Björkman, Stig *97*
Black Book (Zwartboek) 164
Blade Runner 16; *see also* Scott, Ridley
The Blair Witch Project 17, 18, 129, 174, 179
Blais, Isabelle 190
Blanchot, Maurice 9
Blethyn, Brenda 173
Bloom, Claire 64
Boles, George 134
Bordwell, David 49, 51, 70, 71, 156
Borzage, Frank 25, 35, 50, 51, 52, 53, 57, 59, 83, 187; *see also A Farewell to Arms; Liliom; 7th Heaven; Street Angel; Three Comrades*
Brakhage, Stan 125
Breaking the Waves 165
Breillat, Catherine 167
Brent, George 134
Bresson, Robert 111, 120
The Bridges of Madison County 16
Bright, Cameron *130*, 133
Bright Lights Film Journal 2
British New Wave 61, 140
Brooks, James L. 165
Brooks, Xan 139, 141
Browning, Tod 47
Brownlow, Kevin 131, 166
Buckland, Warren 72, 86
Buñuel, Luis 48; *see also Un Chien Andalou; Butch Cassidy and the Sundance Kid* 160

The Cabinet of Dr. Caligari 47
Café Rêve, Montmartre, Paris 3–4
Cahiers du cinéma 83
Cameron, James 16, 161
Cammell, Donald 88
Carax, Léos 114
Carné, Marcel 55
"The Carnival of Death: Perceptions of Death in Europe and the Americas" 4
Carnival of Souls 19, 24, 65–66, 74, 75, 80, 83, 92, 96, 99, 110, 123, 129, 132, 162, 163, 165, 171, 175, *177*, 183, 191; the apport 65; aquatic imagery 66; avant-garde temperament 65–66; early cinema resonance 66
Carousel 59; *see also* King, Henry
Carrez, Florence 111, *192*
Carter, Ann 55
Caruth, Cathy 11, 12, 37, 78, 80
Cassavetes, John 165
Cat People 54, 55; *see also* Tourneur, Jacques
Caught 138; *see also* Ophüls, Max
Cavalcanti, Alberto 165
Cavell, Edith 46
La Caverne maudit (The Haunted Cavern) 41; *see also* Méliès, Georges

Chabrol, Claude 121; *see also Juste avant la nuit; La Rupture*
Chaplin, Charles 34
Chaplin, Geraldine 182
Charcot, Jean-Martin 43, 59
Charity, Tom 129
Chatillez, Etienne 182
Chéreau, Patrice 17, 171
Un Chien Andalou 48, 57, 183; *see also* Buñuel, Luis
Chion, Michel 32, 133, *144*
Christie, Ian 14
Christie, Julie 82, 89, 94, 131
Cimétière Père Lachaise, Ménilmontant, Paris 4
Cinema and Abstraction 108; *see also* Artaud, Antonin
Cinema's Missing Children 2; *see also* Wilson, Prof. Emma
Clarens, Carlos 60
Clarke, Charles G. 59
Clarke, Roger 132
Clayton, Jack 18, 60
Cléo de 5 à 7 118
Clouzot, Henri-Georges 42, 167
Clover, Carol 163
Coates, Paul 119
Coixet, Isabel 165
Collard, Cyril 18
Combs, Richard 79
"complicated mourning" 13, 113, 121, 124
Conway, Tom 55
Cooper, Gary 52
Coppola, Sofia 165
Craig, Siobhan 78
Crawford, Joan 134
Cremer, Bruno 121
Crichton, Charles 165
Cries and Whispers (Fiskningar och rop) 18, 35, 71, 76, 77, 84–88, 92, 95, 96, *97*, 101, 115, 171, 173, 174, 176, 178, 179, 180, 182, 183, 184, 185, 187, 188, 190; color 84–85; emotional confusion 86–87; horror 85; maternal instincts 87; pain 87; visionary temperament 85–86; women 86; *see also* Bergman, Ingmar
Critchley, Simon 100, 104
The Crowd 69; *see also* Vidor, King
Crutchley, Rosalie 63, 64
The Curse of the Cat People 54, 55, 61, 86, 147, 148, 149, 151, 163, *169*, 173, 174, 183, 184; *see also* Wise, Robert

Dalby, Amy 171
Dalí, Salvador 48
Damage 164
Darke, Chris 139, 140, 141
Darrieux, Danielle 52
Davis, Bette 134, 190
Davis, Prof. Colin 21, 132
Davis, Hope 151
Dead of Night 165
Dead Woman 77
Dearden, Basil 165
Death in Classical Hollywood Cinema 4

Death in Venice 158
"The Death of Cinema" 18, 108
Death 24× a Second: Stillness and the Moving Image 14; *see also* Mulvey, Laura
Dedicated to the One I Love 143
Dee, Frances 56
Deleuze, Gilles 4, 25, 26, 27, 28, 29, **30**, 31, 32, 33, 36, 47, 48, 50, 52, 53, 61, **62**, 68, 69, 70, 71, 72, 73–74, 75, 79, 80, **81**, 82, 85, 90, 91, 96, 98, 111, 112, 143, 144, 180, 182
Deleuze and World Cinemas 4
Demme, Jonathan 18
Dempsey, Michael 61, 88, 89, 94
Deneuve, Catherine 190
Deren, Maya 65–66, 99
Derrida, Jacques 9, 38
Descartes, René 28
Destiny (Der müde Tod, Between Two Worlds) 2, 48, 110, 194; *see also* Lang, Fritz
The Devil's Backbone (El Espinazo del Diablo) 147
Les Diaboliques 167
Diamond, Diana 122
Dickinson, Emily 63
Didion, Joan 10, 73
Dieterle, William 57
Dimendberg, Edward 159, 166
Dishonored 52; *see also* Sternberg, Josef von
Dmytryck, Edward 16
Doane, Mary Ann 8, 16, 21, 23, 131, 137
Dobson, Julia 115
Dogme movement 17
Doillon, Jacques 15, 48
Dollimore, Jonathan 10–11
Donnagio, Pino **93**
Donne, John **144**–145
Donohue, Heather 174
Don't Look Now 2, 18, 21, 35, 48, 55, 61, 74, 76, 77, 82, 88–96, 117, 137, 153, 162, 165, 167, 171, **177**, **181**, 182, 186, 188, 191, 193, 195; death-as-fate 88–89, 92; editing 90, 95–96; gender 88, 89–90, 92, **93**, 94, 95; Gothic influence 91–92; incorporation 89; reversion to childhood 94; title 92; water 96
Doolittle, Hilda (H.D) 38, 73
Double Indemnity 164, 167; *see also* Wilder, Billy
Dressed to Kill 162
Dreyer, Carl Theodor 111, 187; *see also The Passion of Joan of Arc*
Duncan, Gem 10, 11, 38, 92, 95, 116, 153
Dunne, Irene 134
Duras, Marguerite 22, 78, 83
The Dying Swan (Umirayuschii Lebed) 46, 187, 194; *see also* Bauer, Evgenii
Dyregrov, Atle 148
Dyson, Jeremy **62**

EastmanColor 84
Eastwood, Clint 16
Ecclestone, Christopher 172
Edison studio 167
Eliot, T.S. 84
Elliot, Alison 135

Elsaesser, Thomas 59, 72, 85
Elsner, Dr Anna Magdalena 3, 4
The English Patient 164
"Envisaging Death: Visual Culture and Dying," Conference 4
Escher, M.C. 153
The European Legacy 4
Evans, David 122
Exchange of Feelings 60

Falconetti, Maria 111, 133, 174, **192**
Le Fantôme d'Alger (A Spiritualist Meeting) 41; *see also* Méliès, Georges
A Farewell to Arms 51; *see also* Borzage, Frank
Fassbinder, Rainer Werner 121
Festen (The Celebration) 16, 18, 24, 172, 180, 195
Field, Todd 29
The Film Journal 164
Film Philosophy 4
"Film Philosophy and Death" Symposium 4
Firth, Colin 149
Fischer, Lucy 117, 165
Fisher, Terence 92
Floyd, Nigel 105
Fontaine, Joan 52, 53
Foucault, Michel 21
Four Quartets 84
Fox, Kate 42, 44
Fox, Margaret 42, 44
Frampton, Daniel 25, 27, 28, 29, 30, 32, 33, **62**, 64, 68, 75, 115, 118, 125
Franju, Georges **81**
Frankenstein 47
Frankenstein and the Monster from Hell 92
Franklin, Pamela 61
Freaks 47, 164
French New Wave, 72
Freud, Sigmund 6, 10, 11, 12, 13, 14, 43, 49, 59, 64, 71, 87, 101, 105, 133, 134, 161, **189**
Freund, Karl 47
Fried Green Tomatoes at the Whistle Stop Café 16
Fritsch, Gunther von 54
Fuller, Graeme 132

Gance, Abel 3, 48
Garmes, Lee 52
Garwood, Jamie 164
Gaudreault, André 44
Genova 2, 7, 25, 29, 147–53, 162, **191**; child apports 147–148; crying 150–151; mise-en-scène 149; mourning film genealogy 153
Germany: Year Zero (Germania, Anno Zero) 71; *see also* Rossellini, Roberto
Gerould, Daniel 23
Ghost 158
Gilbert, Susan 14
Giles, Jane 164
Gilliatt, Sidney 57
Girard, René 171
Gish, Lillian 118, 131, 132
Glazer, Jonathan 15, 133
Godard, Jean-Luc 41

Going My Way 54
Goldberg, Whoopi 40
The Golem 47
Gordon, Christine 55
Gorky, Maxim 104
Gower, Lizzie 22
Grant, Dr. Catherine 4, 195
The Great Gatsby 158
Greenaway, Peter 140
Greenberg, Joel 57
A Grief Observed 9–10, 11; see also Lewis, C.S.
Griffith, D.W. 116, 137, *138*, 186; see also *Orphans of the Storm*
Griffiths, Kate 122
Gromov, Andrei 187
Guattari, Félix 85
Gunning, Tom 44

Hagin, Dr Boaz 4
Hamer, Robert 165
Hamilton, Des 140
Hammer studios 91
Hammid, Alexander 66
Haney-Jardine, Perla 148, 149
Hannah and Her Sisters *97*; see also Allen, Woody
Harding, Ann 52
Harold and Maude 178
Harris, Julie 63, 190
Harvey, Herk 19
Harvey, James 60
Haskell, Molly 51
The Haunting 18, 24, 38, 39, 63–65, 119, 124, 125, 129, 135, 163, 165, 173, 176, *177*, 180, *181*, 182, 183, 184; aesthetic atmosphere 64–65; the apport 64; legacy of woman's picture 63–64; see also Wise, Robert
Hayward, Susan 50, 158, 161
Hazlewood, Lee 141
Heche, Anne 133
Hegel, Georg Wilhelm Friedrich 112
Heidegger, Martin 27, 28, 29, 58, 90, 92, 95
Heise, George 41
Higham, Charles 57
Hill, George Roy 160
Hilligoss, Candace 65, 190
Hiroshima le temps d'un retour 77
Hiroshima mon amour 7, 18, 19, 25, 31, 35, 71, 76, 77–84, 87, 92, 117, *127*, 162, 165, 171, 175, 179, *181*, 182, 183, 185, 188, *189*, 194; acting 81–82; imagery 79–80; language 78; memory 78–79; realist record 83; subjectivity 80; *Vertigo* comparison 83; wandering/searching 80–83; women 83–84; see also Resnais, Alain
Hirsch, Dr Pam 4
Hitchcock, Alfred 2, 53, 74, 83, *138*, 162, 183, 57; see also *Notorious*; *Psycho*; *Rear Window*; *Rebecca*; *Vertigo*
Holland, Willa 149
Houston, Penelope 78, 81
Howard, Arliss 137
Hugo, Victor 111, 120, 128, 139; see also *Tomorrow, When the Meadows Grow*; *À Villequier*

8 Femmes 121, 190; see also Ozon, François
Hurt, Mary Beth *97*
Huston, Danny 131, 134

I Have Loved You So Long (*Il y a longtemps que je t'aime*) 7, 54, 118, 159, 172, 176, 178, 184, 188, 191, *192*, 195
I Walked with a Zombie 54, 55, 56, 173, 174, 179; see also Tourneur, Jacques
Idziak, Sławomir 115
Imitation of Life 59, *93*, 158; see also Sirk, Douglas
In the Bedroom 29, 110, 139, 172, 176, 178, 179, 194
India Song 83; see also Duras, Marguerite
The Innocents 18, 24, 39, 60–63, 75, 80, 87, 92, 122, 125, 129, 132, 135, 137, 146, 148, 163, 165, 170, 173, 174, 175, 180, *181*, 183, 185; abject imagery 63; aesthetic roots 61; apparitions 61, *62*; child apports 61, 63; dramatic atmosphere 61; visionary quality 62
Insignificance 2; see also Roeg, Nicolas
The Instant of My Death 9
"Intellectual melodrama" 26
Interiors 2, 6, 18, 19, 26, *30*, 35, 54, 55, 58, 71, 74, 76, 77, 85, 87, 96–107, 110, 118, 124, 128, 135, 137, 139, 151, 166, 168, 171, 173, 175, 176, *177*, 178, 179, 180, *181*, 182, 183, 184, 186, 187, 188, *189*, 190, 191, 193, 194, 195; death-as-fate 100; Freudian analytical model 101–102; irrevocability 104–105; language 100, 102, 103, 106; mise-en-scène 102–*103*; narrative 98, 105; the sea 99–100; windows 99; writing 103; see also Allen, Woody
The International Society for the Study of European Ideas 4
The Interpretation of Dreams 11–12 see also Freud, Sigmund
Italian Neo-Realism 71, 72

J'accuse 3, 48; see also Gance, Abel
James, Henry 147
James, Nick 118
Jean-Baptiste, Marianne 178
Jeanne Dielman, 23 Quai de Commerce Bruxelles 1080 118
Jenkins, Megs 61
Jessop, Clytie 61
Jeunet, Jean-Pierre 25
Johnson, Richard 64
Jones, Jennifer 57, *192*
Jordan, Richard 101
Jude 172, 174, 176, 179, 185, 187; see also Winterbottom, Michael
Jules et Jim 35, 186
Juste avant la nuit (*Just Before Nightfall*) 121; see also Chabrol, Claude

Kalin, Tom 158
Kandinsky, Vassili 115
Kaplan, E. Ann 134
Karalli, Vera 46, 118

Karina, Anna 84
Katz, Ephraim 51
Kawin, Bruce 84
Keaton, Diane 97
Keener, Catherine 151
Kerr, Deborah 61, 135, 190
Kidman, Nicole 82, *130*, 134
Kieślowski, Krzsztyof 7, 33, 113, 116, 119, 120, 167, 193; see also *Three Colours: Blue*; *A Short Film about Killing*; *Short Film about Love*
Kinematograph 43
King, Henry 57, 59; see also *Carousel*; *The Song of Bernadette*
The Kiss 41, 56, 167
Kissed 47, 56, 87, *146*, 171, 174, 176, 178, 182, 183, 188, 191
Kitses, Jim 159
Klapisch, Cédric 164
Kohner, Susan 59
Kolker, Robert 50, 88
Konigsberg, Ira 159
Kristéva, Julia 145
Kübler-Ross, Elisabeth 9, 29, 150
Kuhn, Annette 49, 145
Kuntzel, Thierry 164

Lacan, Jacques 2, 11, 12, 73
Lake, Tony 76, 77, *93*, 142, 150
Lang, Fritz 2, 48, 59; see also *Destiny*; *Liliom*; *M*
Lant, Antonia 22
Lanzmann, Claude 16
Lapoirie, Jeanne 22
Largier, Luc 77, 82
Last Year at Marienbad (*L'Année dernière à Marienbad*) 26; see also Resnais, Alain
Launder, Frank 57
The Law of Desire (*La Ley del deseo*) 167
Leader, Darian 5, 6, 145
Lebeau, Vicky 95
Leigh, Mike 19
Léon Morin, prêtre *81*
Leone, Sergio 141
Letter to the Clairvoyant 88, 94; see also Artaud, Antonin
Lewis, C.S. 9–10, 11, 23, 25, 38, 56; see also *A Grief Observed*
Lewton, Val 54, 55, 57, 80, 92, *93*, 157, 191
Libération 190
Liliom 59; see also Borzage, Frank
Liliom 48; see also Lang, Fritz
Lindemann, Erich 80, 153
The Loss of Reality in Neurosis and Psychosis 105; see also Freud, Sigmund
Lost in Translation 165
Lovefilm 164
Lumière brothers 41, 42, 131
Lusitania 46
Lust for a Vampire 92

M 48, 166; see also Lang, Fritz
Magnificent Obsession 158; see also Sirk, Douglas
Magritte, René 62, 125

Maguire, Dorothy 56
Malkovich, John 171
Malle, Louis 164
Mamas and the Papas 143
The Manchurian Candidate 158
Manhattan *103*; see also Allen, Woody
Mansell, Janet 171
Manvell, Roger 82
Marks, Laura 16
Marshall, E.G. *97*
Marshall, Herbert 134
Martin-Jones, Dr. David 4
Mason, Hilary 92
Mata Hari 53
Matania, Clelia 92
Mater Dolorosa (*Sorrowful Mother*; *The Torture of Silence*) 48; see also Gance, Abel
A Matter of Life and Death (*Stairway to Heaven*) 58, 187
Maurier, Daphne du 165
McDermott, Kathleen 141
Meet Me in St. Louis 54; see also Minnelli, Vincente
Méliès, Georges 41, 43, 46, 183; see also *Le Caverne maudite*; *Le Fantôme d'Alger*
Mellen, Joan 86
Melville, Jean-Pierre 81
Meshes of the Afternoon 66; see also Deren, Maya; Hammid, Alexander
Miller, Laura 161
Millions Like Us 57, 194
Milne, Tom 88
Minghella, Anthony 15, 164
Minnelli, Vincente 54, 59, 135; see also *Meet Me in St Louis*; *Tea and Sympathy*
Mitry, Jean 159
Modleski, Tania 54, 60, 117
Molnár, Ferenc 59
Moonlight and Valentino 7, 9, 20, 24, 29, 39, 40, 67, 108, 110, 139, 159, 165, 168, 172, 173, 175, 176, *177*, 178, 179, 180, *181*, 186, 187, 188
Moreau, Jeanne 35, 84, 94, 117, 186
Moretti, Nanni 166
Morton, Samantha 82, 89, 94, 131
Morvern Callar (*Le Voyage de Morvern Callar*) 7, 17, 20, 22, 26, 31, 47, 56, 74, 87, 125, 139–147, 159, 160, 165, 166, 171, 172, 173, 174, 176, 178, 179, 186, 188, 191, 193, 195; abject imagery *144–146*; incorporation/introjection 142; Morton performance 140, 141; the sea 147; see also Ramsay, Lynne
Mourning and Melancholia 13, 109; see also Freud, Sigmund
Moviedrome 164
Moviemail 164, 165
Mrs. Miniver 54
Mulvey, Laura 14, 15, 69; see also *Death 24× a Second: Stillness and the Moving Image*
The Mummy 47
Musuraca, Nicholas 55, 56
My Life Without Me 165
Myrick, Daniel 17
The Mystery of the Wax Museum 47

National Film Theatre (NFT) 167, 168
Neale, Steve 45
Nemerov, Alexander 54, 55
Neruda, Pablo 77
New Black: The, Mourning, Melancholia and Depression 5
Night Shyamalan, M. 18
Nikita 114
Nolot, Jacques 123
Nosferatu 47
Notorious **138**; see also Hitchcock, Alfred
Nowell-Smith, Geoffrey 59
Nykvist, Sven 84

Oates, Joyce Carol 8, 31, 80, 123
O'Connell, Vincent 77, 79, 82
"Odorama" 43
Okada, Eiji 77
Olivier, Laurence 53
One Night Stand 18
Ophüls, Max 59, 158; see also *Caught*
Oppenheim, Janet 43, 44
Orpen, Valerie 50
The Orphanage (El Orfanato) 24, 125, 170, 173, 174, 176, **181**, 182, 183, 184
Orphans of the Storm 131; see also Griffith, D.W.
Orr, John 72, 73, 83
Ossessione 167
Ostrowska, Danuta 88
The Others (Los Otros) 24, 25, 63, 129, 165, 170, 184
Our Attitude Towards Death 13; see also Freud, Sigmund
Ozon, François 17; see also *8 Femmes; Regarde le mer; Temps qui reste; Under the Sand; Water Drops on Burning Rocks*

Page, Geraldine **97**, 106, 190
Palma, Brian de 162
Paltrow, Gwyneth 40
Parillaud, Anne 114
Paris 164
Parkes, Colin Murray 29, 67, 69, 70, 82, 109
Pasolini, Pier-Paolo 14, 33, 50, 65, 68, 73, 139, **169**
The Passion of Joan of Arc 111, 133; see also Dreyer, Carl Theodor
Perestiani, Ivan 46
Performance 88
The Perils of Pauline 21
Periz, Ingrid 22
Perkins, Elizabeth 39
Pernel, Florence 112
Persona 86; see also Bergman, Ingmar
Peter Ibbetson 52
Petit Prince á dit 147
Petley, Julian 72
"Phantsascope" 44
Philadelphia 18
Pitié-Salpêtrière, L'Hôpital 43
Plateau, Joseph Antoine 27, 43
Plath, Sylvia 65, 96, 99, 100

The Player 158; see also Altman, Robert
Pol, Gerwin van der 164
Polonskii, Vit'old 187
Ponette 15, 48, 147, 149, 151, 163, 165, 168, **169**, 182, 187, 188, 191, 195
Portal, Louise 171
Portrait of Jennie 37, 57, 58, **62**, 110, 135, 136, 173, 187, **192**
Potter, Sally 140, 162, 171; see also *Thriller; Yes*
Powell, Michael 58
Pressburger, Emeric 58
Pretzel, Paul 104
Private Fears in Public Places (Coeurs) 79; see also Resnais, Alain
Production Code, Hollywood 47
Psycho 158, 162, 166; see also Hitchcock, Alfred
Pursued 160

Queen Kelly 167
Quester, Hugues 118

Rampling, Charlotte 82, 121, 123, **126**, **189**, 190, 195
Ramsay, Lynne 7, 139, 145; see also *Morvern Callar; Ratcatcher*
Ratcatcher 145; see also Ramsay, Lynne
the Real 2, 11, 12, 73, 125, **146**; see also Lacan, Jacques
Rear Window 74; see also Hitchcock, Alfred
Rebecca 53, 63, 108, 135, 138, 165, 171, 183, **192**, 194; see also Hitchcock, Alfred
The Red Desert (Il deserto rosso) 26, 73; see also Antonioni, Michelangelo
Regarde la mer (See the Sea) 121; see also Ozon, François
Régent, Benoît 114
La Reine Margot 17, 171
"Religion and Secularity in Contemporary European Cinema" Conference 4
Remember 147
Renoir, Jean 2
Reservoir Dogs 167
Resnais, Alain 7, 26, 31, 33, 34, 78, 79, 80, 83, 87; see also *Hiroshima mon amour; Last Year at Marienbad; Private Fears in Public Places (Coeurs)*
Richardson, Dorothy 22
Richardson, Tony 167
Rickman, Alan 175
Riley, Michael 90
Riva, Emmanuelle 35, 77, 78, 81, 83, 84, 94, 117, 162
Rivière, Jacques 29
RKO-Radio Pictures 54, 157
Roc, Patricia 57
Roebuck Rudge, John 44
Roeg, Nicolas 2, 18, 35, 88, 91; see also *Don't Look Now; Performance; Walkabout*
Romance 167
Rome: Open City (Roma, Cittá Apertá) 71; see also Rossellini, Roberto
Rossellini, Roberto 69; see also *Rome: Open City; Voyage to Italy*

Rossetti, Christina 147
Rouge 164
Rueda, Belén 174
La Rupture 121; *see also* Chabrol, Claude
Ryall, Tom 157, 159

Sadoyan, Isabelle 113
Sanchez, Emilio 17
Sanders, George 69
Sanderson, Mark 88
Sangster, Jimmy 92
Savage Grace 158
Savage Nights (*Les Nuits fauves*) 18
Saving Private Ryan 3, 16, 19, 20, 161, 187; *see also* Spielberg, Steven
The Scala 164
The Scarlet Empress 52; *see also* Sternberg, Josef von
Scarry, Elaine 86
Schatz, Thomas 165
Schefer, Jean-Louis 27
Schiller, Britt-Maj 128
Schindler's List 16, 19, 161, 187; *see also* Spielberg, Steven
Scholl, Sophie 21
Scott, Ridley 16, *144*; *see also Blade Runner*; *Someone to Watch Over Me*
Scott Thomas, Kristin 172, *189*, 191
Secrets and Lies 19, 110, 139, 173, 176, 178, 179, 180
"Sensing Cinema: History, Theory, Body" Conference 4
7th Heaven 50; *see also* Borzage, Frank
The Seventh Seal (*Det sjunde inseglet*) 165; *see also* Bergman, Ingmar
Seyrig, Delphine 117
Shadowlands 24, 25, 164
Shanghai Express 52; *see also* Sternberg, Josef von
The Sheik 25
The Sheltering Sky 25, 76, 82, 164, 171, 173, 184, 187, 190
Shoah 19
Short Cuts 172
A Short Film about Killing (*Krótki Film o zabijaniu*) 167; *see also* Kieślowski, Krzysztof
A Short Film about Love (*Krótki Film o Miłości*) 113; *see also* Kieślowski, Krzysztof
The Silence (*Tystnaden*) 106; *see also* Bergman, Ingmar
Simon, Ellen 22
Simon, Simone 55
Sinatra, Nancy 141
Since You Went Away 194
Singer, Lori 172
Siodmak, Robert 2, 56; *see also The Spiral Staircase*
Sirk, Douglas 58, 59, 158; *see also Imitation of Life*; *Magnificent Obsession*; *Written on the Wind*
The Sixth Sense 18, 129, 151, 152, 170
Sobchack, Thomas 161
Solomon, Matthew 42, 45

Some Velvet Morning 141
Someone to Watch Over Me *144*; *see also* Scott, Ridley
The Song of Bernadette 57, 187, *192*; *see also* King, Henry
The Son's Room (*La stanza del figlio*) 166, 168
Spacek, Sissy 194
Spencer, Lady Diana 19
Spielberg, Steven 3, 16; *see also Saving Private Ryan*; *Schindler's List*
The Spiral Staircase 56, 57, 147, 184; *see also* Siodmak, Robert
spiritualism 15, 33, 34, 42, 43, 44, 45, 46, 51, 52, 54, 66, 69, 76, 84, 85, 89, 119, 128, 132, 148, 165, *181*, 182, 183
Staiger, Janet 158
Stapleton, Maureen 101
Stephens, Martin 61
Sternberg, Josef von 52; *see also Dishonored*; *The Scarlet Empress*; *Shanghai Express*
Stevenson, Juliet 175
Stewart, Alexandra 123
Stopkewich, Lynne 47
Stormare, Peter 133, 134
Street Angel 50; *see also* Borzage, Frank
Strick, Philip 84, 85
"Stroboscopic Effect" 43
Sutherland, Donald 88
Sylwan, Kari 85

Talking Pictures 164
Tarantino, Quentin 167
Tatie Danielle 182
Tautou, Audrey 176
Taylor, Alma 22
Taylor, Richard 46
Tea and Sympathy 135; *see also* Minnelli, Vincente
Tender Comrade 16
Terms of Endearment 165, 173
Teshigahara, Hiroshi 167
Thérèse Desqueyroux *81*
The 3rd Annual Yale Film Studies Graduate Conference 4
Thomson, David 106, 163
Three Colours: Blue (*Trois Couleurs: Bleu*) 6, 7, 15, 17, 18, 19, 26, 27, 35, 48, 56, 96, 108, 109, 110, 111–120, 121, 128, 131, 135, 137, 139, 146, 151, 159–160, 162, 163, 164, 165, 166, 168, 171, 173, 174, 175, 176, 178, 179, 180, 184, 186, 187, 188, 191, 193, 195; boundary crossing 113, 116; camerawork 114; color 115, 118; demeanor 113–114; image of Binoche 117–118; mother-daughter relationships 116–117; sound 119–120; tactility 118–119; title 112, 115; water 115–117; *see also* Kieślowski, Krzysztof
Three Comrades 51; *see also* Borzage, Frank
Thriller 161; *see also* Potter, Sally
Thulin, Ingrid 85, 86
Time Out 106
Time Out Film Guide 167
Time to Leave (*Temps qui reste*) 35; *see also* Ozon, François

"The Tingler" 43
Titanic (film) 16, 19, 24, 161, 163, 166, 173, 188
Titanic (ship) 38, *177*
To the Lighthouse 38; *see also* Woolf, Virginia
Tom Jones 167
Tomorrow, When the Meadows Grow 120; *see also* Hugo, Victor
Toro, Guillermo del 129
Torok, Maria 80, 89, 90, 124, 142
Totem and Taboo 6; *see also* Freud, Sigmund
Tourneur, Jacques 2, 54; *see also* Cat People; I Walked with a Zombie
The Trial of Joan of Arc (*Procés de Jeanne d'Arc*) 111
Trier, Lars von 165
Truffaut, François 35
Truly, Madly, Deeply 15, 16, 25, 155, *169*, 175, 176, 178, 180, 182, 183, 187, 188, 190
Tudor, Andrew 156, 160
The Turn of the Screw 147; *see also* James, Henry
Turner, Graeme 158
Turner, Kathleen 40
Tushingham, Rita 183
20th Century–Fox studios 60

Ullman, Liv 86
The Uncanny 14; *see also* Freud, Sigmund
Under the Sand (*Sous le sable*) 17, 25, 26, 27, 31, 47, 48, 54, 74, 87, 104, 109, 110, 113, 120–128, 132, *138*, 139, 142, 152, 166, 168, *169*, 172, 173, 174, 176, *177*, 178, 183, 184, 185, 188, 190, 191, 193; abject imagery 125–126, 127; absence/ "presence" 122–123; "complicated mourning" 124; genericity 120–121; Rampling's performance 126; *see also* Ozon, François
Under the Skin 25, 41, 74, 139, 140, 165, 166, 168, 171, 173, 175, 176, 178, 182, 183, 186, 191
Universal Horror 166; *see also* Brownlow, Kevin
Universal studios 47, 61, 158
Universitat Pompeu Fabra, Barcelona, Spain 4
University of Birmingham, UK 4
University of Cambridge 2, 3, 4
University of London 4
University of Sussex 4
University of York, UK 4

Varda, Agnès 118
Variety 56
Verhoeven, Paul 164
Verlaine, Paul 60
Vertigo 83, 165, 173; *see also* Hitchcock, Alfred
Véry, Charlotte 112
A Very Long Engagement (*Un long dimanche de fiançailles*) 25, 176, 182, 188
Videohound's Golden Movie Retriever 167
Vidor, King 69, 70
Vigo, Jean 96, 167
Vincendeau, Ginette 112, 117, 118, 121
Vinterberg, Thomas 16
Visconti, Luchino 167

Les Visiteurs du soir 55
Vitti, Monica 65, 84
Vogue 158
Voyage to Italy (*Viaggio in Italia*) 68–69; *see also* Rossellini, Roberto
Vuillermoz, Emile 33

Walkabout 88 *see also* Roeg, Nicolas
Walsh, Raoul 160
Water Drops on Burning Rocks (*Gouttes d'eau sur pierres brûlantes*) 121; *see also* Ozon, François
Waterston, Sam *97*
The Waves 124; *see also* Woolf, Virginia
Welles, Orson 72
Wells, Dolly 140
Wells, Paul 47, 55
Wert, William van 78
Western 160
Whale, James 47
The Widow Jones 42
Wilder, Billy 2, 70, 164
Williams, Linda Ruth 139, 143, 161
Williams, Sharon 89
Willis, Gordon 101, 102
Wilson, Edmund 54
Wilson, Prof. Emma 2, 3, 10, 12, 40, 80, 111, 114, 115, 152, 166
Wilson, Jim 140
Winger, Debra 164, 190
Winslet, Kate 172
Winston Dixon, Wheeler 8
Winter, Prof. Jay 42, 46, 49, 57
Winter, Jessica 51
Winterbottom, Michael 7, 147, 149; *see also* Genova; Jude
Wise, Robert 18, 54
Woman of the Dunes (*Suna no onna*) 167
A Woman Under the Influence 165
Woman's picture 3, 16, 20, 23, 24, 35, 36, 52, 53, 57, 61, *93*, 99, *126*, 134, 164, 173, 180, 190
Wood, Robin 22
Woolf, Virginia 38, 73, 124, 128, 171; *see also* To the Lighthouse; The Waves
Worden, Dr William 10, 11, 68, 75, *103*, 109, *127*, 150, 151
World War I 13, 37, 38, 44, 46, 47, 54, 166
World War II 57, 67
Written on the Wind 158, 167; *see also* Sirk, Douglas
Wyler, William 54
Wyman, Jane 58
Wyngarde, Peter 61

Yes 171; *see also* Potter, Sally

Zane, Billy 161
Zea, Kristi 22, 102
Žižek, Slavoj 112, 113, 119, 190
Zylberstein, Elsa 172
Zyskind, Marcel 149